The Performance Consultant's Fieldbook

The Performance Consultant's Fieldbook

Tools and Techniques for Improving Organizations and People

Judith Hale

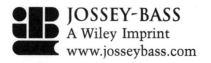

JOSSEY-BASS
A Wiley Imprint
www.josseybass.com

Published by Jossey-Bass/Pfeiffer
A Wiley Imprint
989 Market Street, San Francisco, CA 94103-1741   www.pfeiffer.com

Jossey-Bass/Pfeiffer is a registered trademark of John Wiley & Sons, Inc.

ISBN: 0-7879-4019-4
Library of Congress Catalog Card Number 98-9409

Jossey-Bass/Pfeiffer books and products are available through most bookstores.
To contact Jossey-Bass/Pfeiffer directly call our Customer Care Department within the U.S. at 800-956-7739, outside the U.S. at 317-572-3986 or fax 317-572-4002.

Jossey-Bass/Pfeiffer also publishes its books in a variety of electronic formats. Some content that appears in print may not be available in electronic books.

Library of Congress Cataloging-in-Publication Data

Hale, Judith
    The performance consultant's fieldbook : tools and techniques for
improving organizations and people / Judith Hale.
        p.   cm.
    Includes index.
    ISBN 0-7879-4019-4 (pbk. : alk. paper)
        1. Business consultants—Handbooks, manuals, etc. 2. Employees—
Rating of—Handbooks, manuals, etc. 3. Performance standards—
Handbooks, manuals, etc. I. Title.
    HD69.C6 H35   1998
    658.3'124—dc21   98-9409

Acquiring Editor: Matthew Holt   Interior Design: Joseph Piliero
Developmental Editor: Kathleen Dolan-Davies   Cover Design: Laurie Anderson
Production Editor: Susan Geraghty   Illustrations: Richard Sheppard
Senior Production Editor: Dawn Kilgore

Printed in the United States of America

Printing 10 9 8 7 6

Contents

Preface

*T*his fieldbook tells my story about performance consulting—what it is, why it is important, and how it can contribute to improving performance. Before starting this project I took time to read what others have said about performance consulting. Most of the other books stress why performance consulting is important, but they do not provide the tools consultants need to make it work. Some describe models for analyzing performance problems, but they do not explain how to use those models. They are silent on how to establish credibility with clients and how to build a business case for change. I wanted this fieldbook to give you tools and techniques to get relevant information so that you and your clients could make more informed decisions. Every story in the fieldbook is true, and every tool and technique has been tried and proven effective.

In some ways this book is autobiographical. The ideas and approach to consulting presented here have evolved over twenty-four years of my working with all types of organizations, in both the private and the public sectors. But this fieldbook has also been shaped by my experiences before I even became a consultant, from charting stock market transactions for my dad as a teenager to my education in theater management and my later experiences as a social worker and college instructor.

What came out of these and other experiences was my consulting firm, Hale Associates, which I named after my father. The company logo is composed of three overlapping circles. The circles stand for integrity, ingenuity, and intelligence. Integrity is about honor, honesty, stewardship, and doing the right thing. Ingenuity has to do with getting things done despite limitations. Intelligence comes from having good data; it is not about being intellectually superior.

This fieldbook is inspired by that troika of principles. It discusses

- Maintaining your integrity by insisting on being fact-based, yet accepting other people's points of view
- Using your ingenuity to get good information and to get your clients involved and committed to change
- Applying what you learn to help organizations and people become successful

As consultants we all bring a wealth of experience and learning to our assignments. What we need are processes, tools, and techniques to help us direct our experiences toward producing meaningful results. This is what I've attempted to provide with this fieldbook. I hope you enjoy it and find the information it contains useful and enlightening.

AUDIENCE FOR THE BOOK

This fieldbook is intended for trainers, organizational development consultants, and human resources development professionals, who know firsthand the implications of implementing limited solutions to complex organizational problems. It provides processes, tools, and techniques that these professionals can use, whether they operate as internal or external consultants, to expand their role in their clients' organizations. It offers guidance on how to help clients better understand their organization and develop cost-effective programs to improve performance.

ACKNOWLEDGMENTS

A lot of people helped me put this book together. I want to give special thanks to Dave Haskett, of Johnson Controls, for his willingness to do a quick turnaround on the material. His comments on cost and measures were invaluable. Seth Carey, Chris Appleton, and Chris Duszinski, of McDonald's Corporation, were especially helpful, asking pointed questions and also serving as excellent models. Keith Hall, of SmithKline Beecham, got me to rethink the hierarchy and make it better. It was Dean Larson, of U.S. Steel, who got me to add the thirteenth intervention, measures. Barbara Gough, of UTS, was kind enough to do a fast read and check my logic on the subjects of cost and the work environment. My brother, Steve, and friend Linda Gohlke brought a fresh perspective, as both are naive when it comes to performance consulting. Their comments on the hierarchy and interventions encouraged me to divide these topics into smaller segments, hopefully making them easier to understand.

Many other people offered words of encouragement. Two people were especially helpful: my developmental editor, Joan Kalkut of Empire Communications, and Carla Williams, a longtime colleague. Joan brought to her job the right combination of tenacity (getting me to keep my story lines straight) and suggestions on how to incorporate the tools and techniques into the stories. It was her encouragement that gave me the courage to put forth some of my ideas. Carla Williams, who worked with me for nine years, has seen most of the tools and techniques in action. She knows the stories; but more important, she has a logical way of looking at the world. She built the case for putting the chapter on costs in Part One. Her point was that everything gets down to money, so performance consultants had better understand the economics of consulting and their clients' businesses. Special credit goes to Matt Holt and Kathleen Dolan-Davies, both of Pfeiffer, who helped me navigate through the world of publishing and who provided resources that made this book possible.

A final word of thanks goes to my mother, who endured my many hours at the computer. It was from her and my dad that I learned about personal integrity and doing what you believe in.

April 1998   Judith Hale
Western Springs, Illinois

Introduction

*T*his fieldbook consists of two parts. Part One focuses on the process of becoming a performance consultant; Part Two focuses on processes performance consultants can use to identify barriers to performance, diagnose performance problems, recommend appropriate interventions, and measure results. Each chapter describes processes, tools, and techniques you can use to position yourself as a consultant and provides examples of how to use them. These processes, tools, and techniques are appropriate for both internal and external consultants. The tools are provided on the accompanying disk so that you can modify them for your own work. At the end of each chapter are suggestions on where to learn more.

PART ONE: MAKING THE TRANSITION

Part One is about becoming a performance consultant. Chapter One defines performance consulting and describes what distinguishes it from other types of consulting. It discusses four criteria that set performance consultants apart from other consultants, and it describes a consulting process that communicates what you do and how you work with clients. The process is designed to help you meet the four criteria that define performance consulting. The chapter covers tools and techniques to help you create operational definitions (specifically, of performance consulting) and define and describe your own consulting process.

Chapter Two is about how to move into performance consulting. It includes a detailed transition plan, including advice on how to

- Measure the effectiveness of your consulting process
- Expand your products and services to include performance consulting

- Evaluate your current products and services to identify which ones will hinder your transition (because they drain resources) and which ones to leverage to facilitate your transition

Chapter Three is about how costs are classified and valued. It describes what drives costs and how to manage them. The tools and techniques in Chapter Three will help you determine your own costs and what drives them. There is a tool you can use to value your own time. You can apply these concepts in your work with clients as well, to help them evaluate the cost-effectiveness of their programs and determine the costs of poor performance.

Chapter Four is about how to positively shape people's perceptions of you and the value of your services. The tools and techniques in this chapter are designed to help you

- Get useful information

- Influence clients' decisions and actions

- Assess clients' capability and commitment to change

- Build a strategy for working with clients at different levels of readiness for change

PART TWO: PERFORMANCE CONSULTING

The second part of the fieldbook is about actually doing consulting work. Each chapter describes tools and techniques and includes stories illustrating their use.

Chapter Five is about how the work environment and group norms affect performance. The tools and techniques it offers are designed to

- Identify and discriminate between changes in the organization, changes in a particular job, and changes in an individual that interfere with performance

- Recognize how group norms can negatively affect performance and what to do to improve performance in such circumstances

Chapter Six is about diagnosing performance problems and identifying barriers to performance. Its tools include

- A scorecard you can use to guide discussions about which problems need to be addressed and what will be accepted as evidence of improvement

- A hierarchy that will guide you through a comprehensive process of identifying what interferes with performance

Chapter Seven is about selecting and recommending interventions to improve performance or eliminate barriers to performance. The tools presented here include

- The "families of interventions" job aid
- An "if-then" table for selecting interventions
- A matrix you can use to identify the appropriate combination of interventions based on the cause of a specific performance problem

Chapter Eight is about measures and criteria. It defines what measures, criteria, and metrics are, discusses how to select the appropriate measures, and describes how to evaluate an intervention. It includes the following tools:

- A measures, criteria, and metrics table
- Guidelines for selecting measures
- An intervention worksheet for selecting measures for your interventions

Chapter Nine is about measuring people's performance and evaluating jobs. It provides these tools:

- Guidelines for measuring job inputs, processes, outputs, and outcomes
- A "people performance" worksheet for measuring outputs (productivity) and outcomes (results)
- Guidelines for obtaining behavioral anchors to measure people's performance

WHY THE EMPHASIS ON TOOLS?

The tools used throughout the fieldbook are designed to

- *Function like job aids.* Job aids encourage consistency. By consistently following a set of guidelines, you will build skill and confidence.
- *Provide criteria for developing and evaluating your processes.* Criteria will help you identify which of your processes you need to improve.
- *Provide you with models you can use to improve your interactions with clients.* Models will help your clients better understand what you do and what they have to do to improve organizational and people performance.
- *Help you communicate that you know what you are doing and have processes in place for doing it.* The tools will help you build customer confidence in you and your methods.

- *Give your clients a framework for working with you.* The tools will give clients some indication of what the end state should look like. Knowing what it is you are trying to find out will allow them to focus their attention on the discussion. Without an end state in view, their attention will be on figuring out where you are going and why.

- *Serve as interim deliverables and working documents.* At the end of your meeting you and your client will have a document that describes your decisions and thinking. Your client can then use that document to communicate what the two of you are doing and why.

- *Support presentations.* Either you or your client can use the tools in presentations to explain what you discovered, what you are going to do about it, and how you will measure your results.

- *Develop the client's skills and educate the client on how to improve performance.* The tools model the thinking processes used in discovery, diagnosis, treatment, and measurement. Using the tools will help clients develop their own ability to identify performance problems, select appropriate interventions, and measure results.

- *Focus the client's attention on the process of identifying and solving problems instead of on individuals or faultfinding.* The tools move your discussions to facts, not people.

KEY DEFINITIONS

One of the problems facing any new field is the lack of a common language, so here are some working definitions of the terms used in this fieldbook. You will find that they are in harmony with the terms other performance consulting experts use.

- *Assessment* means finding out what is and is not happening. You engage in assessment to discover *what* the performance is and where there are opportunities for improvement.

- *Analysis* means finding out *why* performance is at the level it is. You engage in analysis so that you can recommend the appropriate intervention or solution to improve performance.

- *Consulting* is the role each of us plays when we engage in assessment, analysis, and recommending interventions.

- *Evaluation* means placing value on situations, activities, and results. Just by paying attention to someone's performance means you have judged it worthy of your attention. The term is sometimes used as a synonym for *assessment* and *analysis.*

- An *intervention* is any purposeful act designed to solve a problem, change behavior, improve performance, increase outputs, or improve outcomes. Interventions include things like introducing programs, adopting new technologies, changing the structure of an organization, redesigning jobs, and training.

- *Measurement* is a subset of evaluation. It is the process of gathering information and comparing what you discover to some criteria to determine if a gap in performance exists or if there has been improvement.

- An *organization* is an entity that employs people. It can refer to a whole entity or a part of it (that is, a company, division, department, function, work unit, or team).

- *Performance* is how well people do work (produce products and services) that is of value to customers and the organization.

- *Performance improvement* refers to the application of specific interventions to remove barriers to performance and encourage the desired performance.

The Performance
Consultant's Fieldbook

Part One

Making the Transition

Chapter 1

Performance Consulting

*I*n their desire to improve organizational performance, managers sometimes seek the help of consultants. They may not fully understand the capabilities and biases consultants bring to their assignments, however. The following story illustrates this point.

FIELD NOTES: SOLUTIONS

A large conglomerate hired Mark to head its unit that manufactures and distributes extrusion metals (used to make window frames, louver blades, I-beams for construction, and storm doors). The main plant was in the Midwest, there was a second plant on the East Coast, and a new plant was scheduled to open in Singapore within six months.

The Midwest plant had lost market share over the previous two years. Its on-time delivery record was poor, and turnover among its sales staff was high. The East Coast plant was just meeting its financial goals, and senior management told Mark they were concerned. It seemed that customer complaints about product quality and missed deliveries were up.

Mark decided to seek the help of a marketing consultant. The marketing consultant recommended a new product image, a new logo, and a new marketing campaign. Mark agreed that a new marketing plan made sense, but he was uncomfortable with the plan because it could take the better part of a year to see results. To see if he could get faster results, Mark sought the advice of a sales consultant. This consultant recommended a sales contest, a new bonus structure, and incentives for achieving sales goals. At about this same time, a senior vice president at corporate headquarters suggested that Mark talk to a management consultant. The management consultant suggested reorganizing the business unit around key customer groups, such as construction, institutional buyers, and re-sellers. Because Mark had been impressed by the successes of the quality assurance department at the company he used to work for, he decided to meet with a quality consultant as well. The quality consultant offered three significant suggestions: set up cross-functional teams; make each team responsible for a whole process, from receiving orders to delivering finished products; and implement statistical process control techniques for each process.

Mark's U.S. sales manager suggested they hire an organizational development consultant to work with the management team. The goals would be to come up with a new vision and mission for the unit and to improve communication within the team. The Midwest plant manager suggested they hire a training consultant to develop training for sales and production personnel.

Mark received a memo stating that the corporation's architectural firm had been hired to do strategic planning for the entire corporation. One of the anticipated outcomes of the strategic plan was a new model for the plants, since the architectural firm was known for agile designs based on manufacturing principles. A human resources consultant recommended studying causes of turnover, implementing a targeted selection program, and doing an employee morale survey.

On his flight to the Singapore plant Mark read about the successes of reengineering. He was particularly impressed by the use of sophisticated information systems designed to shorten cycle times. On his return flight he read another article, about performance improvement consulting. It was then that Mark realized that all of the approaches he had been considering had merit. All of the consultants he had hired had started with a solution, however; none of them had begun with an analysis of what was actually causing the poor performance. Instead, they had all assumed that they had the answer.

Mark's experiences are not unique. Eager for solutions to their problems, organizations act on the recommendations of experts without really finding out what the problem is. Managers are slowly recognizing the need to take a more fact-based, grounded approach to improving performance, however. Changes must leverage real strengths and deal with real weaknesses. This recognition on the part of management presents an opportunity for professionals in training, human resource development (HRD), and other related disciplines to demonstrate how their processes for diagnosing performance problems, selecting appropriate interventions, and measuring results can make a difference. At the same time, professionals in training, HRD, quality assurance, and organizational development (OD) want to shift their role to performance consulting, where they hope to join with management in applying processes designed to find the real barriers to performance. This new role is supported by the American Society for Training and Development, which has shifted its emphasis from training to performance improvement. The National Society for Performance and Instruction even changed its name, to the International Society for Performance Improvement (ISPI), to reflect the new emphasis on improving performance rather than promoting training. Both organizations' conferences, institutes, and publications are aimed at developing a shared understanding of and appreciation for the skills and knowledge required to improve organizational and people performance.

EXPERIENCES FROM THE FIELD: IMPROVING PERFORMANCE

It has been my experience that organizations are fairly erratic about finding ways to improve organizational and people performance. In their search for the optimal size and structure they buy, merge, and sell whole business units. They centralize functions, only to decentralize them later. They buy new technologies, products, and facilities. They distribute assets across unrelated products, only to later consolidate around their name brands. Organizations reengineer their processes, invest in training, and purchase ready-made programs to develop leadership and managerial skills. To reduce costs, organizations reduce the number of jobs by downsizing, outsourcing, and moving jobs to other countries. Many of these actions are done in parallel. Some are in conflict, however, and all are solutions in search of a problem.

To get a better understanding of the kinds of programs organizations take on to improve performance, think about the last two to three years in your own work life:

1. What has your organization done to reduce costs, improve profits, or become more competitive?

2. How many times has it reorganized, bought other companies, or been bought by other companies?

3. How many times has it centralized functions, only to decentralize them later?

4. How many times has your position stayed the same while the people you report to or the department you are assigned to changed?

5. How many times have you moved your office? What were the assumptions behind these moves?

6. What were some of the initiatives your organization embraced to motivate people, satisfy customers, or become more competitive? Were any of those initiatives based on a serious examination of the company's current state? If so, what evidence did the company use to see if the desired result was achieved? Who did the measuring?

7. How successful was the company at implementing changes throughout the organization? Did those changes fulfill the promise of lower costs, higher profits, or competitive advantage? How do you know?

8. What role did you play in any of these efforts? What will it take for you to play a more effective role in the future?

WHAT MAKES A PERFORMANCE CONSULTANT?

When I'm asked to explain performance consulting, I point out that performance consultants

- Are experts in analysis and measurement and provide expert advice, yet also facilitate the client's commitment to taking responsibility for supporting performance

- Play multiple roles

- Are not predisposed toward a particular solution and do not make recommendations until there are data to support them

- Focus on outcomes and measured results

Moving Between Expert and Facilitator

I think of consulting as a continuum (see Figure 1.1). At one end is the expert, whose job is to give advice. At the opposite end is the facilitator, whose job is to manage group dynamics.

Experts who are brought in as consultants usually possess education or credentials in a specific professional discipline. As experts they make definitive statements and express opinions. At this end of the continuum consulting consists of rendering opinions and giving advice. The client's attention is focused on the person expressing the opinion—that is, the expert.

Training and HRD professionals think of consulting in terms of the opposite end of the continuum, however. To them consulting is facilitating. Facilitators rarely give advice, offer opinions, or take a position on any subject; they are perceived as neutral. Their role is to facilitate other people's discovery and commitment to change. So at this end of the continuum consulting is the process of guiding people's discovery and bringing them to consensus. The client's attention is focused on what is happening within the group.

Expert ◄──────────────► Facilitator	
Has discipline-specific knowledge	Knows group processes
Comes with external status	Can manage group dynamics
Has discipline-specific skills	Has interpersonal skills
Offers opinions	Remains neutral

Figure 1.1. The Expert-Facilitator Continuum

To be an effective performance consultant you have to blend the attributes of an expert with those of a facilitator. You must give advice about how to get and interpret the facts and how to improve organizational and people performance. At the same time, however, you must facilitate the *client's* commitment to getting facts, measuring results, and doing the things that support performance. The tools and techniques in this fieldbook are designed to help you move back and forth between expert and facilitator. The tools legitimize your opinions but also encourage your clients to come to their own conclusions and retain ownership of the results. The tools and techniques will focus your clients' attention on the processes of discovery, diagnosis, and measurement, *not on you.*

Playing Multiple Roles

There is another continuum that can be used to distinguish performance consultants from other types of consultants. This continuum goes from critic to doer to spectator (see Figure 1.2). There are people who criticize, people who do, and people who stand around and watch.

Experts are frequently thought of as critics: they tell you what is right and wrong. Facilitators are similar to spectators: they may stand at the front of the room, but they are on the sidelines of the debate. Doers take responsibility for making things happen: they produce. Performance consultants play all three roles, depending on the client's needs and what the client wants to accomplish.

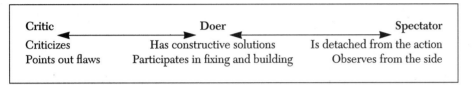

Critic	Doer	Spectator
Criticizes	Has constructive solutions	Is detached from the action
Points out flaws	Participates in fixing and building	Observes from the side

Figure 1.2. The Critic-Doer-Spectator Continuum

Staying Free of Bias

Another thing that distinguishes performance consultants from other consultants is their lack of bias in terms of finding a solution. Other consultants presume the solution rests within their specialty (which is what Mark came to realize). For example, management consultants assume problems can be solved through better leadership and by changing the organizational structure. Quality consultants assume performance can be improved through cross-functional teams and improved processes. Trainers start with the premise that the solution is training. Performance consultants, however, are not biased toward a specific solution. Instead, our approach is to follow a systematic process to determine what contributes to performance and what impedes it. For example, we don't assume, we find out if

- People really have access to the relevant information, and that information is in understandable form
- There are consequences that reinforce the desired behaviors and outcomes
- The organizational environment supports the requirements of the job
- People get consistent, clear directions
- Processes are well-defined and efficient
- Functions and jobs are designed around key processes
- People have the resources and skills they need to be effective

Focusing on Outcomes and Measured Results

As performance consultants, we pay attention to the outcomes or consequences of what is done to improve performance. This means that we measure the outcomes or results of an intervention and assess whether or not performance has improved as a result of it.

I like to think that we challenge our own and other people's thinking. We find out what is really happening so we can bring clarity to situations. We fit pieces together and make sense out of what is going on. This is why it takes special skills to be an effective performance consultant.

DEFINING PERFORMANCE CONSULTING

"Be a leader!" "Be world-class!" "Be customer-focused!" These are just some of the slogans companies use to communicate what they want their employees to do. But if you were to stop people and ask them what each of these slogans means, you would probably get many different answers. The same would be true if you were to ask them what performance consulting is all about. If you want to be a performance consultant, you have to be clear about what it means to *you*. Once you are clear in your own mind about what a performance consultant is, you can develop a transition plan for yourself, because you will know where you are going.

An operational definition is a technique for understanding any new concept (such as performance consulting). Creating an operational definition of performance consulting will achieve three things: it will help you, your colleagues, and your clients come to some shared understanding of just what performance consulting is; it will help you clarify what it takes to be a performance consultant; and it will produce language you can use in your marketing materials.

An operational definition answers three questions: *what, why,* and *how.* When I use an operational definition to clarify a role, I frequently combine it with examples of the typical tasks involved, the required knowledge and skills (sometimes combined as *competencies*), and possible measures of the work performed by people in that job.

In Figure 1.3, an example of an operational definition, performance consulting is defined as a *practice.* You might think of it as a discipline, a role, a process, or something else, however. In this example the reason for the practice of performance consulting (the *why*) is identified as "to optimize performance." You might come up with a different reason, such as to ensure that everyone has what they need to excel, to eliminate barriers to performance, to equip management to better support performance, or to make sure an investment in training pays off by identifying what has to be in place for people to apply what they learn. The example defines the execution (the *how*) of performance consulting as "the application of proven processes." You might see it in terms of

Figure 1.3. Example of an Operational Definition of Performance Consulting

What: Performance consulting is the practice of taking a disciplined approach to assessing individual and organizational effectiveness, diagnosing causes of human performance problems, and recommending a set of interventions. The approach is based on a body of knowledge about organizational and human performance. The outcome is advice on how to improve organizational and people performance.			
Why: To optimize human and organizational performance.			
How: The practice is done through the application of proven processes.			
Typical tasks include:	*Knowledge*	*Skills*	*Expected results*
• Assess individual and organizational performance *(performance analysis)*			
• Identify factors impeding and contributing to performance *(cause analysis)*			
• Select, recommend, and evaluate interventions *(interventions)*			
• Facilitate the development and use of measures and evaluation strategies *(evaluation)*			
• Facilitate the implementation of interventions and the adoption of new behaviors *(implementation)*			

changing your relationship with clients, increasing your scope of services, or shifting from delivery to brokering services. My point is that the label "performance consulting" has to be meaningful to *you.* It should be based on what your clients and organization require of you, should accurately reflect your role in the organization, and should match the four attributes described earlier (being an expert yet a facilitator, playing multiple roles, maintaining a bias-free approach, and focusing on outcomes). Chapter Five provides an example of a job description that integrates all of the elements of an operational definition.

I also find it helpful to look at what the literature says about performance consulting. This does not mean you have to accept what others say, but you do need to know if your understanding of performance consulting differs from others' understanding, and if so, how. For example, the Department of Labor's *Dictionary of Occupational Titles* describes a consultant as someone who "consults with clients to define a need or problem, conducts studies and surveys to obtain data, and analyzes the data to advise on or recommend a solution." This is the *what*. The definition also states that a consultant "utiliz[es] knowledge of theory, principles, or technology of a specific discipline or field of specialization." This is the *how*. Finally, it defines the specific activities (the tasks) a consultant engages in (paraphrased here):

- *Consults* with clients to ascertain and define the need or problem area, and determines the scope of investigation required to obtain a solution

- *Conducts a study or survey* on the need or problem to obtain data required to find a solution

- *Analyzes the data* to determine a solution, such as implementing alternative methods and procedures, changing processing methods and practices, modifying machines or equipment, or redesigning products or services

- *Advises clients* on alternative methods of solving a problem, or recommends a specific solution

In one study the American Society for Training and Development (ASTD) identified the roles HRD professionals play in organizations. I think that four of the roles they identified fall under performance consulting (see Figure 1.4).

When you review all of the roles, you may come to a different understanding of which ones fit under performance consulting. The ASTD also listed thirty-five HRD competencies. Figure 1.5 lists the ones that I think relate directly to performance consulting.

Again, when you review all thirty-five competencies you may come to a different conclusion. The important thing is to be clear about

---

1. *Researcher:* the role of identifying, developing, or testing new information and translating the information into its implications for improved individual or organizational performance

3. *Organizational change agent:* the role of influencing and supporting changes in organizational behavior

4. *Needs analyst:* the role of identifying ideal and actual performance and performance conditions and determining causes of discrepancies between the two

10. *Evaluator:* the role of identifying the impact of an intervention on individual or organizational effectiveness

---

Figure 1.4. The ASTD's HRD Roles That Relate to Performance Consulting.

Note: **The numbers in the figure are the same numbers as on the ASTD's original list. (The text has been paraphrased, however.)**

- What you think performance consulting is

- Why performance consulting is needed

- How performance consultants accomplish what they say they accomplish

- The kinds of things a performance consultant does

- The skills and knowledge required

- How you want your effectiveness measured

FIELD TOOLS: THE OPERATIONAL DEFINITION

It is important to be clear about what you mean by performance consulting, because you will have to explain it to others. Here are some ideas for developing your own definition. Use the worksheet in Figure 1.6 to record your decisions.

1. Whether you are an internal consultant or an independent, external consultant, set up a special planning session.

2. Include staff or colleagues and key customers who support your decision to become a performance consultant or to add consulting to your scope of services. Because you already have a relationship with these people, they should have a vested interest in what services you can provide.

3. Tell everyone that the agenda is to help you (and those who work with you) to define performance consulting.

4. Ask everyone to think about what performance consulting means to them and to be ready to bring those thoughts to the meeting.

5. Once you are together, ask the group these questions:

   • "What does performance consulting mean to you?"

   • "How would my behavior have to change for you to call me a performance consultant?"

   • "If I were to produce a brochure listing my products and services, what would I have to list for you to believe I am a performance consultant?"

   • "Why would you want me to change from what I do now to performance consulting?"

   • "Why would you *not* want me to change from what I do now?"

   • "Who would benefit from my becoming a performance consultant (or adding consulting to my scope of services)?"

   • "Who might *not* benefit from my becoming a performance consultant?"

   • "How would I do my work differently if I were a performance consultant?"

   • "How would my relationships and interactions with clients be different if I were a performance consultant?"

   • "What are the tasks a performance consultant typically does? Which of those tasks are different from what I do now?"

   • "What must a performance consultant know to do these tasks? What must I know that I do not know now?"

   • "What are the skills a performance consultant must have? Which of these skills are different from the ones I have now?"

Figure 1.5. The ASTD's HRD Competencies That Relate to Performance Consulting.

Note: **The numbers in the figure are the same numbers as on the ASTD's original list.**

TECHNICAL COMPETENCIES: having functional skills and knowledge

3. *Competency identification* (identifying the knowledge and skill requirements of jobs, tasks, and roles) requires skill in identifying inputs and assessing their accuracy and completeness.

7. *Objectives preparation* (preparing clear statements that describe desired outputs) requires skill in identifying relevant outputs and proposing criteria to measure their attainment.

8. *Performance observation* (tracking and describing behaviors and their effects) requires skill in identifying what drives or causes behaviors.

BUSINESS COMPETENCIES: having a strong management, economics, or administration base

12. *Business understanding* (knowing how the functions of a business work and relate to one another; knowing the economic impact of business decisions) requires tools for identifying how business functions interrelate and the economic impact of those relationships.

13. *Cost-benefit analysis* (assessing alternatives in terms of their financial, psychological, and strategic advantages and disadvantages) requires tools for identifying direct and indirect costs, judging probability, and weighing trade-offs.

15. *Industry understanding* (knowing the key concepts and variables, such as critical issues, economic vulnerabilities, measurements, distribution channels, inputs, outputs, and information sources, that define an industry or section) is made easier with tools that capture and make public issues so that they can be discussed and the need for better data (versus folklore) determined.

16. *Organizational behavior understanding* (seeing organizations as dynamic, political, economic, and social systems that have multiple goals; using this larger framework for understanding and influencing events and change) requires organizational models and tools for describing the system components and how they interplay.

17. *Organizational development theories and techniques understanding* (knowing the techniques and methods used in organizational development; understanding their appropriate use) requires models and methods and skill in their use.

18. *Organizational understanding* (knowing the strategy, structure, power networks, financial position, and systems of a specific organization) requires skill in gaining access to information and interpreting that information.

- "How might my clients measure the cost benefit of my operating as a performance consultant?"

- "What would I have to have (or buy) to be an effective consultant in terms of resources, skills, client relations, systems, and so on?"

6. Take the results of what you learn and develop an operational definition of performance consulting. Complete as many of the elements (tasks, knowledge, skills, results) as you can.

Figure 1.5. The ASTD's HRD Competencies That Relate to Performance Consulting, *cont'd.*

INTERPERSONAL COMPETENCIES: having a strong communication base

22. *Feedback* (communicating information, opinions, observations, and conclusions so that they are understood and can be acted upon) is helped by having techniques for discriminating useful information and assessing acceptance of that information.

23. *Group process skill* (influencing groups so that tasks, relationships, and individual needs are addressed).

24. *Negotiation skill* (securing win-win agreements while successfully representing a special interest in a decision-making process).

26. *Questioning* (gathering information by stimulating insight in individuals and groups through the use of interviews, questionnaires, and other probing methods) requires skill in selecting and using probing methods that reveal information that is relevant and leads to insight.

27. *Relationship building* (establishing relationships and networks across a broad range of people and groups) requires skill and methods to discriminate relevant from irrelevant cultural nuances and select appropriate behavior.

INTELLECTUAL COMPETENCIES: having knowledge and skill related to thinking and information processing

29. *Data reduction skill* (scanning, synthesizing, and drawing conclusions from data).

30. *Information search skill* (gathering information from printed and other recorded sources; identifying and using information specialists and reference services and aids).

31. *Intellectual versatility* (recognizing, exploring, and using a broad range of ideas and practices; thinking logically and creatively without undue influence from personal biases).

32. *Model-building skill* (conceptualizing and developing theoretical and practical frameworks that describe complete ideas in understandable, usable ways).

33. *Observing skill* (recognizing objectively what is happening in and across situations).

35. *Visioning skill* (projecting trends and visualizing possible and probable futures and their implications).

7. Ask the group to comment.

8. Modify your definition(s) until you are in agreement as to what a performance consultant is.

The definition should describe the business you are in. It should explain what you are about, why you are in business, and how you operate or do business. It should begin the process of identifying the things you do, what you have to know, what you have to be able to do, and how your success or effectiveness might be measured.

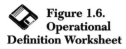
Figure 1.6. Operational Definition Worksheet

What:

Why:

How:

Typical tasks include	Required Knowledge	Required Skills	Expected results *Outputs:*
			Outcomes:

FIELD NOTES: CLARIFYING EXPECTATIONS

Mike worked for a large global company. The firm referred to itself, its franchisees, its suppliers and distributors, and its international investment partners collectively as "the system." Mike was asked to head up a new shared services department at corporate headquarters. The department's mandate was to institutionalize processes throughout the company, its subsidiaries, and suppliers that would improve the system's overall performance. The system's performance was measured in terms of consistent low costs, products that met standards, and increased market shares.

The people assigned to Mike's department had previously worked in training and development, logistics, quality assurance, finance, information systems (IS), word processing, and administration. Everyone in the department carried the title of "consultant specializing in performance improvement"—even those in word processing and administration.

Mike wanted his team to operate as internal consultants with expertise in measurement. When describing what he wanted to see from his team, he said things like, "Consultants stay focused, are politically astute, build alliances, shape performance, remain objective, and measure the financial impact of what they do." His team finally insisted that they all work together to better define what this meant. Figure 1.7 shows how they operationally defined Mike's expectations.

DEFINING YOUR OWN CONSULTING PROCESS

The new field of performance consulting can be confusing, not only to clients but also to those of us who want to play this role. I've found that documenting my consulting process helps me communicate what I do and how it differs from what other consultants do (see Figure 1.8). It also helps me more accurately estimate the time and resources required to fulfill the client's request, and it helps me explain where my involvement is important but might change, depending on the needs of the client. The phases in which I can add the greatest value are Phases I, II, III, IV, and VII. It is in these phases that I and other performance consultants bring discipline and proven procedures to our work that distinguish us from other types of consultants.

Phase I: Defining the Request

Phase I is about scoping out the request, the client's expectations, and the nature of the relationship. The outcome of Phase I is enough information for me to answer these questions:

- *Can I do it?* The request may be outside my area of expertise. I've learned not to try to be all things to all people. Chapters Three, Four, and Five describe in greater detail some of the general skills and knowledge required to be a successful consultant.

- *Do I want to do it?* Every request comes with trade-offs. Some requests, because of their timing, may put other projects at risk. Some requests come with so many constraints attached that they require extra resources just to manage the client and the project. This takes energy away from doing the real work.

- *Do I want to work with these people?* Some people are too busy, distracted, or uncommitted to be involved at the level necessary. Lack of involvement is a red flag, because it reduces the chances that my findings and recommendations will be accepted. Another red flag is being denied access to people who have key information and a stake in what is being proposed. Without the buy-in of stakeholders, the chances that the project will be successful over the long haul is minimal. Furthermore, lack of acceptance and adoption will eventually reflect negatively on the consultant.

- *What is the client's level of sophistication?* Unsophisticated clients increase my costs (by taking more of my time), and I may or may not be able to pass those increased costs on to the client. (Internal consultants can have the same problem, by the way.) Unsophisticated clients require more coaching and direction. This, in turn, requires a greater time commitment by the consultant, whether or not the consultant charges the client for it. Chapter Four has a process for qualifying the client.

Figure 1.7. Operational Definitions of Mike's Expectations

STAYING FOCUSED means having the skill, knowledge, and willingness to

- Discriminate between those actions or decisions that will produce the best outcomes and those that won't
- Act in ways that are more likely to produce the desired outcome, as opposed to ways that won't

Why stay focused? So resources will be directed toward those activities most likely to produce the desired outcomes.

How do we stay focused? By

- Directing resources and attention to things that matter
- Asking hard questions, challenging the relevance of others' actions
- Saying what is really going on, without condemnation

BEING POLITICALLY ASTUTE means having the skill, knowledge, and willingness to find out who influences decisions and actions.

Why be politically astute? So we will be in a position to influence decisions and actions.

How do we become politically astute? By

- Finding out what decision makers attend to and value
- Using that knowledge to establish relationships with them
- Using those relationships to strategically barter information, access, and support, without jeopardizing the business or our professional integrity

---

BUILDING ALLIANCES means having the skills, knowledge, and willingness to

- Identify what type of alliances are appropriate and when they are appropriate
- Define the purpose of the alliance (what we expect from it)

Why build alliances? So we can leverage the resources, intelligence, and power of the larger group.

How do we build alliances? By

- Developing a strategy for entering into alliances
- Sharing expectations with the other members of alliances
- Soliciting their expectations of us
- Setting mutual goals
- Developing a plan of action to advance those goals
- Committing to the plan
- Evaluating the usefulness of our business relationship

Figure 1.7. Operational Definitions of Mike's Expectations, *cont'd.*

SHAPING PERFORMANCE means having the skills, knowledge, and willingness to influence what others do and think.

Why shape performance? So other's actions and priorities will be aligned with what the organization requires to be successful, today and in the future.

How do we shape performance? By

- Sharing our expectations and thoughts
- Giving people accurate, timely, constructive feedback
- Responding to others in ways they will perceive as fair
- Modeling the behavior we expect from others
- Seeking win-win solutions
- Maintaining confidences
- Not misrepresenting others' actions
- Honoring our commitments
- Dealing directly with others

REMAINING OBJECTIVE means having the skills, knowledge, and willingness to remain detached.

Why be objective? So our judgment is not clouded by the emotions and motives of others.

How do we be objective? By

- Distinguishing between emotions, interpretations, facts (evidence), and conclusions
- Not getting caught up in the drama of the moment

MEASURING FINANCIAL IMPACTS means having the skills, knowledge, and willingness to

- Assess the financial impact of decisions or actions on the business as a whole, on business relationships, on other departments, and on other programs and projects

Why measure financial impacts? So we can recognize and act on opportunities to

- Optimize the financial impact of beneficial actions and decisions
- Avoid or minimize the financial impact of negative decisions or actions

How do we measure financial impacts? By

- Identifying and interpreting financial data
- Identifying decisions and actions that have financial implications

Phase I: Defining the request

Qualify the job.
Qualify the client.
Determine expectations.
Define working protocols.
Define roles, relationships, and responsibilities.
Scope out a plan.

Phase II: Fact-finding

Start with hypotheses.
Include all voices.
Use more than one method.
Look for corroborating evidence.
Apply rigor to control bias.
Consider the environment.

Phase III: Analyzing your findings

Compile the results.
Apply analytical techniques.
Look for significant findings and differences.
Identify the costs.
Find out the consequences on costs, satisfaction, image, and so on.
Report the results.

Phase IV: Designing the solution

Describe the audiences (direct and indirect).
Specify the requirements.
Specify the long-term support.
Specify communication and implementation requirements.
Specify the costs and benefits.
Specify other relevant success measures.
Specify the pilot test and rollout plans.
Specify how and who will measure results.

Phase V: Developing the solution

Prepare or secure materials, systems, and other required elements.
Prepare collateral and management support materials.
Prepare public relations materials.

Phase VI: Implementing the solution

Set up an implementation team.
Conduct the pilot test.
Analyze the findings.
Launch the rollout.

Phase VII: Measuring the results

Gather the data.
Compare to preestablished measures.
Report the results.

Figure 1.8. The Consulting Process

- *Is there any chance of making a difference?* Some problems are so complex that a long-range strategy is necessary. Before I accept an assignment, I want to know how long the sponsor and initial project team will stick around and, if they are replaced, whether it will be by people equally committed to the project. Chapter Five describes some of the environmental issues that contribute to performance problems.

- *How much does the current problem cost?* This information is key to determining the worth of the problem and the worth of the solution. Chapter Three is about determining costs, and Chapters Eight and Nine explain valuing and measuring problems in greater detail.

- *What will it take to complete the subsequent phases?* Before I begin an assignment I want to find out if I can (or should) do it alone, if I want the client to provide a team, or if I need to involve other professional resources.

- *How much will it cost the client?* Determining this includes calculating my fee (if you are an internal consultant it includes calculating what your time on the project will cost your organization) and the amount of any other required resources. I use this information to measure the client's return on investment, or payback.

Phase II: Fact-Finding

Phase II is about getting and validating the facts. What distinguishes performance consultants from other consultants is the rigor and discipline with which they gather data. I always point out to the client that I have documented procedures for assessing needs and for each of my data-gathering tactics, to control bias. How much data gathering I do and what type depends on the information I gain in Phase I.

Phase III: Analyzing

Phase III is about analyzing the results of the fact-finding phase. I point out that performance consultants purposefully look for corroborating evidence and that they use descriptive and inferential statistics in their analyses. Again, performance consultants stress their use of proven procedures and the discipline they bring to their work.

Phase IV: Designing the Solution

Phase IV is critical to understanding what resources will be required to develop, implement, and provide ongoing support for the solution to the client's problem.

Phase V: Developing the Solution

Phase V is a natural point for turning the project over to the client or another professional with the appropriate expertise. Nonetheless, I always include this phase as part of the process, because someone has to do it.

Phase VI: Implementing the Solution

Phase VI is another phase in which the performance consultant may or may not play a role. It depends on the nature of the assignment and what resources the client can dedicate to implementation.

Phase VII: Measuring the Results

Phase VII also distinguishes the performance consultant from other consultants. I believe that performance consultants, by definition, have to know how to measure what changed or improved as a result of implementing the solution or program.

There are a lot benefits to defining and describing how you do your work. It helps you communicate the scope of your services. It makes it easier for you to negotiate agreements concerning when you do and do not want to be involved. It helps the client understand all that goes into improving performance.

It helps you place a value on your services. Just as important, having a well-defined process enables you to determine how effectively and efficiently you do your work, by helping you measure the results of it. It is only by measuring your results that you can continuously improve what you do.

FIELD TECHNIQUES: DEFINING YOUR CONSULTING PROCESS

To define your own consulting process, meet with your team and other colleagues who support you in your desire to be an effective performance consultant. Then follow these steps:

1. Review the literature on performance consulting. See if there are any processes you think you might want to adopt or modify to better reflect your vision of how you want to operate.

2. Develop a vision for the role of performance consulting in your organization. Later in this chapter there are suggestions on how to develop a vision and mission statement.

3. Describe the process you use now when working with clients.

4. Identify where you want to add to or change your current process so that it will better support your vision.

5. Decide on how you want to describe your overall consulting process, such as with a flowchart or a list of procedures.

6. Document your consulting process, and share it with supportive clients to get their feedback and confirm that it makes sense to them.

FIELD NOTES: DEFINING THE CONSULTING PROCESS

Mike's vision was for everyone on his staff to operate as internal consultants. As consultants he wanted them to

- Develop and consistently follow a consulting process for working with clients

- Develop subprocesses for defining needs, estimating required resources, providing solutions or services, measuring the cost benefits of those solutions or services, and shifting responsibility to their clients for implementing and maintaining the solutions

- Assess their clients' readiness and commitment to implementing the solutions and supporting the change over time

- Measure the results of their solutions or services in terms of cost benefits

- Measure how efficiently and effectively they handle each assignment

- Measure their customers' satisfaction with their services, the results, and the consulting relationship

- Measure the degree to which their solutions are implemented and their clients retain ownership of and accountability for them
- Continually improve their processes

Mike was particularly interested in measuring how well the team's recommendations were implemented and supported over time. To do this they would first have to assess their clients' capability to support a solution and their commitment to implementing it. In the past the company had invested significant dollars and human resources in developing good ideas and programs. Implementation of those ideas and programs, however, had been uneven, at best. Mike wanted to set up a process that would allow him to separate development accountability from implementation accountability. He and his staff identified the kinds of requests they expected to receive, based on past experience:

- Develop procedures for managers to assess suppliers' financial viability and determine appropriate profit margins
- Develop guidelines for managers to use in identifying cost drivers in a supply chain or product line
- Lead or participate in cross-functional teams charged with major initiatives, since their group has expertise in diagnosis (cause analysis) and measurement
- Arrange and coordinate meetings (miniconferences) for senior management, key suppliers, and partners
- Research trends and do financial analyses
- Prepare presentation materials and produce reports for limited and worldwide distribution
- Participate in developing specifications for information systems to track and communicate the financial performance of key products and specific markets
- Do needs analyses
- Do cost-benefit studies
- Consult on measurement
- Identify the training needs of supply chain and product managers
- Train managers in financial analysis, decision-making tools, word processing tools, and electronic system tools
- Outsource other training requirements

As admirable and challenging as these assignments might be, they would not improve the performance of the system without a commitment by its managers to implement solutions and measure the results. Mike knew he probably could not change the kinds of things senior management or the other departments asked for, but he could change how his department responded to their requests. With this in mind, Mike and his team decided to define how they would do business. They began by developing an overall consulting process for working with management and the other departments (see Figure 1.9).

Figure 1.9. Mike's Consulting Process

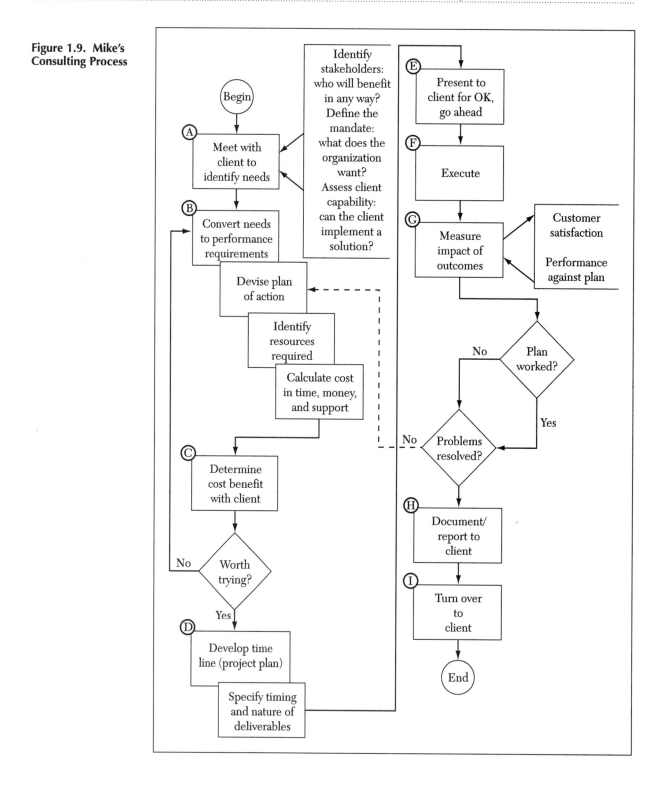

The first activity (labeled A in Figure 1.9) would be to meet with the client to develop an understanding of the client's request. The request could be to solve a problem, develop a product, or provide a service similar to what the team had done in the past. The outcome of those meetings (see B) would be enough information for the team to determine (1) what it would take in terms of resources (time and money) to fulfill the request (that is, the cost) and (2) the client's capability and commitment to following through once the request had been fulfilled. This step would require the team to place some economic value on their time and on any other required resources. The next activity (C) would be to meet with the client to mutually determine whether the potential gain (benefit) would be worth the estimated cost. Together, the consultants and client would determine (1) the worth of the effort, (2) if the client has the resources and commitment to actually implement or execute what is produced, and (3) how the value of the service or product would be determined after it is rendered or implemented.

Once the client and consultants agree to proceed, the next step (D) would be to develop a more detailed project plan, with a time line, milestones, and deliverables. Again, the client and consultant would either agree to the plan and time line (see E) or modify it. The steps under execute (see F) might be extensive or simple, depending on the complexity of the request. For Mike and his team, it was the steps involved in measuring the results (see G) and gaining the client's commitment to owning and managing the project (see I) that had been missing in the past. These were the two steps that would set his department apart from others brought in to fix problems and make improvements.

The overall process required everyone on Mike's team to become expert at establishing shared expectations with clients, assessing clients' readiness and willingness to use what was developed, determining the cost of improving (or not improving) performance, planning and managing projects, and measuring the results or outcomes of what happens. These were the required skills to be a consultant in Mike's department.

Each of Mike's subteams—finance, word processing, training, IS, and logistics—further refined the overall process to make it more germane to the kinds of requests they might handle. The IS team, for example, added a component under F (execute) for testing new application software and proving its acceptance and value before rolling it out across the system. Finance was the subteam that operated closest to the role of experts. They spent most of their time supplying quick answers. However, they wanted to work on more strategic projects. So they decided to sort requests for their services into one of three categories: help desk; business as usual, or regular reports; and strategic assignments. They then set up different processes for each type of request. This allowed the finance group to track what they did and who they did it for and to develop more efficient procedures for measuring their results (see Figure 1.10).

Having a common process (with variations for specific kinds of requests) resulted in a number of benefits. It gave everyone on the team a better understanding of what the others did and what each could contribute that would be of

Figure 1.10. The Finance Team's Process

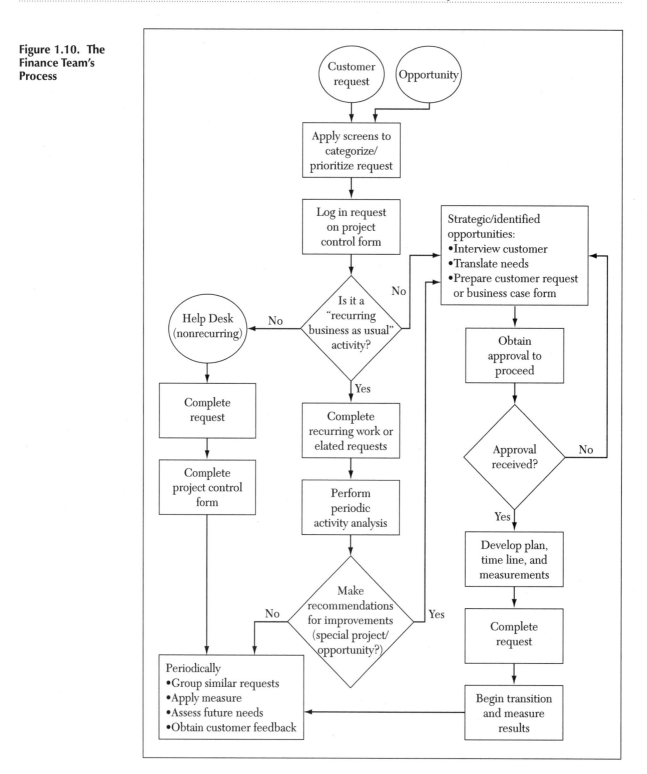

value to the system. It gave everyone a better understanding of what consulting was all about. It even spurred them to learn more about measurement and to improve their consulting skills (especially in facilitation and negotiation). It also gave everyone a basis for measuring their own efficiency and effectiveness.

THE IMPORTANCE OF A VISION AND MISSION

I am a big believer in vision and mission statements and create them for every assignment and project plan. Whenever I get frustrated with the need to develop one more vision or mission statement for myself or a client, I keep this saying, from an unknown businessperson, in mind: "The purpose of planning is to uncover the things we must do today in order to have a future."

I've learned that I have to create a vision to be effective and that a mission statement helps me stay on track. I may or may not share my vision and mission with my client; however, they are an integral part of my process for understanding what the client wants and needs, and they provide a basis for evaluating my effectiveness.

A vision statement describes what you see as the possible and desirable future state of your role or function or of the project or task. A mission statement says what you, the role or function, or the project or task is all about. I always start with the vision and then develop the mission. The sequence doesn't really matter; what does matter is having a sense of the future and being clear about your purpose. Figure 1.11 presents my vision and mission for this fieldbook.

Figure 1.11. Vision and Mission for This Fieldbook

Vision: That training and HRD professionals will be recognized and rewarded for their expertise in performance consulting, through the use of innovative yet practical tools that engage team members and clients in the processes of discovery, diagnosis, problem solving, and measuring results.

Mission: To provide training and HRD professionals with the tools and techniques to

- Move into performance consulting
- Establish themselves as credible members of their company's management team
- Use their current activities (delivery, development, facilitation, and so on) to build their consulting skills and position themselves as capable, savvy businesspeople
- Give management a more comprehensive picture of the factors that impede and support human performance
- Get the information they need to identify, compare, and recommend an array of appropriate interventions that are most likely to achieve alignment between goals and outcomes
- Join with management in measuring the impact or results of interventions

FIELD NOTES: THE FINANCE TEAM'S VISION AND MISSION

Mike's finance team developed the mission and vision statements presented in Figure 1.12. The group's vision indicates their desire to see systems in place that will enable their clients to make wise business decisions on their own. The group hopes for a day when the system's guidelines and information systems and the client's competence level are sufficient that the finance group can permanently get out of the help-desk business.

Figure 1.12. The Finance Team's Vision and Mission Statements

---

Vision: A financial infrastructure that will enable the product managers and their supply chains to make effective business decisions.

Mission: In our efforts to achieve our vision, the financial group will

- Provide leadership on strategic initiatives
- Provide leadership in the development of financial guidelines
- Establish baseline financial and technical competencies for all product managers
- Provide leadership in the development of a business and financial information structure
- Take and communicate a position and provide recommendations on current business issues

---

The group's mission indicates the relationship they want with the client (one of leadership) and what they will do to achieve their vision (provide guidance, set standards, offer expert opinions, and make recommendations).

FIELD TECHNIQUES: SETTING A GOAL FOR YOURSELF

To shift your role from a specific discipline to performance consulting, set a goal for yourself:

1. Look at the consulting continuums in Figures 1.1 and 1.2. Where do you fall on these continuums today? Where do you want to be one year from now? What will you accept as evidence that you have made a change?

2. Review the attributes that distinguish performance consultants from other types of consultants. How closely do these attributes reflect how you are perceived by your clients or how you work with them now? What do you want to change about how you work with your clients and about the type of work you do?

3. Review what the literature says about performance consulting. When can you come up with a definition that works for you?

4. Look at the different consulting processes discussed in this chapter (Figures 1.8, 1.9, and 1.10). Do you have a standardized process for how you consult? What will it take for you to develop a process of your own or adopt a process similar to one of these? How do you want to change the process so that it better fits your situation?

5. Use the operational definition worksheet (Figure 1.6) to define performance consulting for yourself. You might want to develop separate definitions for each task. As you work through this fieldbook, go back and list on the worksheet what you think it is critical for you to know and to be able to do and what you will take as evidence of success. Figure 1.13 lists some of the competencies I think performance consultants need. Play with it, build on it, and make it work for you.

6. Develop a new vision and mission for your role or function.

SUMMARY

If you want to be a performance consultant, then you have to define performance consulting for yourself. You have to develop a process for how you will do business. Just calling yourself a performance consultant is not enough. You need a process, coupled with procedures, tools, and techniques, that

- Integrates the attributes of an expert with those of a facilitator
- Puts you in a position to join with clients as a partner
- Allows you to monitor, measure, and improve your own effectiveness
- Enables you to efficiently and effectively deliver all of your services
- Helps you measure the results of your services

WHERE TO LEARN MORE

Kaufman, R., Thiagarajan, S., and MacGillis, P. (Eds.), *The Guidebook for Performance Improvement* (San Francisco: Jossey-Bass/Pfeiffer, 1997). This guidebook contains six sections: Origins, Direction Finding and Goal Setting, Analysis, Design and Development, Implementation, and Evaluation. It presents the ideas and perspectives of thirty-one authors and is a basic book for the performance consultant.

Robinson, D. G., and Robinson, J., *Performance Consulting* (San Francisco: Berrett-Koehler, 1995). This is one of the earlier books on performance consulting. On page 6 the authors define performance consulting as "the process by which we can work with management and others to identify and achieve performance excellence linked to business goals."

Stolovitch, H., and Keeps, E. (Eds.), *Handbook of Human Performance Technology* (San Francisco: Jossey-Bass, 1992). This handbook contains six sections: The Fundamentals of Human Performance Technology, The General Process of Human Performance Technology, Human Performance Interventions of a Noninstructional Nature, Human Performance Interventions of an Instructional Nature, The Professional Practice of Human Performance Technology, and The Future of Human Performance Technology. Sections 2, 5, and 6 relate to the ideas in this chapter of the fieldbook.

Self-management:

- Make accurate self-assessments (test yourself).
- Have self-confidence (establish a presence).
- Have self-discipline (maintain a sense of priority).
- Maintain an efficiency orientation (always look to do it better).
- Manage your image (maintain external status).

Interpersonal:

- Maintain social objectivity (remain detached).
- Establish rapport (build connectedness).
- Engage in group processes (play the task and social roles).
- Cultivate social power (build alliances).
- Be spontaneous (act freely in the here and now).
- Generate cognitive dissonance (purposely provoke reflection).
- Be politically savvy (know whose agenda it is).
- Make use of reciprocity (trade favors without losing integrity).

Communication:

- Describe abstract concepts (create models; make analogies).

Reasoning:

- Maintain perceptual objectivity (view events from multiple perspectives simultaneously; engage in heuristic or systemic thinking).
- Engage in conceptualization (identify and recognize patterns in an assortment of information and develop a concept that describes the patterns or structures; think inductively).
- Use concepts diagnostically (test information by systematically applying it to a concept; think deductively).
- Practice logical thought (place events in a causal sequence).
- Be proactive (provoke activity to some purpose).
- Be concerned with impacts (assess impact on multiple elements).

Performance Management:

- Interview, observe, and survey (gather data).
- Analyze descriptive, inferential, and financial data (determine significance and correlations).
- Analyze language, symbols, behavior, norms, and rituals (understand social systems).

Figure 1.13. My List of Consulting Competencies

Chapter 2

The Transition

Some training and HRD departments find the transition to performance consulting difficult. There are a number of reasons why the journey is not a simple one. For example, it requires changing how you operate, learning a different set of skills, and revisiting your own premises about what you can and cannot do.

FIELD NOTES: FALSE STARTS

Doug changed the name of his department from Training and Development to Training and Performance. But he did little else. When people asked him what was now different about what his department did, he had difficulty answering. Doug lacked a clear picture of what performance consulting is and a plan for making the transition to it. As a result, nothing in his department really changed.

Doug's situation is common. Training departments often try to move into performance consulting simply by changing their name. Although a name change can help, it is not enough. You have to be able to explain what performance consulting is, why you are moving to it, and how you will operate differently as a result of the change. You have to offer the products and services a performance consultant provides, measure what you do and how you do it, and promote your new services. You have to have a plan.

When I'm asked about how to make the transition to performance consulting, I talk about the importance of having a plan. The plan should include

- *A destination.* It is hard to arrive anywhere without a destination in mind. Defining performance consulting and preparing a vision and mission statement for yourself will complete your picture of where you are headed. A vision describes how your world will be once you have successfully completed your mission. A mission statement explains what you are all about, what you do, and the business you are in.

- *A list of available resources.* Every trip requires resources. In this case resources include your consulting processes and procedures, your current products and services, your skills and knowledge, and your relationships.

- *A strategy.* This is your game plan for getting to your destination. Your game plan might be to leverage your resources, for example, or to get out of what you are doing now so that you can redirect your resources toward performance consulting. Another game plan might be to build strategic alliances. You might come up with other strategies as well.

- *Measures.* Measures will help you prove that taking on the new role of performance consultant has been a benefit to your organization and your clients.

The process of developing and carrying out a plan is not particularly linear, but having a destination in mind at the beginning helps. Once you have decided on a destination you can think about how you will get there, what resources you will need to get there, and how to measure your success once you've arrived. For example, if your strategy is to leverage your resources, then those resources have to be well established. If your strategy is to build strategic alliances, then you may not have to do anything to your resources. If your strategy is to stop what you are doing now so that you can redirect your resources, then you may have to find someone else to take over what you no longer want to do. If your strategy is to expand your services, then you may have to develop yourself so that you can take on new responsibilities. What is important is to look at where you are now and decide what is a reasonable course of action for yourself. You can't always finish one step before going on to the next. Instead, as you learn and gain success you may have to circle back and pick up some steps you bypassed earlier.

FIELD TECHNIQUES: MAKING THE TRANSITION TO PERFORMANCE CONSULTING

Here are some things you can do to move from your current role to that of performance consulting (notice that the things covered in Chapter One, making definitions and mapping out processes, occur early in the plan):

Choosing a Destination
- Define the role of performance consulting.
- Develop a vision and mission statement.

Identifying Your Resources

- Define and describe your process for how you will do business (that is, how you will interface with your clients).

- Identify the products and services you now offer, those you want to offer, and to whom you want to offer them (this is covered in this chapter).

- Develop tools and techniques to help you build skill and confidence in your new role (this is covered in Chapters Three and Four).

- Refine your processes for and approaches to discovery, diagnosis, treatment, and measurement (you will find models you can use and modify for this purpose throughout the fieldbook).

- Identify what resources you will require to be effective (additional processes, skills, systems, and so on).

Developing a Strategy

- Continue to learn about the dynamics of organizational and people performance, what organizations can do to improve performance, and how to measure performance and results.

- Build strategic alliances with key staff (such as finance, legal, and marketing managers) and with line personnel from the organization's core business.

- Identify a willing customer with a need, and build your confidence by taking on projects that are just at the edge of your comfort zone.

- Manage your relationships and image.

- Market and promote your services and successes.

Defining Measures

- Establish your performance standards.

- Measure the results of what you do and the interventions you recommend.

- Measure your own efficiency and effectiveness.

It is important to start with your destination; however, you will probably move back and forth from resources to strategy to measures and back to resources again. For example, this chapter jumps ahead to measures (setting performance standards) and then goes back to resources (defining your products and services).

FIELD NOTES: MAKING THE TRANSITION

Kelly was head of a centralized training department at a large insurance company. The company had experienced layoffs in the past, and training was one of the first departments to be eliminated. Kelly did not want to go through that again. She believed that by limiting her department's services to training, she and her staff would be at risk for future layoffs. She wanted to expand their services to include consulting on how to improve people performance. She knew such a transition would not be easy. Her staff were all trainers. Her line managers only asked for training. Her students only wanted classroom training. Yet the cost of training was increasingly under attack. Neither she nor her clients could show how training made a difference to the company. She had to change what her department did and how it operated so that the value they added to the company could no longer be questioned.

She began by redefining what her department did and how it would do business. She and her staff built a new vision and mission for the department. Next they changed the name of the department to Learning and Performance Improvement. They expanded their list of products and services to include analysis, coaching, and consultation on evaluating performance. The process of building a plan gave everyone a much deeper understanding of what they did, what they wanted to do differently, who they wanted to serve, and what they had to do to make the change real. Their next step was to learn more about assessment and measurement. They defined their processes and added new tools to help them operate more efficiently. They found a friendly and willing client. They tried out their processes and tools. They became known as performance consultants.

ESTABLISHING YOUR OWN PERFORMANCE STANDARDS

About the same time that you are working on your plan, you should begin to think about how you want your work to be evaluated. There will come a time when someone will ask you about the value of performance consulting, and you will be better off if you have already set up your measures of success. Your consulting process and plan should help you come up with some performance standards. Without standards you cannot compare your performance today with what you did in the past and what you do in the future. You do not have to know what your assignment is to set your performance standards. Instead, set standards based on your process and the tools and techniques you will use to carry out your assignments. Figure 2.1 lists the standards I use.

With these standards as my guide, I can measure how well my processes, tools, and techniques have enabled me to be

1. *Efficient:*
   - How quickly did I scope out a job and determine what it would take, in terms of time and money, for me to deliver the requested product or service?

Figure 2.1. My Consulting Process Standards

My *efficiency standards* set targets for

- The time required to scope out a job and determine what it will take to deliver on the request
- The time required to fulfill a request (cycle time)

My *responsiveness standards* set targets for

- How much time passes before I respond to a request
- How much time passes before I start an assignment

My *accuracy standards* set targets for

- Allowable differences between cost and time estimates and actual expenditures
- Allowable differences between what I expect an assignment to be and what it actually turns out to be

My *effectiveness standards* set targets for

- Acceptable levels of client commitment, cooperation, and confidence
- How well my interventions accomplish what I intend them to accomplish

My *cost standards* set targets for

- The cost-benefit ratio of my services
- The cost-benefit ratio of the interventions I recommend

- How long did a project actually take? (What was the cycle time?) Even if the cycle time for a project is longer than it should have been because of events beyond my control, measuring it gives me information that will help me improve how I handle what is under my control on the next job.

2. *Responsive:*

- How long was it before I got around to actually meeting with the client to find out what the request was?
- How much time passed before I actually got started on the assignment? Again, delays may be beyond my control, but they still add to my costs. Tracking this information puts me in a better position to negotiate for faster turnarounds on approvals, reviews, and so on in the future.

3. *Accurate:*

- Did my estimate of how much of my time the assignment would take differ significantly from what it actually took?
- Did I acquire an accurate understanding of the job in the beginning, so that my surprises were few? Every job brings with it the possibility of unanticipated complications. It is only by comparing what I thought at the beginning of a job with what I knew at the end that I can improve my process for qualifying jobs and clients.

4. *Effective:*

- Did I gain the client's commitment to proceed? Did I secure the client's cooperation throughout the project? Did I build the client's confidence in what I did and how I did it?

- Did the solutions I suggested work? Again, a lot of variables can come into play when it comes to implementing a major program. If I don't measure my results, though, I'll never know how well I managed the variables that were within my control or helped the client manage those within its control.

5. *Cost-effective:*

- Did the client feel that the investment in my services was worth it?

- Did the benefit gained from the solution or intervention exceed the cost? When clients get my bill, I want them to think only about the value they received. Even internal consultants should be sensitive to this. Your services did cost your client: whether you are an external or an internal consultant, you want your clients to feel that their needs were met and that your involvement was worth what it cost them.

You can use the following suggestions to develop standards that will help you measure how effective your processes are and how well your suggestions meet your clients' requirements.

FIELD TECHNIQUES: MEASURING WHAT YOU DO NOW

1. Create an intake process for meeting with clients to scope out each assignment or request.

2. Create a mechanism (a time log, calendar, or project plan) for tracking how long it takes you to develop an understanding of the client's request, develop a proposal or work plan for the client, execute each step of the plan, and measure the results of what was done.

3. Track your time over one month or for at least one assignment.

4. Classify the time you spend on each phase or specific step of your process in terms of efficiency, and use this information as a point of comparison for future work (that is, as a baseline).

5. Identify phases or steps for which you think you could develop better procedures or improve your skills to reduce your cycle times or make better use of your time.

6. Set standards for yourself in terms of how efficient or effective you want to be.

7. Continue to track your time, and compare it to your standards or baseline.

8. Continue to identify those phases in which you think you could work more efficiently.

9. Redesign your process or improve your procedures in ways that help you become more efficient.

**FIELD NOTES: MEASURING THE
CONSULTING PROCESS AND ITS RESULTS**

Because each of Mike's subteams (training, finance, IS, logistics, and word processing) now followed a common consulting process, Mike could develop a way to evaluate everyone's performance. To do this Mike developed a table of consultant behaviors and results (reproduced in Figure 2.2). The column heads (across the top) list the five areas of performance Mike wanted to evaluate. The first column lists different levels of consulting proficiency, starting with least proficient (the top row) and progressing to most proficient (the bottom row). The examples in column 2 illustrate how consultants at various levels of proficiency use processes, from not at all (in the case of the least proficient consultants) to systematically and expertly (in the case of the most proficient ones). Columns 3 and 4 deal with how well a consultant estimates the resources required to fulfill a request and then assesses his or her estimates against what is actually required. The last two columns are about how effective a consultant's subprocesses are at measuring customer satisfaction and determining cost-benefit ratios for the work performed.

The rows list behaviors and outputs that Mike used as baselines to measure performance. The first three rows list behaviors and results that reflect inadequate performance. The fourth row lists behaviors and results that Mike would accept as evidence of meeting expectations. The last row lists behaviors and results that indicate the consultant exceeds expectations. To exceed Mike's expectations, a consultant had to use well-defined, efficient processes that resulted in services that met customer needs and added value to the system.

The operational definition that the team had come up with based on Mike's definition of consulting (Figure 1.7), the picture of the consulting process they produced (Figure 1.9), and Mike's list of performance measures (Figure 2.2) gave everyone a better understanding of the behaviors and results Mike was looking for.

ALIGNING YOUR PRODUCTS AND SERVICES WITH YOUR NEW ROLE

Once you have a destination in mind and a plan drawn up, the next step is to take a hard look at what you do and compare it to what you *want* to do. I find that people who work in training and HRD have usually inherited what they do. They may have initiated and developed some of their programs, but for the most part their department's programs were in place when they were hired. I also find that people don't know why they do what they do. The reasons, or business drivers, behind their programs have long been forgotten.

Level of proficiency	Using systematic processes	Estimating efficiently
Not visible. **You are not meeting expectations.**	You do not use a systematic process in your work with clients.	You lack a process for predicting the resources required to fill requests.
Visible. **There is room for improvement.**	You may follow a systematic process on one or two major projects.	You may follow a process to predict what is required.
Stable. **You're close.**	You follow a systematic process on all major projects.	Your process for predicting what is required can be completed within one week.
Capable. **You meet expectations; you've got it!**	You always follow a systematic process in working with clients.	You use a regular process to predict what will be required to fulfill each request in terms of time and expenses.
Optimum. **You exceed expectations as part of your regular way of doing business!**	You are considered an expert at performance consulting.	You can estimate the cost to diagnose a performance problem (not including required outside resources) and recommend appropriate interventions within twenty-four hours.

Figure 2.2. Mike's Expectations for Consulting Proficiency

Business drivers are the reasons why organizations agree to fund the development and delivery of programs and services. Most programs and services are offered for one of two reasons:

1. They are created in response to some business need.
2. They are created because someone in the organization wanted them and got the funding under the guise of meeting a business need.

Programs and services that are created in response to a business need include things like

- Job-specific training that is implemented because there is no other cost-effective way for people to learn the job. These programs are offered to new hires and people who are transferred or internally promoted, because

Estimating accurately	Assessing customer confidence	Measuring results
You have no process for comparing what you predicted would be required to what was actually required.	You have no way to clearly demonstrate customer satisfaction.	You cannot show your clients a clear cost-benefit relationship.
You may follow a process to track actual requirements.	You may follow a process to determine customer satisfaction (such as a survey).	You may follow a process to determine costs and benefits.
You track actual costs in total.	You follow a process to determine customer satisfaction, with particular emphasis only on the quality of your work.	You follow a process to determine benefits and costs over time (ongoing maintenance costs, administrative costs, execution costs, and so on).
You have a process to compare your predictions with reality.	You have a process to assess customer confidence, by measuring benefits achieved, deadlines met, and overall customer satisfaction.	You have institutionalized a process for doing cost-benefit analyses.
You demonstrate continuous improvement in your ability to diagnose problems, recommend interventions, and measure results.	You are asked to do nontraditional work and are perceived as an expert in measurement.	You quantify the benefits of interventions to the organization and have a system to predict future benefits.

Figure 2.2. Mike's Expectations for Consulting Proficiency, cont'd.

the job or task is not easily learned through traditional academic or on-the-job programs.

- Mandated programs that are in place because there is no other cost-effective way to satisfy some regulatory requirement. These programs are offered so the organization can comply with some law or regulation. Examples are safety programs and other programs used to certify or maintain certification.

- HR programs initiated because they are an integral part of a process, such as new-hire orientation, performance appraisals, and performance management.

- Programs used to support or deploy an organizational strategy. Examples include new-technology efforts, applying quality improvement principles to work processes, shifting work away from individuals and toward cross-functional teams, and working with customers to identify their requirements.

- Skill-building programs offered in response to an identified skill deficiency, such as in financial analysis, coaching, or developing standards. Career development programs may go here, too.
- Product or market support programs created to support the selling of new products or the servicing of new markets.

FIELD TECHNIQUES: IDENTIFYING BUSINESS DRIVERS

Before you can align your products and services to the needs of the organization, you need to examine why the organization maintains the programs and services it now has. Start by asking these questions:

- Why was this program created or this service offered?
- Has the need been satisfied? If not, is there a better way to satisfy the need? If yes, then why is it still being done?
- Who would be affected if the organization no longer offered the program or service? How would they be affected?

FIELD TOOLS: PRODUCT PORTFOLIO WORKSHEETS

Before you can become something different, it helps to examine what you do now and assess the demands it places on you. There are two worksheets here for doing that. Product Portfolio Worksheet 1 (see Figure 2.3) gives you an overall picture of your current products and services, that is, the business you are in today. Product Portfolio Worksheet 2 (see Figure 2.4) gives you a picture of how well your current and future products and services will perform.

Together, these worksheets will help you better understand

- Your current and future products or services
- The business reason, or driver, behind each product or service you provide
- The people who depend on your products or services
- The resources required to deliver those products or services
- What, if any, products or services you can eliminate or devote less resources to
- What, if any, products or services would bring greater value if delivered differently
- Where you can develop a business case for changing what you do or improving how you do it

Both worksheets will help you identify opportunities to modify and improve what you do. You can use both worksheets to examine your current products or services and any new ones you add as a result of moving into performance consulting.

Products and Services	Customer	Business Driver	Methods (how delivered)	Resources Required
1.				
2.				
3.				
4.				
5.				
6.				
7.				
8.				
9.				
10.				

**Figure 2.3.
Product Portfolio
Worksheet 1**

Product Portfolio Worksheet 1

Use Product Portfolio Worksheet 1 to

- Clarify and gain consensus on what you do now, for whom you do it, why you do it, and the resources required to deliver your current products or services

- Reach consensus on what it is you want to do in the future, for whom you want to do it, why you want to do it, and the resources your proposed products or services will require

- Communicate to clients what you do today and what you want to do in the future

The worksheet is a simple matrix. The column headings that I find most useful are (1) some description of the product or service, (2) a description of the client or user, (3) a definition of the business driver, (4) a description of how the product or service is currently delivered, and (5) an account of how many resources it requires. You can modify the columns to meet your own needs.

Depending on the number of programs or projects you are responsible for, you may want to fill out a different worksheet for each program type (training, facilitation, consulting, services), each client, each different curriculum, or each delivery mechanism. Here is how to use the worksheet:

Part 1								
1. Program or service	2. Customer	3. Driver	4. Dates	5. Percent of market	6. Delivery	7. Frequency	8. No-shows and cancellations	9. Owner

1. What is the name of the program or service?

2. Who are the customers?

3. What was the initial reason behind the service? What problem was it designed to solve?

4. When was it originally introduced? When was it last updated?

5. What was the size of the target market? How many have been served to date?

6. How is it delivered (electronically, by contract personnel, by professional staff, by the customer, on the job)? Who does the delivering (an instructor, a supervisor, a vendor, a local college)?

7. How frequently is it offered or performed (daily, weekly, quarterly, when asked)?

8. What is the average level of participation (class size)? What is the trend in no-shows or cancellations?

9. Who owns the program (your organization or a vendor)?

**Figure 2.4.
Product Portfolio
Worksheet 2**

1. *List the program, product, or service* you currently offer. Be sure to include services like contracting, managing projects, selecting vendors, preparing documents of understanding, screening vendors, training trainers, qualifying trainers, registering students, administering student files, producing and maintaining course materials, scheduling, and managing facilities and equipment.

2. *List the customers* for your products or services.

3. *List the business driver* behind each product or service. For example, is it mandated, connected with turnover, or required for certification?

4. *Briefly describe how you deliver* the product or service at present. For example, is it delivered one-on-one or in a classroom setting? Is it delivered electronically, or is it self-administered? Is it offered at a local college or outsourced to a vendor?

Part 2						Part 3		
10. Rating						11. Measures used	12. Resources	13. Comments
Q	IC	DC	E	L	O			

10. You and the people who help you administer, schedule, and deliver the program or service should individually and then together rate it on a scale from 1 (worst/least positive) to 5 (best/most positive) for each of these factors:
    - quality (Q)
    - indirect costs (IC)
    - direct costs (DC; together IC and DC tell you your delivery cost)
    - how easy it is to provide (E)
    - how well it is linked to business drivers (L)
    - overall customer response (O)

Note: a rating of 2 or below means attention or action is needed.

11. How do you measure or judge the value of this program or service? For example, is it by the frequency of the request, customer feedback, the revenue it generates, the fact that it is required by a regulatory agency, or something else?

12. What is the overall resource commitment required to deliver this program or service?

13. This is a place for everyone involved to say whatever they want about the program or service.

**Figure 2.4.
Product Portfolio
Worksheet 2,** *cont'd.*

5. *List the resources required* to deliver it. Be specific about the number of people required and the amount of time they spend. For example, who does the work required to deliver the product or service? How much time do they spend doing it? Which and how many people are qualified to do it?

Once you have a picture of what it is you do and why, discuss these points with your colleagues or clients:

- Whether or not it is appropriate to continue delivering this set of products or services. You might ask, for example, Is there still a business driver behind each service? What would be the consequences if we stopped providing a certain service or committed less resources to it?

- How you might reduce the amount of resources it takes to deliver your current set of products. For example, you might ask, Where are there opportunities to outsource? Where are there opportunities to make better use of technology? Should we have the client do it instead of doing it ourselves? What would be the consequences if others did it?

- Which of your current services would you definitely *not* provide if you were in the business of performance consulting?

- What services would you add if you were in the business of performance consulting? Include things that you wish you could do but do not do because you lack the skills, customer relationships, or resources to be successful.

- How would you have to operate differently if you were performance consultants?

- What internal support systems and processes would you want to add or improve so that you could be effective as a performance consultant? For example, can you track your costs now? Do you have a way to value your time? Do you have a formal process for doing needs assessment?

If you get stuck because you are thinking about *how* you can offer new products and services instead of *what* you want to offer, consider how you might leverage your current set of products to support your transition to performance consulting. For example, you might ask, Which of our current products or services give us legitimate access to influential people? Which ones allow us to develop the skills and confidence required to move more into consulting? Which ones give us access to critical information that a consultant should know?

Create a new worksheet that lists the products and services you want to offer in the future. Include who your clients will be, the business drivers behind what you would like to offer, the resources that will be required, and whether or not you have those resources now.

FIELD NOTES: ALIGNING PRODUCTS AND SERVICES

Deborah was hired to be the new director of training at a national communications company. The company asked her to change the focus of the training department from technical training to performance improvement. She started by learning more about her staff, what they did, and what their capabilities were. Next she met with key line managers from the field and found out what they expected of her and her people. She also asked the staff directors at the home office what they wanted from her department. Learning what her field and home office customers wanted gave Deborah a lot of ideas about how her department could better contribute to the company. For example, she saw the need to adopt a more efficient delivery system; to work with managers to reduce turnover; to propose a more effective, targeted selection program; to coach managers on how to better support new hires; and to develop expert systems to more efficiently accommodate regulatory changes.

She knew that to make these changes she would have to find out what resources the department had and how it used them. Deborah and her staff decided to take a closer look at exactly what it is they did. Together they created a worksheet, where they recorded what they did; their customers, stakeholders, and sponsors; the drivers behind their services; how their services were delivered, and the amount of resources their services consumed. Figure 2.5 shows what they came up with.

It was clear from the exercise that Deborah's trainers were consumed with supporting new-hire customer service training (note the resources devoted to the first two services). The few people who were left were dedicated to coaching managers, delivering technical training beyond what was covered in the new-hire program, and participating in corporate projects.

Deborah and her staff then reviewed what their field customers wanted. They had learned that the managers at the call centers wanted more competent trainers; more sales training; shorter learning curves for new hires (it was taking them from four to five months to get up to speed at the time); and a more efficient way to keep customer service representatives current on product changes, regulatory changes, and competitor information.
Managers of home office functions like finance, IS, and quality assurance wanted reduced turnover (it was as high as 30 percent in some departments); help with message design, to reduce the risk of lost revenues and fines from giving inaccurate billing information to customers; an expert system that would reduce the time to train call center personnel; advice on designing procedures and help screens; and ways to get information to the front line faster, at less cost, and in a form that could be understood and readily accessed.

Deborah and her staff then created a second worksheet. This time they listed the products and services they thought they must offer to get customers to accept them in their new role. They included services such as

- Developing tools clients could use to improve performance (such as a process for supporting sales, a model for coaching, standards for trainers, and a better hiring process)
- Developing cost models that they and their clients could use to determine current costs and do cost-benefit analyses
- Serving as subject matter experts in learning, performance, message design, electronic delivery systems, and expert systems
- Administering and monitoring (through new technology) training registration, schedules, and learners' course completion
- Serving as team leaders for major corporate initiatives

Figure 2.6 lists their new products and services.

Products and Services	Customer	Stakeholder
1. Deliver new-hire product training	Customer service reps (CSRs)	Supervisors and center managers
2. Deliver new-hire sales training	CSRs and supervisors	Center managers
3. Deliver product training	CSRs and supervisors	Marketing
4. Deliver updates on procedures	CSRs and supervisors	Methods and procedures
5. Deliver management skills training for HR	Supervisors	Center managers and HR
6. Facilitate meetings, on request	Center managers	Center managers
7. Coach managers on sales, on request	CSRs and supervisors	Center managers
8. Maintain the accuracy of technical training content	CSRs	Center managers
9. Participate in corporate projects	Corporate office	Varied, based on criteria for participation

Figure 2.5. Deborah's Portfolio of Current Products and Services

Product Portfolio Worksheet 2

Product Portfolio Worksheet 2 is particularly well suited for evaluating programs and services from Worksheet 1 that you want to examine in greater detail. Depending on how many there are, you may want to fill out different worksheets for different client groups or curricula. The worksheet will help you

- Decide what programs or services still bring value
- Identify what you can do to improve those programs or services or reduce the cost of providing them
- Better manage the life cycle of your programs and services
- Identify which programs or services are worthy of additional time or money for improvement

Product Portfolio Worksheet 2 (Figure 2.4) has three parts. Part 1 lists some variables or factors to consider for each product or service you offer or

Sponsor	Driver	Methods	Resources
Sales VP	Turnover and growth	Instructor-led classes and multimedia	Forty instructors, full time
Sales VP	Turnover and growth	Instructor-led classes	20 percent of five consultants' job
Sales VP	Steady stream of new products	Instructor-led classes	30 percent of two consultants' job
Internal audit	Constant change in regulations	Memos and announcements	100 percent of one designer's job
HR	Turnover and growth	Training trainers, evaluating trainers, scheduling trainers	Contract trainers
Sales VP	Shift to a more team-oriented culture	In-person contact	20 percent of two consultants' job
Sales VP	Shift to a sales culture	In-person and phone contact	20 percent of two consultants' job
Sales VP	Changes in product attributes	Team member or leader review	80 percent of two designers' job
			20 percent of three to five consultants' job

Figure 2.5. Deborah's Portfolio of Current Products and Services, *cont'd.*

plan to offer. This includes some of the same information as on Worksheet 1. Part 2 has spaces for you and the other people who support your products or services to rate them based on their quality, costs, and other criteria. Part 3 lists measures used in evaluating the products or services, the resources they require, and comments from anyone involved. You can customize the first two parts to meet your needs.

Part 1: Variables. The first time you use the worksheet, be sure to record the appropriate information for each of the variables or factors listed (see the numbered list of questions at the bottom of the figure).

Part 2: Ratings. Use a Likert scale to rate the program or service according to those criteria. A Likert scale is a five-point scale used to rate something. What distinguishes it from other scales is that it allows people to give neutral or noncommittal ratings (by selecting the midpoint, or 3, on the scale).

Products and Services	Customer	Driver	Methods	Resources Required
1. Manage the delivery of new-hire product and sales training	Call centers	Lower cost of training	Instructor-led courses; multimedia courses; coaching of trainers	Scheduling software; qualified trainers; trainer coaches
2. Deliver ongoing product and procedures training	Call centers	Changes to products and procedures	Instructor-led courses; self-administered training; on-line help; job aids	Scheduling software; qualified trainers; trainer coaches
3. Screen and brand vendor training	Call centers and HR	Lower cost of training	Repackage and confirm they meet instructional criteria	Criteria; evaluation process; contracting process
4. Select and qualify contract trainers to deliver HR's training	HR and call centers	Improve quality; control costs	Train and certify trainers	Training standards and certification process
5. Facilitate meetings	Managers	Faster results	Use facilitators	Qualified facilitators
6. Coach managers to improve sales and performance	Call centers	Retention; higher sales goals	Use consultants	Qualified performance consultants
7. Do needs assessments and organizational reviews	VPs	Higher sales goals	Partner with HR, IT, finance, and so on	Well-defined process; survey technology
8. Develop performance measurement tools	VPs	Align merit with results	Partner with HR, marketing, and so on	Evaluating and measuring processes and tools
9. Consult on technology, job, and message design	Call centers	Lower costs; speed	Lead teams and consult	Contracting process
10. Update and maintain training	Call centers	Fines	Use instructional designer	Authoring system

Figure 2.6. Deborah's New Products and Services

When you create the scale, be consistent as to which value is positive (the 1 or the 5); do not switch back and forth.

Part 3: Evaluation and Resources. Part 3 of Product Portfolio Worksheet 2 is about evaluation and resources. On it you can indicate

1. How you evaluate each program now (for example, using Kirkpatrick's levels 1, 2, 3, and 4, or some other method).
2. The amount of resources you must commit to it (include equipment, space, administration, testing, setup, materials, instructors, other qualified personnel, and so on).

Part 3 also includes a space for general comments.

FIELD TECHNIQUES: EVALUATING THE WORTH OF WHAT YOU DO NOW

Using Product Portfolio Worksheet 2, follow these steps to help yourself evaluate the worth of your current products or services:

1. Ask yourself what you want to know about what you do now. (Use your answer to come up with the variables you want to consider.) For example, do you want to know
   - Which products or services consume the most resources?
   - Which products or services cost more to deliver than the value they generate?
   - Who your customers are for each product or service?
   - Whether you have exhausted the market for a given product or service?
   - If there are other customers for a product or service?
   - If your customers really value a certain product or service?
   - What percentage of your customers use each product or service?
   - What the driver was behind each product or service, whether that need has been met, and whether the product or service is the best way to meet that need? How to find out this information?
2. Based on your answers, create a worksheet and include a column for every variable.
3. Fill out the portfolio as best you can. Solicit input from customers where appropriate. Pay attention to what you do *not* know about a specific program or service, especially if you do not know how much it costs to deliver or support.

4. Ask others who are directly involved in supporting the service to rate it according to the variables you have selected.

5. Ask them to add any comments they want.

6. Once you have gathered the information, question the worth and value of each program and service. Look for indicators that the worth or value is less than it might be. For example, is it costly to deliver? Is the link to the organization unclear or weak? Is the number of cancellations and no-shows high?

7. Identify those products and services that would benefit from changing the delivery system, the number of offerings, when the product or service is offered, how it is offered, and so on.

8. Identify those products and services you can stop offering or outsource.

FIELD TECHNIQUES: FINDING A WILLING CLIENT

You may find that you already offer many of the products or services listed in your new product portfolio. However, if there are some that you have not offered or lack experience with, think of a client who might be willing to give you that experience. This is what Kelly, who worked for the insurance company, did. You probably already have well-established relationships with your clients. If you do,

1. Select one that you think will be responsive to your assuming the new role of performance consultant.

2. Begin by explaining what it is you want to accomplish.

3. Explain why you think the client would benefit from your doing this or participating in some way.

4. Ask if there is an issue or problem the client would like to have a better understanding of.

5. Ask if there is an initiative, team, or problem where your skills in analysis, measurement, or facilitation would be of value.

6. Negotiate for your involvement.

7. Develop a charter for the assignment, and clarify what the deliverables might be.

8. Identify or develop some measures for your performance and the deliverables.

9. If appropriate, build a project plan, with a defined time line and milestones.

10. Fulfill the request.

11. Evaluate the results and how you went about completing the assignment.

12. Share the results with your own colleagues so that you can improve. Share them with other potential clients so that they can see the possible value to them of your products or services.

USING THE PRODUCT PORTFOLIO WORKSHEETS WITH CLIENTS

You can use the techniques I have described so far not only to help yourself be more effective in your practice but also with your clients, to help *them* be more effective in what they do. The processes of defining what they are all about and how they do business, measuring their performance and that of their products or services, and so on are the same. For example, I use the operational definition to help my clients and their customers come to a shared understanding of their respective roles, responsibilities, and practices. The definition serves as a reality check for all concerned. It can help both you and your clients tell people who you think you are and what you are all about. Your customers can then judge whether or not this description is supported by your behavior and the results you produce.

You can modify the product portfolio worksheets for use with your clients as you see fit. To use the worksheet with a client, use a similar process as you would for yourself. For example, help the client come up with a list of questions about its products and services, such as

- Who are our customers?

- Is this the business we want to be in?

- Do our customers value these products and services?

- What other products and services do our customers want?

- Are we cost-effective and competitive?

- What do we really want on this list that would allow us to add even greater value to our organization?

FIELD TECHNIQUES: BUILDING YOUR PLAN

To make the transition from what you do now to performance consulting,

- Look at the elements of your plan. Identify those elements you want to act on, and give yourself a deadline to do so. Add other steps that you think will help. How far along do you expect to be one year from now? What will you accept as evidence that you are making progress?

- Review the standards and measures in Figures 2.1 and 2.2. If you were to evaluate yourself against any of these criteria, where would you fall today? What do you have to do to begin exceeding your clients' expectations?

How might you use these measures to support your plan to move to performance consulting? How would you change these measures to better reflect your situation? How easy would it be for you to start using measures like these?

- Look at the product portfolio worksheets (Figures 2.3 and 2.4). How might you modify these worksheets to capture the information you want about what you do now? How might you use the insights you gain from these worksheets to build a case for becoming a performance consultant? Are you currently offering services you should not be or services that should be provided by someone else? What resources would be freed up if you were to change what you do and how you do it?

The acts of evaluating your current products and services, assessing their worth against some predefined criteria, and questioning the reason for them are the kinds of things a performance consultant does. If you don't think so, review the list in Chapter One of the four things that distinguish performance consultants from other consultants. Congratulations, you are now on your way to becoming a performance consultant!

SUMMARY

It takes more than a name change to make the transition to performance consulting. You have to mold a plan, define measures of success, and develop the kinds of products and services a performance consultant offers. Most important, you have to start acting like a performance consultant. The easiest place to start is with yourself. In the process you will increase your skills and better understand your new role.

WHERE TO LEARN MORE

Block, P., *Flawless Consulting* (San Francisco: Jossey-Bass/Pfeiffer, 1981).

Fuller, J., *Managing Performance Improvement Projects* (San Francisco: Jossey-Bass/Pfeiffer, 1997).

Lippitt, G., and Lippitt, R., *The Consulting Process in Action,* 2nd ed. (San Francisco: Jossey-Bass/Pfeiffer, 1986).

Reddy, W. B., *Intervention Skills: Process Consultation for Small Groups and Teams* (San Francisco: Jossey-Bass/Pfeiffer, 1994).

Chapter 3

Costs

One of the most overlooked prerequisites of effective consulting is the ability to understand the economics behind poor performance. Unlike trainers, consultants must be able to quantify the costs of a client's current processes and practices as well as determine the costs and benefits of their own recommendations. Here is what happens when neither the client nor the consultant understands costs and what drives them.

FIELD NOTES: COST OF SALES

The VP of finance at a large corporation confronted the VP of sales over the rising costs of sales at their company. Until then no one had ever talked about the cost of sales. Everyone knew the sales cycle: down in the first two quarters, up in the third quarter, and way up in the fourth quarter. The company didn't launch its sales campaigns until the end of the third quarter, and it based its sales reps' bonuses on their fourth-quarter sales. But the sales reps were expected to entertain clients, take them to lunch, and travel to their offices all year long. The subject of cost of sales never came up. Sales reps were never even given any information about what it costs the company to make a sale.

The VP of sales turned to the director of training and demanded that he provide a workshop on territory management at the next regional sales meeting. The VP told the director of training what the content would be and how the success of the program would be measured. No one asked how he knew that poor territory management was the reason behind the "high" cost of sales. Because the training wasn't budgeted, the director of training argued that the cost of the session should go in the budget for sales, not the budget for training.

The circumstances described in this story did not suddenly emerge. The company's sales costs were driven by business practices that had been considered quite acceptable for years. Unlike Mark, in Chapter One, who wondered how he could best improve the financial performance of his Midwest plant, the VP of sales at this company seems uninterested in finding out which costs are high and by how much, if they are high for all sales staff or just a few, or even what the real problem is. The director of training seems interested only in not having the cost of the workshop show up in his budget.

EXPERIENCES FROM THE FIELD: UNDERSTANDING COSTS

I'm often asked to speak on the subject of evaluation at national conferences. The questions I'm most frequently asked concern how to prove return on investment (ROI) and how to do a Kirkpatrick's level 4 evaluation (that is, how to prove that the training solved the business problem or improved performance). Just like performance consultants, clients often must struggle with how to estimate the value of a product or service or prove its worth. My experience is that trainers, HRD professionals, and consultants and their clients are often faced with similar problems: they don't understand how to value, or quantify, the problem they want to solve in economic terms, and they don't have systems in place to isolate costs and determine what causes them. These problems are compounded by the fact that people think they are supposed to know these things, as if this information were just hanging around waiting for someone to notice it. It's not that easy. Here are some things I've learned over the years that I have found very valuable when working with clients:

- *Organizations classify their costs depending on their unique needs, and they don't all do it in the same way.* Furthermore, organizations vary significantly in their ability to accurately isolate costs and identify what causes them. Find out exactly how your clients identify and classify their costs.

- *Not all costs are valued the same.* Some are looked on less favorably than others (specifically, indirect, fixed costs).

- *Costs don't just happen; they have a cause.* The customers, business practices, processes, or people that cause them aren't necessarily the ones charged with or held accountable for them, however. Find out what or who caused the cost you're investigating, not just who gets blamed for it or is held responsible for reducing it.

- *Cost management is about managing the causes of costs.* You have to manage the cause, or cost driver, to reduce, avoid, or eliminate the cost.

- *Most efforts to reduce costs don't; they just shift costs around.* Find out what the implications of your recommendations are for others before you claim they will reduce costs.

How Organizations Classify Costs

There are different types of costs; yet, we talk as if all costs are the same. There are some universal rules and guidelines for classifying costs; yet, how an organization classifies specific costs depends on that organization's unique needs. You need to understand how your organization or client classifies costs so that you can isolate which costs your services are expected to reduce and compare the cost of doing something with the cost of doing nothing. This information is key to your being able to quantify a problem and justify your recommendations for change. Following are some rules of thumb concerning how organizations classify costs.

Organizations classify costs depending on the type of business they are in and what they want to do with the information. For example, companies typically start by distinguishing product or service costs from the cost of selling the product or service, the cost of support services, and management costs (that is, the costs of running the business; see Figure 3.1).

Organizations further classify their costs within each of these major categories. The headings or labels under which a company or business unit classifies costs usually represent its larger cost components. For example, service organizations almost always distinguish salaries from overhead. Capital-intensive businesses almost always separate out depreciation costs. (Depreciation is defined later in the chapter.) Manufacturers separate the cost of making their products from the costs of selling, servicing, warehousing, and shipping them and the costs of managing the business (see Figure 3.2).

Organizations pay attention to the costs that affect profits, pricing, and bonuses. For example, manufacturers pay attention to the cost of

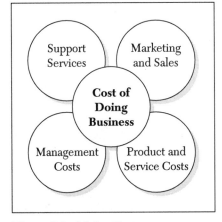

Figure 3.1. Major Cost Classifications

- The *raw materials* used to make their products, because raw materials are frequently the largest part of a product's cost. Manufacturers want to know when the cost of raw materials changes and what causes the change, as this cost directly affects their ability to price products competitively and make a profit. They also pay attention to whether or not raw materials add hidden costs because they require extra handling.

- *Processing or assembling* the raw materials (specifically, the costs of labor, equipment, materials, tooling, and testing). Labor can be a significant part of a product's cost; therefore companies pay attention to how much and how well they are using their workers as well as to how much they are paying them. Poorly scheduled, untrained people can add unnecessary costs.

- Their *plants and facilities* (specifically, the cost to acquire, operate, and maintain them, including depreciation, utilities, insurance, and taxes). Because

**Figure 3.2.
Manufacturers' Major
Cost Components**

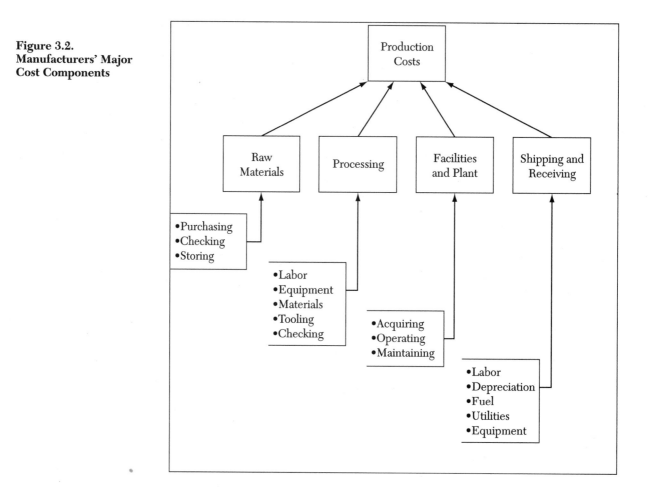

facility costs are significant, companies pay close attention to what percentage of their facilities is dedicated to producing products. Underutilized space can increase the overall cost of a company's products and services, forcing an increase in its prices or a lower profit margin.

• *Warehousing and shipping* the product (specifically, labor, depreciation, fuel, utilities, insurance, taxes, pallets, and refrigeration). These costs, too, get added to the price or reduce the profit margin.

All companies are particularly concerned with the cost of sales and the cost of service. Figure 3.3 shows what is typically thought of as the cost of sales, and Figure 3.4 shows the items that usually make up the cost of service. Your clients may include other or different costs, however.

Determining the cost of running the business (see Figure 3.5) is more complex, because what is included depends on the type of organization and its reason for tracking some costs and not others.

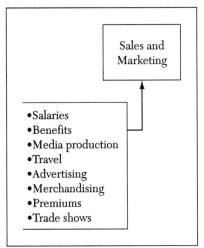

Figure 3.3. Cost of Sales

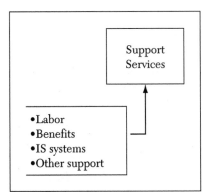

Figure 3.4. Cost of Service

How Organizations Value Costs

Businesses do not treat all costs the same. They look on some costs more favorably than others. The kinds of costs most companies look on more favorably are those that are easier to isolate, control, and pass on to customers; these are generally incurred in direct proportion to the amount of business being done. The kinds of costs that businesses look on less favorably are those that are harder to isolate, control, and pass on; these are usually incurred independently of the amount of sales.

Rule No. 1: Find out how your clients classify their costs and how they distinguish direct costs from indirect costs.

Organizations pay attention to

- *Direct and indirect costs.* Direct costs are easier to isolate and can be linked (and charged) to a specific customer, product, or service. For example, the cost of raw materials, fuel for delivery trucks, and technicians who make service calls are all direct costs. Indirect costs are harder to isolate and link to a specific customer or product; therefore they are spread across products and customers. Indirect costs include things like sales, marketing, management, human resources, and administration. Indirect costs are frequently referred to as overhead.

- *Variable and fixed costs.* Variable costs fluctuate based on the volume of work being done (raw materials costs are variable, for example); therefore they are somewhat controllable. Fixed costs, such as depreciation, do not fluctuate and are thus less controllable. Some costs are partially fixed and partially variable. The cost of electricity is an example: companies use electric power all the time (the fixed portion), but they use more power when production lines are up and running (the variable portion).

The Relationship Between Direct, Indirect, Variable, and Fixed Costs

Most, but not all, direct costs are variable costs. Examples of direct costs that are variable include the cost of raw materials and the cost of production labor (regular and overtime wages and benefits). You can attribute these costs to a specific product or service, and you most likely incur them only when you have business (you don't buy raw materials without customer orders, and you can lay workers off when business is down).

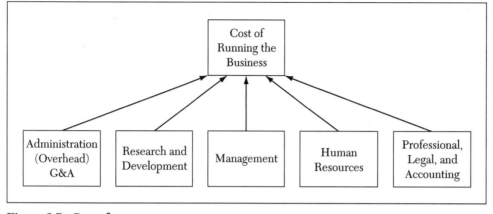

Figure 3.5. Cost of Running the Business

There are a few direct costs that are fixed. For example, consider depreciation on the equipment used to manufacture products. You can attribute the cost of the equipment to the product it produces (making it a direct cost), but you still have the cost (depreciation) whether the equipment is running or not (making it a fixed cost).

Most indirect costs are also fixed costs, because companies continue to incur them regardless of the amount of sales or production. Changes in the volume of work have minimal effect on them. When organizations want to cut costs they usually start by looking at their fixed indirect costs. Examples of fixed indirect costs include management costs, which include management salaries and benefits and perhaps facility costs for management offices, and overhead, or general and administrative (G&A) costs. G&A costs include administration costs; insurance costs; real estate taxes; the cost of licenses; interest expense; rent and leasing costs; the cost of heat and other utilities; depreciation and amortization of assets not easily linked to specific products, services, or customers; marketing and advertising costs; research and development (R&D) costs; training and HR costs; and accounting and legal costs. (Administration, marketing and advertising, R&D, training and HR, and accounting and legal costs include costs for salaries and benefits, facility use by the specific function, and depreciation on equipment used by the specific function.) Figure 3.6 briefly defines and provides examples of variable direct costs, fixed direct costs, and fixed indirect costs.

Depreciation is a reduction in the value of a producing fixed asset because of wear and tear from normal use. Examples of assets that are depreciated include facilities (buildings) and capital goods (equipment and vehicles). Companies with high depreciation costs (like manufacturers) are more capital-intensive. *Amor-*

Type of cost	Examples
Variable direct costs: allocated to specific products, services, or customers; fluctuate with the volume of work performed	• Raw materials • Labor used to build products or provide services • Consultants contracted to develop or facilitate programs • Vendor courses • CSRs' overtime
Fixed direct costs: allocated to specific products, services, or customers; do not fluctuate with changes in the volume of work performed	• Depreciation of capital equipment used to make specific products or dedicated to servicing specific customers • CSRs (salary, benefits, and percentage of facility use) who are dedicated to a specific product line or customer group and whose hours do not fluctuate with business volume • Supervisors whose departments are dedicated to one business line, product, or customer • Professional staff dedicated to one business line, service, or customer • Corporate university facilities or dedicated space
Fixed indirect costs: not dedicated but spread across products, services, and customers; do not fluctuate with changes in business volume	• Management salaries and benefits • Staff salaries and benefits • Corporate office expense

Figure 3.6. Examples of Costs

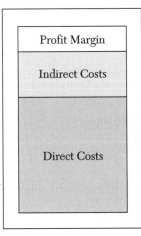

Figure 3.7. Components of Price

tization is the gradual reduction in the book value of a nonproducing asset that has a limited life. The original cost is spread over the life of the asset. Examples of assets that are amortized include patents, copyrights, and franchises.

What Businesses Include in the Price of a Product or Service

The price of a product or service includes its direct costs plus some portion of the business's indirect costs plus some margin for profit (see Figure 3.7). Organizations strive to reduce their costs so that they can maintain or lower their prices (to become more competitive) without reducing their profit margin.

Rule No. 2: Find out how your organization, department, or client classifies its costs. Find out what costs, if any, are considered direct versus indirect. Whether you are a direct or an indirect cost, find out how your time, space, and equipment are valued and thus allocated, or spread.

FIELD TECHNIQUES: LEARNING HOW YOUR ORGANIZATION CLASSIFIES COSTS

I've given you only a very simple explanation of costs, but it's enough for you to begin to have a conversation with your client's or organization's finance department. You have to find out how your client or organization classifies costs, why it uses that particular method, and how well it can isolate its costs. Here is a technique for doing so:

1. Meet with someone in the accounting or finance department and ask how the organization classifies costs.

2. If your client or organization uses broad categories like overhead, management, G&A, and so on, ask what costs go into each category and who decides what costs go where.

3. Ask which costs are considered direct and which are considered indirect.

4. Ask which costs are fixed (less controllable) and which are variable (controllable).

5. Ask which costs are the larger cost components.

6. Ask how changes in business volume affect costs and which costs are most affected.

7. Ask how the organization recovers its fixed costs when volume or business is down.

8. If the organization is capital-intensive, ask how it allocates and recovers depreciation when volume or business is down.

9. Ask which costs the company attributes to you or your department (salaries, facilities, equipment, and so on) and how it classifies them. If some of your costs are considered direct, ask to which products, services, or customers they are linked. If some or all of your costs are considered indirect, ask on what basis they are spread across customers, lines of business, or products (that is, equally or in proportion to usage).

FIELD TOOLS: VALUING TIME

Sometimes consultants and clients do not know how to value their time. Thus even if they are able to eliminate activities or become more efficient, they don't know how to assign a value to the time they have saved. Figure 3.8 provides a worksheet for figuring out how much your time and your client's time is worth.

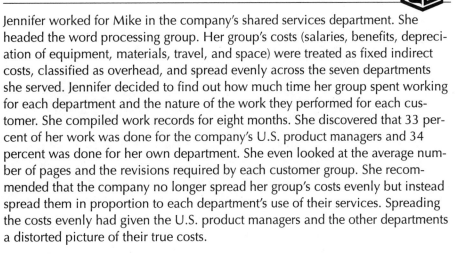

**Figure 3.8.
A Formula for
Valuing Time**

1. Identify an appropriate pay grade and select the annual salary at the midpoint of that grade.

   Enter that figure here. _____

2. Divide that figure by the number of available hours in the year (see below). ÷ 1,800

   Enter the result here. _____

3. Add a percentage for overhead (an indirect, fixed cost). A commonly used number is 35 percent. × 1.35

   This is your hourly rate. = _____

This formula gives you an hourly rate you can use to value your time and your client's time. Once you know the formula you can change its assumptions based on the realities of your situation. The figure of 1,800 work hours per year is derived from this formula:

52 weeks a year × 40-hour workweek	= 2,080 hours
Less minimum vacation time (2 weeks)	− 80 hours
Less an average 11 personal days and holidays	− 88 hours
Less typical number of training hours	− 50 hours
Less typical time spent in meetings	− 40 hours
Less typical miscellaneous and sick time	− 22 hours
Available hours per year	= 1,800 hours

FIELD NOTES: SPREADING FIXED COSTS

Jennifer worked for Mike in the company's shared services department. She headed the word processing group. Her group's costs (salaries, benefits, depreciation of equipment, materials, travel, and space) were treated as fixed indirect costs, classified as overhead, and spread evenly across the seven departments she served. Jennifer decided to find out how much time her group spent working for each department and the nature of the work they performed for each customer. She compiled work records for eight months. She discovered that 33 percent of her work was done for the company's U.S. product managers and 34 percent was done for her own department. She even looked at the average number of pages and the revisions required by each customer group. She recommended that the company no longer spread her group's costs evenly but instead spread them in proportion to each department's use of their services. Spreading the costs evenly had given the U.S. product managers and the other departments a distorted picture of their true costs.

COST MANAGEMENT

Cost management is about taking direct action to reduce, avoid, or eliminate costs. The term *cost management* is actually somewhat misleading. What you manage is not costs but what *causes* them (this is similar to time management, where you manage what you do with your time, not the time itself).

Rule No. 3: Find out what drives, or causes, your costs.

Here is what causes costs:

- Companies engage in activities to create products and deliver services.
- These activities consume resources (time, materials, space, and equipment), and resources cost money.

Activities are directed by a product or service's requirements, the processes used to create the product or provide the service, customers' requirements, and business practices. By linking resources first to an activity, then to the product or service, and eventually to the requirement, process, customer, or practice, you can trace the true source of the product's or service's costs. By identifying what drives unnecessary activity (such as an unnecessary requirement of the product or the customer, a poorly designed or executed work process, or poor people performance), you can find ways to eliminate or reduce the amount of activity and thus reduce costs. Thus you can reduce costs either by eliminating activities or by reducing the amount of resources they consume.

Rule No. 4: Look for hidden costs.

Hidden costs is the term I use for those costs an organization either does not or cannot isolate. Hidden costs fall outside the organization's system for isolating and tracking costs. Such costs frequently get shifted between groups: the group that gets charged with a hidden cost may not be the group that created it. For example, when sales reps fail to get complete or accurate information about new accounts, the cost of getting that information is shifted to someone else, like accounting or customer service. The failure to get complete or accurate information in the first place increases the cost of sales, but that portion of the cost is hidden or buried in overhead because it is shifted to accounting or customer service. This is why Jennifer wanted to track her department's activities to specific customers. She wanted to know which customers drove her activities and thus her costs. She discovered that five of her customers were paying more than their fair share and two were getting off easy.

UNNECESSARY COST DRIVERS

You or your clients have unnecessary costs when

- Product or service requirements are excessive.
- Processes are not well designed.
- The customer's requirements are not fully understood and this results in doing more work than required (rework) or doing work the customer doesn't value.
- The information, equipment, space, or tools to do the job are insufficient or inappropriate.
- People lack skills.
- People's behaviors force others to incur costs (that is, they shift costs to others).
- Jobs or tasks could be done with less costly resources, such as through automation or outsourcing.
- Management does not provide adequate direction, resulting in unnecessary activity.

Rule No. 5: To manage costs, you must identify and isolate them, find out what they are made up of, and find out what causes them.

Once you know what caused a cost you can change the requirements (product, service, or customer), improve your processes, or eliminate practices that shift it around.

FIELD TOOLS: ISOLATING AND MANAGING COSTS

Some of the tools organizations use to isolate costs and find out what drives them are

- *Activity-based costing systems.* Not all accounting systems are designed to help manage costs. In fact, most accounting systems are designed only to report costs. Activity-based costing is an accounting system specifically designed to identify costs and support cost management.
- *Statistical process control* (SPC). SPC identifies variance within products, pinpoints what causes it, and suggests ways to improve processes to eliminate all predictable causes of variance. (Variance is the degree to which individual products deviate from a standard. It results in rework, which adds unnecessary costs.) SPC identifies the causes of variance: poor people performance; bad process design; deficient equipment, tools, or materials;

inaccurate or incomplete information; and so on. It helps you focus on things that will actually reduce variance and not just shift costs to other parts of the company.

- *Process mapping and analysis.* Clients do this to identify and describe all the elements that go into a process (that is, to make the process visible) so that they can identify which elements are unnecessary or contribute to excess costs.

FIELD TECHNIQUES: FINDING COST DRIVERS AND HIDDEN COSTS

When you meet with your client's or organization's finance or other managers, ask them

- How they track costs
- Which cost management techniques they use, why they use them, and how effective they are
- Which costs they want to manage (direct, indirect, fixed, or variable)

When your clients talk about wanting to reduce costs, ask them

- Which costs they want to reduce and what systems they have in place to determine what those costs are now
- If they can effectively isolate costs and if they can distinguish between direct, indirect, fixed, and variable costs
- What seems to be driving their costs (product requirements, customer requirements, inefficient processes, poor people performance, and so on)
- What departments, work groups, or individuals are doing now that increases indirect or fixed costs

---

FIELD NOTES: REDUCING THE COST OF NONCOMPLIANCE

Deborah's boss sent her a memo that said her department had to reduce the cost of noncompliance by 35 percent by the end of the year. The first thing Deborah did was meet with her boss and the head of finance to get clarification. She wanted to know

- Whose costs she was expected to reduce. (It turned out to be customer service and field sales.)

- What this would mean in dollar terms. (She had to cut out $5 million.)

- How the cost of noncompliance was currently calculated. (It was an arbitrary process. The VP of finance and her boss had added the direct costs [salary] and indirect costs [percentage of overhead] of the customer service reps and field sales reps together and guessed that there was 35 percent waste in the system.)

- What the causes of noncompliance were. (They didn't know, but they assumed that it was because people didn't know how to do certain aspects of their job.)

One of Deborah's first tasks was to get management to better define noncompliance, what they would take as evidence of improvement, whose noncompliance they were concerned about, and who would bear the cost of reducing it (the perpetrator or someone else). She was told to focus on noncompliance in the call centers and among the customer service reps (CSRs) in particular. The cost of the CSRs was classified as overhead. It was considered a fixed indirect cost. The customer service centers' costs were spread across all products and markets. However, a small portion of their costs was considered part of the cost of sales (for example, when the CSRs took customer orders). This part was direct (it could be attributed to a specific product or service) and variable (it was driven by the number of customers who called wanting to buy). However, no one had tracked what portion of the CSRs' time was spent taking sales orders and what percentage was spent answering service calls. Deborah began by finding out what percentage of the CSRs' time was spent resolving customer complaints, correcting billing errors, checking the status of shipments, and so on (in other words, mistakes caused by breakdowns in other departments). The source of this type of noncompliance was not the CSRs. She also wanted to know the percentage of time spent on callbacks that were required because a problem had not been resolved the first time, because this represented noncompliance by the CSRs. Once she knew the scope of the problem she could place a value on it and find out the root cause. Deborah wanted to know whether the cause of the callbacks was poorly designed order forms, the company's practice of rewarding people for fixing problems, or a lack of consequences for the true offending party. She wanted to know what the real costs were, what drove them, and what she could feasibly do to reduce them. She found out the average salary of the CSRs and came up with a dollar value for each CSR work hour. She would use this figure to determine whether what she did reduced the amount of time spent on non-value-adding activities. She took the time to better understand the organization's ability to isolate costs and manage costs, because she anticipated that the following year the company would ask her to drive down the cost of compliance (that is, of doing the job right the first time).

IMPROVING PROCESSES AND PRACTICES TO REDUCE COSTS

Poorly designed (or poorly executed) processes add unnecessary costs. Processes include all the activities, decisions, and resources (equipment, information, time, money, and people) used to

- Take an input (for example, a customer request, a course evaluation, a new training requirement)

- Add value to that input by changing it in some way (by engaging in activities that transform the request into a new product or more useful information)

- Produce an output the customer wants (a training course, a report with recommendations, modified materials, and so on)

Processes vary in size and scope. There are processes within and across departments and functions. Some processes are considered primary, because they are linked to the core business. These include processes such as receiving, producing, marketing, selling, servicing, and distributing products and services. Other processes are considered secondary, because they are performed by departments that are considered part of overhead. These include such processes as purchasing, HR management and development, and information systems management.

Rule No. 6: Understand business processes and practices.

Business practices are a business's regular way of doing things. One could argue that they are simply a part of the business's processes; however, I consider them separately as practices because that's how my clients think of them. Inefficient practices are cost drivers because they consume excess resources. Poorly designed practices shift costs to other parts of the organization or result in hidden costs.

MANAGING COSTS IN PERFORMANCE CONSULTING

Before you can help clients manage their costs, you have to understand your own costs and manage them. One way to do this is by describing, evaluating, and improving your processes and practices.

When you describe a process you identify all of the activities, decisions, and resources that make up the process. You also find out what drives the process; that is, is the process performed in response to a customer requirement, a program requirement, or a business requirement? The description communicates what is done and in what order, which resources each activity consumes, and how time is spent.

There are different ways to describe a process. Whichever method you use, you want the description to capture the following information:

- The activities that occur
- The resources consumed by each activity
- The activities' relationships to one another (that is, which are done sequentially and which are done concurrently?)

Once you have described a process you will be in a better position to question

- What the process does, how it does it, and why it does it
- What information the process uses and where that information comes from
- What information the process produces and who uses it
- What technology the process uses, what resources that technology requires, and the cost of those resources

A process or practice adds unnecessary costs if it uses too many resources, uses resources that cost too much, or produces products or services that do not meet customer expectations.

To improve a process you must first make it visible; this means you should describe or map the process. Then you will be in a position to identify the resources consumed and the cost of those resources. You will also be in a better position to identify where and how activities or tasks shift costs to other processes, departments, or suppliers.

FIELD TOOLS: PROCESS OR TASK PERFORMANCE WORKSHEET

Use Figure 3.9 to help you evaluate your own processes or tasks. Like the product portfolio worksheets in Chapter Two, this worksheet is meant for you to customize so that it will capture the information you currently do and do not have about what you do and how you do it.

The worksheet will help you determine which processes or tasks you need to formalize better so that you can determine if and how they add unnecessary costs. The worksheet drives discussions about

- How well-defined your processes or tasks are
- How capable you are at measuring what your processes or tasks cost
- How many resources your processes or tasks consume
- Which ones add unnecessary costs
- The value added (or not added) by doing what you do in the way that you do it
- How you will measure any improvements you make

1. Process	2. Purpose or reason	3. Resources required	4. Cost	5. Criteria					6. Comments
				D	E	N	V	U	

1. What is the process or task you are evaluating?

2. Why is it done? Whose need does it meet?

3. How many resources does it take? How many people or what percentage of time is dedicated to or involved in this process or task?

4. What does it cost to perform this process or task in terms of dollars, time, or resources?

5. Ask each of your colleagues or key customers to independently rate the process or task according to the following criteria (add criteria to meet your needs). Use a Likert scale (1 being very positive, 5 being very negative, and 3 being noncommittal or indifferent) or some other scale.

   • How well is the process or task described or documented? (D)

   • How efficient is the process? (E)

   • How well does it meet customer or department needs? (N)

   • How much value does the customer or department gain from this process or task? (V)

   • How easy is this process or task to use or do? (U)

6. Add any other comments. Based on everyone's understanding of the process or task, which ones are worthy of improving?

Figure 3.9.
Process or Task
Performance Worksheet

FIELD TECHNIQUES: IMPROVING YOUR PROCESSES AND TASKS

Create a process or task worksheet of your own, or modify the one in Figure 3.9 to suit your own business. Then follow these steps to complete it:

1. *List your processes or tasks.* Meet with the people you work with. Together list those processes and tasks you would like to better understand in terms of time, resource costs, output, and value. Look at the product portfolio worksheets from Chapter Two to get ideas about what you do and for whom you do it. For example, some services are processes themselves. Other services require intake procedures to identify the customer's requirements. All of your services should have a process for evaluating customer satisfaction and your effectiveness. To help you get started, think about how you

   • Identify customer needs

   • Scope out customer requests

   • Select contractors and vendors

   • Maintain current training courses

   • Evaluate your products and services

   • Register and administer people who attend your programs

   • Manage and maintain facilities (meeting rooms, classrooms, computer systems, and so on)

   • Train and develop your own staff

2. *Identify their drivers or customers.* Why are these processes or tasks required? Whose needs are they meeting? You may want to revisit Product Portfolio Worksheet 1, where you listed what you do and for whom you do it.

3. *Identify the resources they require.* Again, look at what you put in Product Portfolio Worksheet 1. Ask how many people (employees or contractors) are engaged in each process. Ask what percentage of their time they dedicate to these activities.

4. *Determine their costs.* Put a value on the resources you identified in Step 3. What are your direct costs for each process or task?

5. *Rate them.* Set some standards or expectations for your process or task management. Measures might include how well you describe or document the tasks or processes, how well you understand what and how many resources they consume, how well people use them, how easy they are to use, and so on. Rate your performance for each process or task, based on the management criteria you selected.

6. *Identify opportunities for improvement.* Focus your attention on those processes or tasks for which you can identify ways to reduce costs, once you understand them better.

FIELD NOTES: REDUCING FIXED AND HIDDEN COSTS

Linda, the director of training and performance improvement at her company, was concerned that so much of her staff's time was spent marketing training programs instead of consulting on performance improvement initiatives. One day she decided to question what drove her department to stay in training (selling instructor-led workshops) instead of moving more into performance improvement. She looked at her budget with this question in mind.

The company evaluated Linda's performance based on her ability to recover her costs. Most of her costs were in facilities. Her department owned six buildings, all of which had classrooms set up especially for instructor-led courses. Linda suddenly realized that she was not in the performance improvement business but was in the real estate business. She was selling classrooms to cover a fixed cost. With this realization she put all six buildings on the market, sold them, and leased classroom space as it was needed. She changed her fixed cost for classroom space to a variable one. She got out of the real estate business, which allowed her to direct her staff's efforts toward performance improvement.

Kelly hired contractors to deliver training to field offices. One day she looked at her instructor costs (variable direct costs charged to specific programs) and noticed that all of her instructors charged essentially the same fee. All received similar evaluations from students. On the surface it looked like each instructor added the same amount of cost to deliver a course. When she discussed the instructors with her administrative assistant, however, she discovered that one instructor was very difficult to support. This instructor always lost materials, requiring second shipments. She wouldn't set up the classroom, which meant a local administrative person had to come in early and set up the room. She wouldn't check out the computers, overhead projectors, or any other equipment, so a technician had to be on call during her classes. She didn't have her classes break or go to lunch on schedule, which caused traffic jams in the cafeteria and made students in other courses late in getting back to class. What Kelly realized was that her direct cost per instructor may have been the same, but their indirect costs were not. This instructor was actually much more expensive than the others, and her higher cost was being born by others in the company. Kelly decided to rethink her evaluation of this instructor.

Russ's manager asked him to reduce his operating budget for the coming year. His two largest fixed costs were salaries for full-time staff and depreciation on medical equipment purchased for use during training. He asked that all staff track their time for a month and note what they were doing and who they were doing it for. He discovered that three administrative staff members spent approximately 60 percent of their time rescheduling people for classes, including "no-shows" (people who didn't show up for training and later called to get in another class). Russ thought their time could be better spent on activities that added value. He documented the cost of rescheduling students and went to his boss with a recommendation on how to reduce this cost. The departments of the no-shows suffered no financial consequences for their behavior, but it increased Russ's costs significantly. Russ wanted this cost to be borne by the offending students' departments, not his.

Next Russ looked at depreciation. The company's business policy stated that when a department used a product the company made, that department had to purchase the product. Therefore Russ's technical training group had to buy the equipment it used to train field technicians to install and repair equipment. Some of this training equipment cost over a million dollars. Russ couldn't resell the training equipment, because he had to be able to train technicians on all models of equipment. The cost of delivering technical training was charged to the field service department; however, this did not include any costs associated with the training equipment. Russ went to his finance department to discuss the implications of leasing the equipment instead of buying it.

FIELD TECHNIQUES: HELPING CLIENTS IMPROVE THEIR PROCESSES

If you participate on a process improvement team as part of your performance consulting services, here are some things you can do to add value to the team's activities:

1. Facilitate the mapping or describing of processes. Be sure to help the client identify all the activities involved and assign a value to them. Be sure to clarify how costs are classified and assigned (to a department, product, service, customer, or spread).

2. Facilitate discussions about which activities add value and which ones do not. Identify which activities should be eliminated because they are redundant or unnecessary, consume too many resources or unnecessary ones, or cause other processes to engage in activities that do not add value.

3. Help the client identify where it can use fewer or less-costly resources and still achieve the same or better outcomes.

4. Work with the client to identify where any false economies might exist because current processes or business practices shift costs to other processes or departments.

5. Ask if there are any policies, standards, or requirements that result in activities or the use of resources that do not add value, add unnecessary costs, or shift costs.

6. Ask about the technology used by each process and whether or not it results in non-value-added activities or the use of unnecessary or too-costly resources.

Once you and your client have identified what drives the cost of the client's processes, you can decide whether or not to redesign them or better manage their cost drivers.

SUMMARY

Performance consultants must understand costs, what drives them, and how they become hidden or get shifted around. Unnecessary costs are the result of poor people performance, poorly designed processes, misunderstood customer requirements, and non-value-adding business requirements. Besides helping your clients, understanding costs will also put you in a better position to define your own costs and prove that your activities add value. If the training director in the story at the beginning of this chapter had better understood costs, he could have helped the VP of sales isolate the company's sales costs, identify their causes, and develop a plan to either eliminate or reduce them. If the VP of sales had better understood how to make managing the cost of sales an integral part of his job (and thus a criteria for judging his performance), he could have avoided his confrontation with the VP of finance.

WHERE TO LEARN MORE

Cokins, G., Stratton, A., and Helbling, J., *An ABC Manager's Primer: Straight Talk on Activity-Based Costing* (Montvale, NJ: Institute of Management Accountants, 1992). This book comes highly recommended by my clients as readable and useful.

Cooke, R., *36-Hour Course in Finance for Nonfinancial Managers* (New York: McGraw-Hill, 1993). This book also comes highly recommended by my clients, who found the ideas informative and useful.

Gill, J., *Understanding Financial Statements and Financial Analysis: The Next Step* (Menlo Park, CA: Crisp Publications, 1990). A practical little book about the fundamentals of understanding financial reports.

Hawkins, P., *The Ecology of Commerce* (New York: HarperCollins, 1993). This is a very interesting little paperback. The most important chapter is Chapter 9, "The Opportunity of Insignificance." The chapter brings to life how in our efforts to reduce costs we only shift them around and burden others.

O'Guin, M., *The Complete Guide to Activity-Based Costing* (Englewood Cliffs, NJ: Prentice Hall, 1991). This is one of the better books on cost management. It is very readable. You don't have to read the whole book, but do pay attention to the first four chapters. I use the concepts in this book in my own business and to help clients better understand when they are shifting costs instead of reducing them.

Stack, J., *The Great Game of Business: Unlocking the Power and Profitability of Open-Book Management* (New York: Doubleday, 1992). This is a very insightful paperback about business economics and how an educated workforce can drive out costs.

Stalk, G., and Hout, T., *Competing Against Time* (New York: Free Press, 1990). There are a lot of books about reengineering and process redesign; this one is very readable and includes excellent examples. The rules on pages 76 and 77 force you and your clients to think about the implications of not understanding how work gets done and which activities have value. The book helps you understand how the design of jobs and work processes can add unnecessary activities (and time), which increases hidden costs.

Chapter 4

Credibility and Influence

Performance consulting requires more than knowing how to design needs assessments and participate in cross-functional teams. It takes a special mindset, combined with political and image management skills.

FIELD NOTES: THE NEED FOR CREDIBILITY

Doug was the director of training at his company. He complained that he couldn't get management to change the company's career development policies, simply because they would not listen to him. He believed the reason they wouldn't listen to him was because his position was too low. Doug knew he would have greater influence if only the company would give him a promotion.

Marilyn headed the training unit at one of her company's field offices. She complained that managers from corporate headquarters would come in and tell her and the other field training managers what to do. Although she saw opportunities to add value to the company beyond training, she hesitated to offer her ideas because she was not from corporate.

Having position power and being part of the corporate team can make it easier to be an effective performance consultant. These things are not required, however, and they don't guarantee that your voice will be heard or your ideas considered. The ability to influence other people's decisions and actions requires a combination of position, expertise, courage, and skill.

EXPERIENCES FROM THE FIELD: BEING CREDIBLE

Whenever I'm asked about how to get people of higher status to accept me as a professional, I use the analogy of a recipe. The essential ingredients are

- *Relevant information.* Know your stuff, and know the client.
- *The courage to speak up.* Believe that what you have to offer is worthy of your client's consideration.
- *Interpersonal skills.* Make people comfortable.

The spices are

- *Trust (with verification).* Assume people's good intentions, but challenge their information and seek corroborating evidence. Remember that opinions and myth are not facts, and hope by itself won't make things happen.
- *Political savvy.* Never forget whose agenda it is, and make sure that person comes off looking good.
- *Dissonance.* Make people uncomfortable enough that they will pause and consider new information.
- *External status.* Make sure your clients know that people outside their group or organization think well of you.

The cooking instructions are

- *Establish a presence.* Manage your image.
- *Remain impartial and objective.* This doesn't mean you shouldn't form an opinion; just don't take sides. Remember that everyone can be right at the same time.
- *Stay focused.* Never lose sight of where you want the client to go and why. Don't confuse being liked or accepted with the goal of improving performance.

It is difficult to separate the key ingredients from the spices and the preparation. It takes all of them to produce a tasty dish.

THE ESSENTIAL INGREDIENTS: INFORMATION, COURAGE, AND INTERPERSONAL SKILLS

Information

In an article in *Performance Improvement* (September 1996), Byron Stock states that the two top obstacles to performance improvement are lack of information and lack of measures. Training and HRD departments may be particularly vulnerable. They are way down the information chain in many organizations. They are the last to know and the last to be involved and are generally called upon after others have already decided on a solution. Unfortunately the solution may not be based on a thorough understanding of the factors that influence performance. Training and HRD professionals have to move up the information chain if they are going to operate as performance consultants.

For some people, asking to be included in decision making seems pushy or even illegitimate. The problem then seems to be how to gain involvement in a way that feels legitimate. One strategy is to contribute useful information at every opportunity. Another strategy is to establish relationships and set up systems that will give you timely access to information. These strategies work together, because getting information depends on having information to share, and having information allows you to get more.

When I'm asked how I stay current so that I will have something useful to contribute, I tell people about what I learned from studying David McClelland's research on what makes people in the foreign service effective (McClelland, D. C., and Dailey, C., *Evaluating New Methods of Measuring the Qualities Needed in Superior Foreign Service Officers* [Boston: McBer & Co., 1973]). The discriminating factor was not having graduated from a specific school but the ability to engineer opportunities to get useful information.

Relevant information—information that helps people make more informed decisions—is a valuable commodity. Sometimes the information people find most useful is the old or proven principles, which is why it helps to be grounded in the fundamentals of performance improvement. Other times, however, people want information about what is going on now, because they like to feel they are "in the know." A question I'm asked frequently is, "What are other companies doing?" Rather than answer that question directly, I find that talking about what other companies have learned proves that I know my stuff better than talking about what they are doing does. This was reinforced recently by an article I read in an internal company management magazine. The article was about an innovative safety program. The program, which touted the use of peer pressure to support safety goals, certainly made sense. Later I asked a manager at the company how well the program was working. He quickly blurted out that the program was a bust because it pitted coworkers against one another, and rather than turn on one another, the company's workers simply chose to ignore the program. In the end the program was unenforceable and a waste of money. Obviously it would be misleading to simply share with a client what this company did without also pointing out what it learned from the experience.

Courage

When I'm asked about the courage to speak up, I often refer people to a little test I found in a book called *Guide to Personal Risk Taking* by Richard Byrd (New York: AMACOM, 1974). The test listed sources of personal power such as seniority, desirable personal traits, interpersonal skills, professional friendships, confidence, expertise, access to information, and so on. Byrd's premise is that the more personal power you have, the less you need to rely on position power to take risks; the less personal power you have, the more you need to toe the party line. When I first took the test I was interested to find that some of the factors that determine personal power were outside my control, such as seniority and the desirability of my personal traits. However, most of the factors were within my control, such as improving my interpersonal skills, increasing my store of information, and building relationships.

In fact, most of the factors are interdependent. If you are willing to take responsibility for one, such as relationships, the success you have there will affect the others. For example, improving your interpersonal skills leads to friendships, which lead to information; better information leads to expertise, which leads to confidence; greater confidence leads to the courage to create opportunities.

I've also learned not to be afraid of criticism. Schaller, in his book *Getting Things Done* (Nashville, TN: Abingdon Press, 1986), includes the willingness to accept criticism as one of the thirteen essential characteristics for leading and influencing others. Senge, in *The Fifth Discipline* (New York: Doubleday, 1990), also comments on the willingness to be criticized. When you speak up, it is less important to be right than to force reflection and examination. The truth is that staying silent also has consequences, as it reduces your chances of being included in the decision-making process. Think about what it takes to be a professional athlete. These people know everyone is watching them and that their every move will be criticized. When an athlete executes a successful play or maneuver, everyone cheers; but when he fails, everyone's a critic. Yet, without the athletes there would be no game. Only by joining in the game can you put yourself in a position to influence the outcome.

If you want to influence someone, you have to stick your neck out. I once saw an inspirational poster advertised in an airline magazine. The poster had a picture of a golf ball, with a fairway in the background. Under the picture was the caption "You'll miss every shot you never take." Speaking up when it matters is a risk. So when I'm considering the need to speak up, I reflect on Byrd's personal power test and recall the importance of doing the things that will raise my score. If I create opportunities to stay informed I can take more risks, because my comments will be grounded in facts. If I strengthen my relationships, people will be open to at least considering my comments.

Interpersonal Skills

Interpersonal skills are a combination of nonverbal and verbal communication skills and social and cultural sensitivity. As with physical beauty, it is often apparent from other people's reactions whether or not someone has interpersonal skills. Some people are able to establish a rapport with people of one social group but not with those from another group. The key variable is the ability to pick up on social cues concerning which behaviors are acceptable and then to adapt your behavior to that of the group. I don't know of any shortcuts to obtaining interpersonal skills. They are developed by interacting with people of different backgrounds and different levels of interpersonal skills. At a minimum, you have to be aware of your own behavior, observe how people interact, and be willing to take responsibility for establishing relationships with others.

There is no substitute for the right ingredients. Good information, the courage to speak up, and effective interpersonal skills are essential to gaining other people's trust. These are elements you can acquire and develop with education and experience. It is hard to compensate for their absence, however, even with superior skills in needs assessment and measurement.

FIELD TECHNIQUES: GETTING INFORMATION

Here are some things you can do to acquire relevant information about your client or organization in a timely manner:

1. Listen carefully to find out what the business is doing and to understand the politics behind its choices.

2. Learn your customer's business—what it does and how it does it. Find out what its products are, who its customers are, and who its competitors are. Find out where it stands financially and how it makes financial decisions.

3. Get to know the librarian at your company, your local public library, or a local college or university. Indicate your interest in and need for quick access to timely information. Talk about how the two of you can work together. Find out what the librarian will expect of you, and honor your side of the agreement.

4. Scan the business section of your newspaper. Pay particular attention to news about technological developments and your clients' or organization's competitors, suppliers, and key customers.

5. The *Wall Street Journal* contains the latest information on the legal front. Take a quick look for snapshots of emerging legal precedents.

6. If you don't already have one, introduce yourself to a broker. Periodically ask him or her for financial information about your clients and their major competitors, suppliers, and customers. Learn how to read a prospectus, an annual report, and financial statements.

7. Commission the ASTD to do a literature search for you about trends in training, training delivery, and performance improvement. Watch for the big theme issues of the journals *Training, Training and Development,* and *Performance and Improvement* and their counterparts in personnel journals.

8. Subscribe to research journals or find another way to review them, such as at your local public library, at a college library, or on-line. Scan their tables of contents. Look for research studies about technology, change, productivity, and improving performance. Some of the journals I find useful are *Kappan, American Psychologist, Performance and Instruction Quarterly, H.R. Quarterly,* and *Human Resource Management.*

9. Pay attention to the best-seller lists in the *New York Times Book Review.* Look for books about new management theories, corporate success stories, and quick cost-cutting solutions (taking over a market, increasing productivity, and so on). Also check the book section in your Sunday paper for reviews of new business books. Your customers may not have read them, but they will know about them. You do not have to read each book in its entirety, but do try to scan the salient chapters or at least read the abstract.

10. Develop professional relationships with colleagues from other organizations. Join professional organizations such as the ASTD, the ISPI, and the Society for Human Resource Management (SHRM). Use those relationships to set up user groups and special task forces to share information and commission studies.

11. Create opportunities to learn and polish information-sharing techniques. For example, submit proposals to present at local and national conferences, join committees, volunteer to be a greeter at local meetings, and submit articles to business organizations' local chapter newsletters.

12. Learn to do searches on the Internet.

**FIELD NOTES: DEVELOPING
THE ESSENTIAL INGREDIENTS**

Deborah had now specified her department's vision and mission, described its products and services, defined its processes, and established measures to evaluate those processes. The next step was to meet with her staff to develop a plan for getting information about what was going on in the company more quickly. The team decided that they needed a better way to get information from within the company, information about their market, and information about new developments in performance improvement. The plan they came up with called for them to create strategic relationships, establish carefully selected professional affiliations, subscribe to targeted journals and newsletters, and become more skilled at using the Internet.

They decided they wanted to establish strategic relationships with their company's finance and marketing departments. These relationships would be key to finding out early what programs the company was funding, which managers were seeking funding, and what new products and marketing campaigns were under development. Early access to this information would allow the team to recommend simultaneous creation of help screens, funding for training, and funding for just-in-time documentation. All that was needed was to create an opportunity to build the right relationships.

To learn more about new developments in performance improvement, two members of Deborah's team decided to contact other, noncompeting organizations in their area to see if they would be interested in getting together to share what they were doing. They contacted the major employers in the area, and ten companies decided to participate. The companies created a purpose statement for the group and some guidelines concerning when and how often to meet, who to invite, and how they would share information. Deborah's group's rationale for arranging these meetings was that finding out what other companies were doing would not only help them personally, it would also make it easier for them to build a relationship with the people in their own finance and marketing departments.

THE SPICES: TRUST, POLITICAL SAVVY, DISSONANCE, AND EXTERNAL STATUS

Trust

One of the things I've learned is that people tell the truth. However, their truth is based on what they know, what they've heard, and what they've surmised. During the time that I was a commercial arbitrator I learned a lot about facts and hearsay. I also came to understand that most people do not distinguish between the two. There are many ways to get a more accurate and complete picture of a situation; however, they all require some political savvy. It helps to remember that

- People base their conclusions and opinions on what they have experienced and what they have heard others talking about.

- Perceptions are real, but they are not the same as facts.

- People, especially senior managers, do not want to be embarrassed because of something they could have known but didn't.

Here are a few things you can do to verify what you're told:

- Find out if people's conclusions are based on one incident or if they have corroborating evidence.

- Ask questions to help people see the difference between direct evidence and hearsay. For example, ask, "How exactly did you find out that information? Did you come across it yourself, or did someone tell you about it? Is this a one-time event, or has this happened before?"

- Point out whether what you are hearing is hearsay, folklore, or a deduction based on direct observation. For example, say, "Oh, so you're basing your conclusion on what Joe told you. Boy, I sure would like to see that for myself! I get nervous when I have to rely on someone else's interpretation of what happened without seeing some additional information." Or ask, "So, you saw the numbers yourself?"

Political Savvy

In chess there is a play called the gambit, a move designed to get your opponent to expose his or her queen. An analogous move exists in social settings. For example, you might tell a story or make a comment that exposes some weakness or frailty about yourself, such as your discomfort, despair, or fatigue with a certain situation. The other person has three choices. He or she can match your exposure with a similar one about himself or herself, ignore what you said, or discount what you shared. If the person responds with a mutual admission (such as, "I know, I get pretty exasperated myself and wonder if it's all worth it"), there is evidence of some regard for your position. If the person ignores your disclosure, you need additional information before you can conclude that the person will give your ideas serious consideration. If the person discounts your disclosure, you have initial evidence that he or she will discount your ideas as well.

I use the concept of the gambit in business settings (where the conversation is usually less personal than in the preceding example) to test how well my ideas are being accepted, how open the client is to critical discussion, and how people in a group work together. For example, if someone mentions the mistakes made during the development or launch of an earlier program, I listen to how the conversation unfolds. Others in the room might point out what was learned and how that can be used in the current situation, or they might ignore the comment or contradict or discount the remark. Their comments provide valuable cues to how I should proceed.

In other situations I will share stories of common mistakes and false starts and then listen to how my audience receives the stories. Again, they might match them with a story about their own false starts, ignore them altogether, or discount them as lacking foresight. If my or other people's ideas are discounted, I know I have to work harder at influencing decisions.

Dissonance

Dissonance is another technique I use to get people to pause, reflect, and reconsider. Most people are familiar with dissonance in art. The artist will show water falling the wrong way or stairs going around in circles. Some well-known comic strips use dissonance as the basis of their humor (for example, *Doonesbury, Non Sequitur,* and the now-deceased *The Far Side* and *Calvin and Hobbs*). Teenagers create dissonance by challenging social customs (a friend of mine calls the teenage years the age of costumes, hair, body jewelry, and so on). People who fit in and behave as expected do not generate dissonance. People who toe the party line do not cause dissonance. Dissonance occurs whenever our sense of the expected is disrupted. In business settings you can create dissonance with new or unexpected information (for instance, by introducing an unexpected thought, a new interpretation, or a different perspective). You can create dissonance by telling a story or using an analogy that gets people to think about a situation in a new way. Your goal is not antagonism, unpleasantness, or (like a teenager) to be noticed. Your goal is to get people to be open to new perspectives and possibilities while not losing face.

The importance of being willing to accept criticism and opposing views is illustrated by a story my father once told me. He believed you could judge the health of an organization by the degree to which its leaders allowed at least one person in their ranks who was different. My father called it "looking for the guy in the brown suit." In the 1940s and 1950s corporate leaders were all male, they all wore navy or black suits, their shirts were white, their ties were plain, their shoes were black oxfords, and their socks matched their pants. Dad always looked for the guy with gravy on his tie, the guy whose jacket didn't match his pants, who wore loafers instead of oxfords, or whose shirt was blue or pink. Dad's premise was that if the leaders could not tolerate deviation from the dress code, they probably wouldn't entertain constructive arguments. Today "brown-suiters" are the conscience of the organization. Much of the work of the performance consultant is to act as a conscience. We are the ones who raise the issues of proof, facts, and fallout. I am a brown-suiter and proud of it.

External Status

Status within an organization depends on the person, the organization, and the norms of the group. Common sources of status are degrees, specific experiences, and ties to leadership. For example, in a chemical engineering firm a degree in chemical engineering carries a fair amount of status; if your organization's leaders come from a military background, having served in the armed forces will bring you some credibility, at least initially; organizational leaders with a background in the social services will probably look favorably on Peace Corps experience; and so on.

Status outside the organization is similar to internal status. Although having the same academic and life experiences as organizational leaders certainly helps, external status comes more from associations with people, agencies, and ideals that the organization looks upon favorably. Examples include

- A formal relationship with a professional, industry, or community organization

- Being cited positively in the business or industry press

- Having had a professional relationship with other groups your organization wants to be like or learn from

- Having access to influential people in the press, industry, or community

Verifying information, being politically astute, creating dissonance, and using status are the instruments needed to leverage your information. They are what will help you get an audience. Moreover, they are what you will use to find out what is really going on.

FIELD TECHNIQUES: DEVELOPING POLITICAL SAVVY, DISSONANCE, AND STATUS

Here are some suggestions for learning to become appropriately skeptical, to become more politically astute, to instill dissonance, and to acquire external status:

1. Always look for corroborating evidence.

2. When you hear secondhand information, point out that it is hearsay. Ask for direct evidence or where to find it. For instance, ask, "Who has read the report" (or seen the numbers, heard the comments, and so on) "and would be willing to give us his or her interpretation of what happened? Could we see the report ourselves?" Engage the client in conversations about who benefits (and how) from the perpetuation of hearsay and who is affected (and how) when you operate from facts instead.

3. When there is a dispute over the accuracy or interpretation of some information, try to get each party to assume the other person's role or position and then interpret the information from that standpoint.

4. Find out the real sponsors of ideas and programs. Find out what they have to gain if their ideas are accepted and what they might lose if they are not.

5. Exemplify as many of the client's characteristics, norms, language, values, and so on, as you can. But don't be exactly like the client; a little deviation helps, as long as it does not conflict with the client's values.

6. Observe what happens when one person in a group challenges assumptions or tries to promote critical dialogue about an issue. You will learn who has the most influence in the group, how open the group is to opposing ideas, and to what degree the group is in real consensus versus silent compliance.

7. If there is something that everybody thinks is obvious but really isn't and no one asks about it, raise the question under the guise of being new to the group, needing to explain it later, or wanting to get a richer picture of the situation. If no one supports your request, negotiate to talk about it after the meeting with one or two people.

8. Establish some source of external status. It won't carry you over the long haul, but it will help you in the beginning.

FIELD NOTES: LEARNING TO COOK WITH SPICES

Deborah was in a meeting with two of her peers. During the conversation her peers began to argue over which one of them was responsible for certain items in the budget. The argument was getting more and more heated, and they began to accuse each other of deliberately trying to duck their responsibilities. Deborah interrupted with the statement, "I think you two are operating from different data sets." It got them to pause long enough for her to continue. "You are both referring to what sounds like the same financial report, but you understand the company's finances too well to be this far apart on the same report. Is it possible that you are actually referring to different reports that happen to go by the same name? Why don't the two of you get a copy of the report you are talking about so we can all look at it together?" They reluctantly agreed. When they returned they discovered they had indeed been talking about different financial reports that happened to have the same name.

Chris, one of the consultants in finance who reported to Mike, was meeting with the head of accounting, Frank, and the head of production, Brian. The goal of the meeting was to come up with recommendations about how to improve communications between the two departments to reduce administrative costs.

They decided to map how information flowed between accounting and production, starting from the ordering of raw materials to the billing of customers for receipt of finished goods. Frank and Brian began to argue over what information existed, where the information went, how it got there, how often it was transmitted, and in what form. The two men were becoming more and more polarized. They looked to Chris to take sides. Chris interrupted with, "You're both right and you're both wrong. You're right based on what you know. You're wrong because you only have part of the picture." She suggested that they each spend one day at the other's site. While there, each one was to observe only, with no criticism allowed. The assignment was to find out exactly what information the other one worked with. The three of them agreed to meet again in two weeks after Frank and Brian had completed their assignments. Frank and Brian learned that they each worked from different—and incomplete—information. They returned with a stronger conviction that the new information system had to provide both of them with a more accurate picture of administrative costs.

THE COOKING INSTRUCTIONS: ESTABLISHING A PRESENCE, REMAINING IMPARTIAL AND OBJECTIVE, AND STAYING FOCUSED

Establishing a Presence

I remember a TV interview with Marilyn Monroe. She was asked why she didn't wear hose or jewelry. Her answer was something about wanting people to focus on her overall sensuality, not her hair or jewelry. She considered comments about her hair (or dress, or any discrete item) to be evidence that she had not managed her image well. I've often used her philosophy as a model for myself. Although I'm not interested in selling sensuality, I am interested in selling useful information—and myself as an expert. I want my clients to experience our collaboration as an instrument that helps them make sense out of what is happening in their work environment. I want them to know that I have only their best interest in mind. Therefore I'm careful not to send distracting or conflicting messages. Distracting messages happen when we say things that get people to question our motives, when our materials are unclear about who we are and what we do, and when our materials contain conflicting messages about the business we are in.

Another thing I learned about managing my image is to get to the point quickly. A few years ago my brother told me he was looking for material for his "elevator conversations," since he frequently had only those few seconds in the elevator to communicate the value of his department. He had to quickly establish a presence, negotiate for resources, and get permission to proceed. Therefore he wanted a few phrases, facts, visuals, or stories that would quickly convey his successes, breakthroughs, results, and dilemmas.

I've thought of that conversation often. At times we all want and need an audience with the right people. So many times, however, we ask for a ninety-minute or two-hour meeting—and time is the most valuable resource people have. Asking clients for their time is a very costly, even painful, request. When we take others' time to tell our story, we're meeting our needs, not theirs. It takes skill to immediately establish a presence, get to the point, say what you mean, and ask for what you want. Clients appreciate it when you respect their time.

Remaining Impartial and Objective

Another thing I've learned is to be impartial. When you take sides someone loses, and people don't let go of their losses. They just go into hiding and wait for another opportunity to bring up the issue again or get even. Therefore, try to make everyone a winner.

I've learned to begin with where the client currently sees the situation, not with how I want them to see it. This means I have to accept their assessment of the situation and their solution to the problem. I always acknowledge—aloud—that they have taken the time to think through the problem and have arrived at a logical conclusion. Once I'm sure they know that I accept their ideas, I can

- Present new information they may not have been privileged to receive but should know

- Talk through another interpretation of the situation, under the guise of making sure I fully understand their perception of the situation

- Talk about how much better they would look if they were to let their solution evolve into one that incorporated the opposing view (in cases where there is an opposing view). I tag on something to the effect that they and their adversary are smart enough to come up with a really innovative solution that will make them both look good.

- Solicit the help of their peers to come up with a way for them to change their position and save face.

Staying Focused

Although it is important not to take sides, it is just as important to express your opinion, as long as it is based on a solid understanding of the situation. As an expert you are expected to have an opinion. I've also learned, however, that it is important for people to save face.

A few years ago I was asked to bid on a multimillion-dollar job. I was told the client had made up his mind and not to present any other suggestions. The client had attended a trade show and seen an example of how a company had changed its culture and saved money through the use of new technology. The client asked the vendor, "Can you do this for us?" A more appropriate question would have been, "What has to be in place for us to experience the same results?" Very few people will admit that they can't do something (especially a salesperson). I believed the client's idea wouldn't work in his organization. I got my facts together about hidden costs associated with his favored solution and what it would take to implement it. I called one of the client's best friends and quickly related my understanding of the situation, presented the problem, and said, "Your friend could be making a decision with negative career consequences. I need your help to get him to at least consider these other factors, in a way that helps him save face. He bought into this idea with insufficient information. Let him know it's okay to change his mind when the change is based on more complete and accurate information."

I've also learned that some of the strangest things can divert people from the task at hand. Instead of focusing on the problem, its implications, and how to solve it, people often waste energy on irrelevant issues. Introducing new language that is not part of the client's vocabulary is an example of something that can throw a client off track. Clients talk about costs, problems, missed opportunities, and solutions. They talk about reorganizing, implementing programs, and changing selection criteria. They do not talk about *interventions;* that's our word, and *performance technology* is our label. If you want your ideas to be heard, use your clients' language, don't ask them to learn yours. Language can be a barrier if people feel left out because they aren't familiar with the lexicon. This is true whether you are discussing chemistry, finance, marketing, manufacturing, electronics, or performance technology. When you introduce new or unusual language, the focus of the conversation shifts away from healthy debate to something else. It may, in fact, shift to questions about your credibility. Staying focused on the task, not on you or your profession, helps assure clients that your only motive is their best interest.

FIELD TECHNIQUES: ESTABLISHING A PRESENCE, REMAINING IMPARTIAL AND OBJECTIVE, AND STAYING FOCUSED

Here are some things you can do to create a presence and thus enhance your credibility and sphere of influence:

1. Create a logo, a visual image for your practice or department.

2. Create a slogan or a few phrases that quickly say what you are all about.

3. Volunteer to be on your client's team or committee as a scribe or coordinator. Once there, be sure to contribute; don't just sit on the periphery. Fill the task and social roles as needed.

4. Produce solutions, recommendations, and programs that the client will see as adding value. Talk through implementation issues, downstream costs, and the implications of your suggestions for other systems.

5. Document your results in terms of increased revenues or reduced costs. Be willing to share the glory.

6. Develop and practice your elevator conversations. Be clear about what you want to accomplish, and always think about your audience. Ask yourself what they want to know and why they want to know it. Give them only what they need. If they ask for more, give it to them, but let the client drive the agenda.

FIELD NOTES: FOLLOWING THE COOKING INSTRUCTIONS

Deborah wanted a strategic alliance with the VP of finance. She asked if they could meet for ten minutes. She went in with a ten-minute overview covering who she was, her department's mission, and what she wanted from the meeting. She included two stories illustrating how the lack of her early involvement had added costs. One of the things she wanted was for finance to know her department's capabilities and to establish an ongoing, mutually beneficial relationship. The two of them communicated regularly from then on, mostly during ten- to fifteen-minute meetings.

Kelly, the head of training at a large insurance company, continued to meet with her staff to discuss some of the problems they were having gaining acceptance as performance consultants rather than trainers. Kelly was particularly troubled by how hard it was to get access to senior management. The group wondered why it was so hard to gain acceptance in their new role, despite their expertise in needs assessment and facilitation. They wondered why external consultants could come in and immediately be accepted as credible. After studying ASTD's competencies, they asked themselves, "What are the skills and knowledge behind these competencies? What do we have to do differently?" And most important, they asked, "What do we have to change about ourselves to be effective in this new role?" It became clear to Kelly that they all needed to become more politically savvy and to learn more about influencing decisions. They also needed to learn more about marketing their services.

Kelly called Dave, a colleague at another company whom she had met at a professional meeting. Dave had put together a full-scale marketing plan for his training department. His plan included

- Changing the name of the department from Training to Performance Development.
- Creating the slogan "A Small Investment for Big Returns" for the department and putting it on all department materials.

- Putting together a short, seven-minute briefing his staff could deliver covering what they have done and are doing, their plans for the future, and the drivers behind their services.

- Reorganizing the department to more closely align it with the core business.

- Arranging for department staff to work in the field for three to six months (although his company greatly valued field experience, Dave's staff did not come from the field).

Kelly knew she could implement parts of Dave's plan. She also recognized that her staff had no marketing strategy and little presence outside of her department. She and her staff met to come up with image-enhancing ideas. They assembled a portfolio of the informational materials her department produced. When they looked at it, they discovered there was no one look, no logo, nothing that immediately said any of it came from their department. Instead, the materials simply described the department's processes, with no information about the results or benefits it provided its clients. Kelly quickly arranged a meeting with marketing to learn how to better communicate the department's message.

FIELD TOOLS: QUALIFYING THE CLIENT

So far this chapter has focused on building your own credibility and influence. The irony is that sometimes your clients will need to do the same for themselves. Clients can be unsophisticated about how to get good information and about knowing when to speak up. They may lack interpersonal skills and political savvy. They may have trouble staying focused on what is important. As a professional you can develop your own skills, but as a consultant you must learn to work effectively with your clients no matter how skilled they are.

A few years ago I was asked about my process for qualifying my clients. The question led me to document what I intuitively look for when I first meet a client, the information that helps me decide if I want to do the job and what it will take to work effectively with the client. Based on my reflections I compiled a survey, provided here in Figure 4.1, which you can use to assess your clients' sophistication and to distinguish your issues from theirs. Using this tool will help alert you to the factors you will have to manage if you are going to be effective in your relationship with the client.

Read over the questions before you meet with your client. Identify the issues you want to clarify in your early interviews, when you are still scoping out the job and deciding what resources (time and people) it will take to fulfill the request. You and your colleagues can answer the questions separately and then share your answers. You can then use your answers to develop a strategy for working with the client. Figure 4.2 lists some suggestions for how to proceed.

**FIELD
TECHNIQUES:
STRENGTHENING
YOUR CREDIBILITY
AND INFLUENCE**

If you want to be credible and better influence your client's actions and decisions, then you need to develop your own plan:

1. Begin by coming up with ways to build on and enhance the essential ingredients. That is,

   • Come up with ways to get the *relevant information.* Stay in the know; find out what is going on and who is behind what initiative.

   • Have the *courage to speak up.* Ask for an audience. Present information you believe is worthy of being considered, while managing the risk of speaking up. Assess how much influence you have now and what you can do to get more by improving your interpersonal skills, developing relationships, increasing your expertise, and so on.

   • Continue to develop your *interpersonal skills.* Cultivate your skill at building relationships and your ability to gain others' trust.

2. Work on the spices. That is,

   • *Trust people, but always verify* the information they give you.

   • Develop your *political savvy.* Find out what people's hidden agendas are, and always try to make the right people look good.

   • Strategically *create dissonance* when people are entrenched or polarized, to get them to pause long enough to incorporate new information or rethink their position.

   • Increase your *external status.* Do things that help build your professional reputation.

3. Perfect your cooking. That is,

   • Learn to *establish your presence* and manage your image.

   • Practice *remaining impartial,* but do not hesitate to express a well-founded opinion.

   • Periodically ask where the discussion and the action is going, to *stay focused* on what matters.

4. Learn to consciously assess where you clients are, how sophisticated they are, their attitudes, and how committed they are to the project at hand. Use that information to come up with a strategy for working with them effectively. In the process you will further enhance you credibility and influence.

Client Capabilities and Commitment

1. To what degree has the client defined the problem?

   Not clearly   Can't tell   Very clearly
        1   3   5

   Comments_____

2. To what degree are the different groups within the client's organization in consensus about the problem?

   Polarized   Wide variance   In consensus
        1   3   5

   Comments_____

3. To what degree has the client defined the solution or how to handle the problem?

   Not clearly   Can't tell   Very clearly
        1   3   5

   Comments_____

4. To what degree are the different groups within the client's organization in consensus about the solution or how to handle the problem?

   Polarized   Wide variance   In consensus
        1   3   5

   Comments_____

5. How well does the client understand what is meant by *competent performance?*

      Naive   All over the map   Sophisticated
        1   3   5

   Comments_____

6. How well does the client understand how skills, knowledge, and values relate to competence?

      Naive   All over the map   Sophisticated
        1   3   5

   Comments_____

7. How well does the client understand what research is already available about competence and performance?

      Naive   All over the map   Sophisticated
        1   3   5

   Comments_____

8. How well does the client understand the organizational factors that influence performance?

      Naive   All over the map   Sophisticated
        1   3   5

   Comments_____

9. How do people feel about the project?

   Resistant   Not sure   Supportive
        1   3   5

   Comments_____

10. How willing is the client to consider new possibilities and take risks?

   Mind made up   All over the map   Open
        1   3   5

   Comments_____

11. How skilled are the client's people at working as a team?

   Unskilled   Wide variance   Very skilled
        1   3   5

   Comments_____

12. How skilled are the client's people at representing customer groups?

   Unskilled   Wide variance   Very skilled
        1   3   5

   Comments_____

13. How skilled are the client's people at managing projects?

   Unskilled   Wide variance   Very skilled
        1   3   5

   Comments_____

14. How skilled are the client's people at processing written information?

   Unskilled   Wide variance   Very skilled
        1   3   5

   Comments_____

15. How skilled are the client's people at processing statistical information?

   Unskilled   Wide variance   Very skilled
        1   3   5

   Comments_____

Figure 4.1.
Qualifying Survey

16. How skilled are the client's people at processing oral information?

Unskilled	Wide variance	Very skilled
1	3	5

Comments_____

17. How skilled are the client's people at building communications plans?

Unskilled	Wide variance	Very skilled
1	3	5

Comments_____

18. To what degree has the client already determined who will do the work?

Entrenched	Unclear	Open
1	3	5

Comments_____

19. To what degree has the client already determined how the work will be done?

Entrenched	Unclear	Open
1	3	5

Comments_____

20. To what degree has the client already determined how much the work is worth?

Entrenched	Unclear	Open
1	3	5

Comments_____

21. How well adapted are the client's systems to gathering customer intelligence?

Not well adapted	Wide variance	Sophisticated
1	3	5

Comments_____

22. How well adapted are the client's systems to analyzing data?

Not well adapted	Wide variance	Sophisticated
1	3	5

Comments_____

23. How well adapted are the client's systems to disseminating information?

Not well adapted	Wide variance	Sophisticated
1	3	5

Comments_____

24. How well adapted are the client's systems to identifying trends and drivers?

Not well adapted	Wide variance	Sophisticated
1	3	5

Comments_____

Demographics

25. What business is the client in?

26. What are their business drivers?

27. Who's their competition?

28. Where do they stand in the market?

29. How are they organized? What is their organizational structure?

30. How many employees do they have?

31. Who is involved in this effort?

32. Who will be most affected by the effort?

33. Does the project have a sponsor? Who? Where is he or she in the organization?

34. Is the team in place?

35. Has the client developed a score card or defined criteria to measure the results of this project? If so, what are the criteria and standards? How do they plan to get the information they need to determine if they have achieved their objective?

36. Is the project budgeted?

37. Do they have a timetable for the project?

38. What software do they use now that might be appropriate for this project?

39. How geographically spread are the team, the customers of the project, and the organization's decision makers?

40. Is this project part of a larger goal?

If the client organization	Then
Is very clear or has defined the problem	• Confirm how they came to the conclusion they did. • Look for evidence that they were thorough in their process.
Is not clear or has not defined the problem	• Work with them to develop a process, or suggest a process for defining the problem.
Is not in agreement	• Plan to meet with representatives of the differing views to confirm what it is they disagree about. • Use that information to bring them to consensus or to come up with a new view that they can all support.
Is naive or is all over the map	• Plan to bring all the players to a similar level of understanding about what supports competent performance and what undermines it.
Is resistant to the project	• Add to your strategy a process for overcoming resistance and getting buy-in.
Is skeptical	• Find out what the source of the skepticism is.
Has its mind made up	• Find out about what, and the reason behind this position. • Acknowledge the legitimacy of the position, but if you believe it is unproductive, create enough dissonance to introduce doubt (while complimenting them for being conscientious). • Then give them the information they need to come to a more informed conclusion. You may want to ask a neutral party to be the one to introduce the new information.
Is unskilled	• Add coaching or training, teaming, project management, data analysis, and so on, to your process.
Is open to who will perform the work and how it will be done	• Add facilitating discussions about who might do the work and how to define your process.
Is entrenched, and you or others disagree	• Find out their reasoning. • Acknowledge their rationale. • If the entrenchment is based on old hurts or wounds, make public the reasoning. • Identify who gains and who loses from the decision. • Create enough dissonance to get them to reconsider. • Recommend a solution that still satisfies their needs. • Negotiate for them to join with the others to come up with a process they can all support.
Does not have systems suited for the project	• Explain the implications of this deficiency in terms of costs and time. • Work with a design that accommodates the systems in place, or help the client negotiate for additional resources.

Figure 4.2.
If-Then Table:
Developing a Strategy
from the Survey Results

SUMMARY

Doug and Marilyn, in the stories at the beginning of the chapter, were looking to their organizations to legitimize their roles and to gain a voice in decision making. Having position power and being close to the action can help, but they do not take the place of having an effective image and a reputation as a credible professional. These are things only you can do. The ideas in this and the previous chapters offer you a template for building a presence in your organization.

WHERE TO LEARN MORE

American Society for Training and Development, *Models for HRD Practice* (Alexandria, VA: American Society for Training and Development, 1996).

Byrd, R., *Guide to Personal Risk Taking* (New York: AMACOM, 1974) and *C&RT: The Creatrix Inventory* (San Francisco: Jossey-Bass/Pfeiffer, 1986). The second title is a self-assessment inventory designed to help people explore how their personal characteristics help and hinder their work success.

Iverson, K., *Plain Talk* (New York: Wiley, 1997).

Langdon, D., *The New Language of Work* (Amherst, MA: HRD Press, 1997).

Schaller, L., *Getting Things Done* (Nashville, TN: Abingdon Press, 1986).

Senge, P., *The Fifth Discipline: The Art and Practice of the Learning Organization* (New York: Doubleday, 1990).

Stolovitch, H., Keeps, E., and Rodriguez, D., "Skill Sets for the Human Performance Technologist," *Performance Improvement Quarterly,* 1997, *10*(1), 97–123.

Watzlawick, P., with Weakland, J., and Fisch, R., *Change: Principles of Problem Formation and Problem Resolution* (New York: Norton, 1974). This book and Watzlawick's other works, particularly *Ultra-Solutions: How to Fail Successfully* (New York, Norton, 1988), are excellent at explaining how our own mental models of the world and ourselves prevent success. *Change* is especially constructive on learning how to look at situations from a different perspective (which leads to breakthroughs) and stay focused on solving the real problem. Start with the second half of the book, which is full of wonderful examples. The first half of the book explains how to apply mathematical models to understand human relationships.

Westgaard, O., "Describing a Performance Improvement Specialist, The Heurist," *Performance Improvement,* 1997, *36*(6), 10–14.

Part Two

Performance Consulting

Chapter 5

Environment and Norms

*N*ot only do performance consultants need a special set of skills, they also need specialized knowledge. For example, they need to understand how work environments and social systems in organizations shape performance. Here is an example of what can happen when these things are not understood.

FIELD NOTES: ENVIRONMENTAL PITFALLS

The bank was considered a model of sound banking practices. Its main branch was an architectural wonder, with soaring marble columns and a grand Roman portico. The bank's employees were known for being stoic, polite, and obedient. They were shocked and humiliated when the TV news announced that their bank was on the brink of failing. The bank's senior management had been speculating on risky investments. Day after day the feature story in the local newspaper was about possible fraud and malfeasance at the bank and the need for stronger government controls on the industry. Every day brought disturbing new developments, like the firing of an experienced auditor over a dispute about investment practices. Humiliating cartoons were showing up on the office walls. The bank's employees found themselves facing embarrassing questions from neighbors and colleagues. The questions about why it had happened seemed unending. Why hadn't someone spoken up, challenged what was happening, reported it to the government?

The new management decided a culture change was needed. Employees soon received a memo telling them to lighten up and that telling jokes was appropriate behavior. This was followed by advertisements in which the bank was depicted as a buffoon. Morale dropped to an all-time low, and incidents of serious illness increased among the bank's midlevel managers. The bank was in serious difficulty, and the new management did not understand how deeply the betrayal of trust by the old senior management had undermined their employees' self-esteem. There was no simple solution.

EXPERIENCES FROM THE FIELD: ORGANIZATIONAL DYNAMICS

Before I present guidelines on how to do performance consulting, it's important that you understand some of the underlying principles of organizational dynamics. It's been my experience that clients and peers do not always have the same understanding of how the work environment affects performance. One reason for this is that we come from such different backgrounds. My standing joke is that at least all accountants have studied debits and credits and all doctors have studied anatomy. The performance consulting profession isn't so lucky; performance consultants' professional and academic backgrounds vary significantly. And even those of us who have degrees in human resources, education, or business cannot assume we all studied the same concepts, since those academic programs are shaped more by the philosophies and strong personalities of popular professors than by a codified body of knowledge.

Therefore, before getting into the processes of assessing needs and selecting interventions, I think it is important to explain two concepts on which those processes are based. Please think of this chapter as a primer. My intent is to give you an understanding of my thinking behind the tools presented in the later chapters.

I taught graduate courses in management for the Insurance School of Chicago for fourteen years. The courses were part of the insurance industry's chartered property and casualty underwriting (CPCU) and management programs. In addition to finance, the courses stressed management theory, analytical decision-making models, and organizational behavior. Every term brought a new textbook, which meant I got to read a lot. In the early 1980s I had the opportunity to hear Richard Boyatzis and David McClelland speak on their methodologies for defining competence. They presented a powerful case that competence depends on context (that is, the work environment). This helped me understand what was going on in the insurance industry. Insurance companies often hired one another's employees. The assumption was that if an underwriter held the CPCU certificate and was a good performer at one company, he or she would perform equally well at another company. This proved not to be the case. Companies forgot to consider that each one had it own policies, products, procedures, and culture. Earning the CPCU designation and having experience in underwriting was not enough to ensure that a person could perform well in different environments. With this observation in mind I created two models for understanding how environment affects performance. The first model concerns the work environment, and the second is about group norms.

THE WORK ENVIRONMENT

Three variables have to come together, or be in harmony, for an individual to achieve optimum performance in a particular job. These variables are

1. The resources of the organization, including its mandate, technology and systems, and financial strength

2. What the job is expected to produce (the outputs)

3. What the individual knows, can do, and is willing to do

The more the three variables overlap, the greater the chance that optimal performance will occur. The further apart they are, or if one of the three is not in sync with the other two, the greater the likelihood of marginal or poor performance. I call the area of overlap the "zone of competence" (see Figure 5.1).

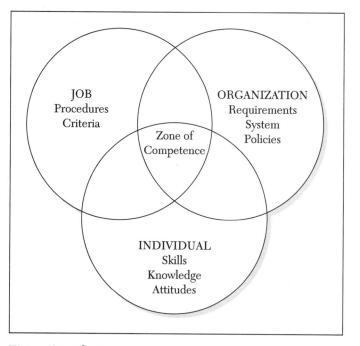

Figure 5.1. The Zone of Competence

The Organization

People performance depends on what the organization can offer. The term *organization* can describe a whole company, a division within a company, a department, a function, or even a work group or team. For example, companies have reputations, and so do departments and teams. Companies have financial and other resources, and so do departments and teams. Companies are more or less attuned to developments in the marketplace, just as departments and teams are more or less attuned to developments in their company. Whether you are dealing with an entire organization or just a work group, its customer profiles may not be clearly defined and its customers may not have similar needs. No matter its size, an organization shapes what its people do and how they do it. Organizations shape performance through their culture and values, their leadership and guidance, their information systems, their core processes and technologies, their product mix and customer profiles, their economic strength, and their reputation in the marketplace.

These elements make up the characteristics of an organization. When people join the organization, they are either attracted to or accept its characteristics. People who can accommodate or adapt to the organization's characteristics will usually be successful there. When these characteristics change, however, whether by choice or in response to outside forces, the balance between the organization, the job, and the individual gets disrupted. This balance can only be restored if the elements of the job or the capabilities of the individual also change.

The Job or Task

The activities and duties that make up a job or task also shape performance. People's performance is affected by

- How well the organization has defined their roles, responsibilities, and relationships
- How well it has designed the rules, procedures, and processes associated with their job or task
- How efficient and appropriate the technology used in the job is
- How mature and functional the business relationships they must deal with are
- How clear, accurate, and timely the information they must work with is
- How similar and reasonable their customers' expectations and needs are

These elements make up the characteristics of the job. Some jobs and tasks have well-developed, thoroughly documented procedures; others do not. Some jobs put people in long-established, mature relationships; others do not. Roles and relationships are well-defined for some jobs but less so for others. A change in procedures, relationships, or any of the other elements disrupts the balance. Whether the change is looked on positively or negatively, the organization and the individual have to adapt to restore the balance. If they do not adapt, performance suffers.

The Individual

Different people bring different skills, knowledge, emotional and physical capacities, and motives to their jobs. Their performance can be enhanced or threatened when there are changes in their capacity (intellectual, physical, or emotional) or personal motives. For example, people who go to school may find their old job less fulfilling. People who find themselves with increasing personal or family responsibilities may be less enamored with a job that requires a lot of travel. People who are faced with increasing complications from chronic health conditions may find it harder to execute certain procedures or to use more sophisticated technologies. Again, when people's capacities and capabilities change, the balance is disrupted. To restore the balance the organization might dedicate more resources or redesign the job.

What is important is to separate changes in the work environment from those in the job and those in the individual performing the job. Because the organization, the job, and the individual are all always adapting, this can be very difficult to do.

FIELD NOTES: CECIL AND THE COMPUTER

Cecil requisitioned fuel for the military. He had been responsible for calculating the fuel requirements of the U.S. Air Force during World War II, the Korean War, and the Vietnam conflict. To do his job Cecil had to solve complex mathematical problems. Remember math story problems from high school? *A train leaves Los Angeles traveling eighty miles per hour. You leave Washington, D.C., driving fifty miles per hour. Who will get to the Mississippi River first, you or the train?* Cecil had to solve problems something like those, only much more complex. He had to consider things like

- Where the military's fuel storage tanks were located all over the world, their capacity, and how much fuel they contained at any given time
- How many planes there were of every type, how much fuel they consumed, where they were stationed around the world, and where they had to be
- How many fuel tankers there were, where they were located, how much fuel they had on board, how fast they could travel, and how far they had to go
- How many storage tanks were destroyed or could possibly be cut off
- Where ground forces were, how many there were, and how many miles they were from surface and air support

Cecil had to come up with contingency plans for various "what if" situations, like *what if we lose this many tankers?* or *what if it takes the tankers this long to get somewhere?* or *what if these landing strips are too damaged for planes to land?* He had to consider all of these factors and figure out how many planes could be kept in the air, and for how long, in a variety of situations.

People's lives were at risk. The demand for accurate calculations was critical. The military depended on its intelligence sources and its suppliers for information. The computing power we take for granted today did not yet exist. Whenever there was a threat of an international incident, Cecil was not allowed to come home. He was taken to a heavily secured area, where he would remain for days at a time. Cecil was given the information he had to work with orally or through written intelligence reports.

The job required highly developed skills. Cecil had to solve complex math problems without the benefit of today's technology. He had to be a quick and good thinker. Because he had only attended school through his sophomore year in high school, he had never been formally trained in the language of mathematics. He could not read algebraic formulas. As a consequence he could not communicate how he calculated an answer. He could only tell you what the answer was, and that was all he was asked to do.

Twenty-five years after Cecil first started in the job, the air force put in a "big" computer and hired ten people with Ph.D.'s in mathematics. The Ph.D.'s and Cecil were given the same problems. The Ph.D.'s converted their information into formulas and gave the formulas to computer programmers, who then built programs for the computer. Cecil and his two helpers worked as they always had. Cecil would meet periodically with the Ph.D.'s and compare answers. Even though Cecil always knew the answer, these were difficult times for him. He could not talk to the Ph.D.'s in their language. He didn't know how to translate his thinking into formulas computer programmers could use. He only knew the answers. The introduction of the computers had changed his job and the skills required to be effective in it.

⊙ FIELD TECHNIQUES: ISOLATING ENVIRONMENTAL CHANGES

Assume that people's performance has deteriorated in your client's organization. To understand whether or not changes in the job environment have affected their performance, you would start by watching them do their work. To find out if anything has changed, you would pay attention to

- *Where they get the information they use, what form it comes in (electronic, oral, written, and so on), and the language or symbols it consists of (words, icons, tones, colors, and so on).* You want to know if a new technology or reporting relationship has changed some aspect of the information people use to do their jobs.

- *The equipment and tools they use.* You want to know if the equipment people use to do their jobs requires a certain level of strength, manual dexterity, fine motor skills, or visual and auditory discrimination. If people's performance has changed, find out if their tools or equipment have changed and if those changes require new skills.

- *The workplace layout, air quality, noise level, and lighting quality.* A change in layout can disrupt relationships and work habits. Poor air quality and ambient noise can contribute to fatigue. Shadows and glare can contribute to mistakes.

You would then use this information to support your recommendations about what has to change in either the work environment or a specific job to restore balance and productivity.

FIELD NOTES: ADDING A NEW PRODUCTION LINE

Russ, who works in HRD at a medical manufacturer, was assigned to a team to find out why production errors were up at one of the company's production centers and to come up with recommendations on how to improve performance. The center in question made plastic tubes for lotions, ointments, and salves. Russ asked to spend a day at the plant. He wanted to see how it operated and to have a chance to talk to the production line crew. Two people worked the lines each shift. The lines had to be cleared, cleaned and sterilized, and recalibrated for each type of tube and at the end of each shift. The same workers had been with the center ever since the plant had opened five years ago. Another person worked the swing shift and covered for the others when they were ill or on vacation.

Russ saw that there were six production lines in the plant. The newest line had been added two months ago. Russ noticed that the equipment used on four of the lines came from different manufacturers. He also learned that the procedures for setting up, calibrating, and line clearance were significantly different depending on the equipment manufacturer. The crew pointed out that there were a lot of things different about the equipment. For example, the dials were in different places, some instruments had digital readings and others were analog dials, some had two-way valves and others had three-way valves, the color red meant off on one line but signaled a problem on another, and so on. The number of variables the crew had to deal with had more than doubled over the last five years. Russ used this information to support his recommendation that an industrial engineer be hired to see if some of the variables could be removed. He also wanted the engineer's opinion on whether or not more people should be hired. He recommended that visual symbols and job aids be added to each machine to cue the crew in the proper sequence of steps for clearance, cleaning, and calibration. Removing or reducing the number of variables and adding resources (people and job aids) would help restore balance.

VARIABILITY IN JOBS

Jobs with the same output requirements may not really be the same. Varying circumstances or situations can make the same job very different for different employees. For example, an employee at a field location may face different conditions than an employee doing the same work at corporate headquarters. Different geographical locations can change a job significantly. Salespeople assigned to different territories may face different markets. Their customers may not have the same level of sophistication, the same buying power, or the same needs. Their sales managers may be more or less skilled at coaching. Some may service very concentrated markets, reducing the need to travel. Others may service very dispersed markets, requiring greater travel or skill at using electronic communications systems. Yet, because the salespeople all represent the same products for the same company, people will be inclined to think that their jobs are the same. Well, the job may be the same, but the conditions under which the work is done are different.

Building engineers who service HVAC (heating and air conditioning) systems for small retail businesses face very different circumstances from engineers who service hospitals or laboratories that require uninterrupted service and consistent humidity and temperature. Even though these differences may be understood, they are sometimes overlooked when companies reassign (even promote) a high performer. The ability to perform a job well under one set of circumstances does not always translate to a different set of circumstances.

If nothing has changed in the work environment, yet performance among group members is not the same, look for variability in the job. Pay particular attention to the conditions the different group members work under (ask them, or go see for yourself). You want to investigate

- *The working conditions.* Are they the same for everyone in the same or a similar job? Look at number or frequency of disruptions, sophistication of processes, and so on.
- *The relationships the job requires.* Are similar relationships required for everyone in the same or a similar job? Look at protocols, culture, business norms, language, and so on.
- *The job's inputs.* Are they the same for everyone in the same or a similar job? Look at information, customer requirements, and expectations.
- *The geographical location.* Is it the same for everyone in the same or a similar job? Consider the effects of distance from headquarters and of working in different time zones.

If you discover that people in similar jobs actually work under very different conditions, describe the differences and somehow make them public or go on record concerning the differences. Then recommend that the organization either (1) eliminate or reduce the differences by adding resources or (2) equip people to better deal with the differences.

FIELD TOOLS: THE CONTEXTUAL JOB DESCRIPTION

Traditional job descriptions usually list job responsibilities and the preferred education and experience. They are used to support hiring, selection, and salary decisions. My experience is that traditional job descriptions are either silent about working conditions or describe them minimally. To address this deficiency I developed a tool for creating job descriptions that considers the conditions of the job (see Figure 5.2). The tool serves as a job aid and worksheet for describing a job and its work environment, in particular.

You can combine the contextual job description with an operational definition of the job (see Figures 1.3 and 1.6) to get a more comprehensive picture of what it takes to be successful in the job. Just as with many of the previous tools, the contextual job description is best completed in collaboration with the client and someone in the job. As a performance consultant your job is to facilitate the processes of discovery and of gaining consensus. The benefits of the tool come from these processes. The tool encourages people to question their assumptions about jobs and about what influences job performance.

Figure 5.2.
Contextual Job
Description

1. What is the job's mission and purpose?
   - What business need was it created to satisfy?
   - How would the organization be affected if the job were eliminated?
   - Who within the organization would be affected?
   - Would the effect be positive or negative?
2. Who are the job's customers? Who depends on it and needs it to be done well?
3. What are the underlying and sometimes unspoken assumptions that determine how performance will be evaluated? What demands of the job's work environment require extra skills and knowledge?
4. Who are the people, teams, or groups that a person doing the job has to get along with?
   - What relationships must an employee establish or maintain to be successful in the job?
   - With whom must they be established, and how accessible are the necessary people in terms of time and distance?
   - How different are the people doing the job from one another and from those with whom they must have relationships (in terms of their values, norms, language, knowledge, skills, status, culture, and so on)?
5. What do the people in the job have to produce or deliver to be considered effective? On what basis is their performance evaluated: efficiency? quality of the relationships gained or sustained? quality of the work? cost of the work? cost benefit derived from the outputs of the job? customer satisfaction? revenue generated (indirectly or directly)?
6. What are the typical tasks that make up the job?
7. What do people have to know to do the job?
8. What skills do people have to have to be effective in the job?

FIELD
TECHNIQUES:
ISOLATING
DIFFERENCES IN
JOB CONDITIONS

To identify a job's conditions and determine if conditions differ for different employees, start by asking questions that will reveal some of the unspoken assumptions various people have about the circumstances under which the people doing that job must work:

1. Ask employees in the job and their bosses to describe the people, teams, or groups the employees have to work with, in terms of
   - Their values, norms, language, knowledge, skills, social status, and business sophistication
   - How much they differ from one another
   - How much they differ from the employees in the job
   - Which of these differences require additional skills or knowledge on the part of the employees

2. Ask the employees and boss to explain the business reason for the job. Why is the job done? What need was it created to satisfy? How would the organization be affected if the job were eliminated? Who would be affected, and how?

3. Ask the employees what they have to produce or deliver to be considered effective. On what basis is their performance evaluated: efficiency? quality of the relationships gained or sustained? quality of the work? cost of the work? cost benefit derived from the outputs of the job? customer satisfaction? revenue generated (indirectly or directly)? some other measure?

From this information you can gain an understanding of the job and the circumstances under which the people who do it work.

FIELD NOTES: MOVING TO THE INTERNATIONAL DIVISION

Mike was asked to find out why his company's U.S. product managers' performance dropped significantly when they were transferred to the international division. The product managers were responsible for product safety and brand integrity for specific products. As U.S. managers they had been assigned suppliers and supply chains. A supply chain consisted of all the companies involved in getting a product to the store. The companies at the start of a chain produced the raw materials for a product. Companies in the middle of the chain converted the raw materials into the finished products. The companies at the end of the chain packaged and distributed the finished products.

Mike found that a traditional job description already existed for the international product managers and that the job responsibilities, educational requirements, and performance expectations were the same as for the company's domestic managers. Product managers had to have a degree in science. Most of the managers' degrees were in agronomy, animal husbandry, and microbiology. The performance criteria for both jobs measured how well the managers' suppliers reduced their product costs, ensured uninterrupted supply, protected brand integrity, and maintained product safety. Mike decided to focus on the underlying assumptions and environmental conditions of the job.

He met with some of the U.S. product managers and their key suppliers. He learned that they worked with sophisticated, long-term suppliers. Many of the suppliers had been with the company for over twenty years. The relationship between the suppliers in each supply chain was also well established. The U.S. product managers spent most of their time encouraging their suppliers to embrace the principles of process improvement and to improve business transactions among themselves to eliminate unnecessary costs.

Next he met with some of the international product managers. He learned that in many international markets, local suppliers did not exist. As a result the supply chains were a combination of local, regional, and international firms. The product managers were expected to find local manufacturers and teach them how to make the products. Because the company had rigorous product quality standards, the managers frequently had to help local suppliers secure lending to upgrade their production lines. As a result of these factors, the international product managers had to know local lending practices, the import regulations and protocols of a variety of nations, the transportation options and requirements within and across various international borders, several different languages, and the nuances and protocols of different business cultures. They had to be able to deal in multiple currencies, negotiate agreements among suppliers to accommodate varying rates of inflation, decide which currency to do business in (as some worked in countries with very high inflation), get people from different countries with long histories of hostility to cooperate with one another, and assess their suppliers' ability and willingness to comply with the company's business ethics.

Mike decided to develop new job descriptions for both groups that would focus on the job's conditions, not just its tasks. Figure 5.3 is the job description he produced for international product managers. Mike recommended that the company better prepare managers for international assignments through training and by increasing corporate support and backup.

Figure 5.3. International Product Managers' Job Description

Job Title: International Product Manager

Purpose:

- To provide leadership, stewardship, training, direction, information, and feedback to zone staff, management, and suppliers
- To provide expertise in the areas of standards, raw materials selection, processing, packaging, distribution, manufacturing, and regulatory compliance
- To lead a coordinated effort to link the independent segments of the supply chain (suppliers, distributors, stores) in ways that result in the best value to the system, while providing ongoing tactical distribution support to all markets

Givens:

- There is wide variance in supplier and in-country personnel abilities and technologies, technical expertise, and resources.
- Effective relationships are required with people of different countries, values, languages, ethics, business practices, and norms.
- International product managers are expected to operate independent of backup resources, while preserving product quality, safety, integrity, and supply.
- The ability to demonstrate and perform any step in the process, from raw materials to finished product, is required and expected.
- The job requires the ability to operate within a wide range of political and economic environments.

- International product managers must exemplify the principles of TQM in their own practices, such as by evaluating and continuously improving company processes, being customer-oriented, exhibiting leadership, making fact-based decisions, and so on.

Required Activities:

- Direct the quality assurance needs within the zone.
- Develop trained professionals in the local countries.
- Locate and develop suppliers who understand the company's standards, as evidenced by their quality and prices.
- Set direction and priorities in conjunction with in-country management.
- Perform product and supplier evaluations.
- Maintain knowledge and skills in the technical areas of product technology, sensory evaluation, safety programs, and good manufacturing practices.
- Develop, oversee, and revise specifications and policies related to suppliers.
- Maintain awareness of legislative issues regarding world trade to help local suppliers understand the potential impact on their operations.
- Commit to and exemplify the department's philosophy and values.
- Support the achievement of departmental objectives.
- Strive for continuous improvement in all activities.
- Maintain competitive awareness.
- Perform all required administrative functions.

FIELD TECHNIQUES: ISOLATING CHANGES IN PEOPLE

In situations in which people performance is down but job conditions are relatively equal and nothing has changed in the workplace, it's time to focus on the people. You want to find out if either their physical capacity or their personal motives have changed. This is best done in collaboration with someone from HR. You will also need to ask supervisors to cite specific, fact-based examples of the change in performance.

Performance consultants rarely get involved with performance problems related to specific individuals; however, you may want to offer your skills in facilitation and negotiation to help clients experiencing trouble with specific employees. You can facilitate discussions with supervisors about whether or not performance expectations and concerns over the change in performance have been communicated to the employee. You can help in negotiating with the employee to seek medical or other professional help. You may want to join with HR to help managers understand how to address performance problems due to changes in employees' physical or emotional health. Whatever role you play, you will have to be very astute about discriminating between people's conclusions (what they think has happened) and what has actually been observed firsthand. Here are some guidelines:

1. Meet with the supervisor to find out exactly what has changed. If the supervisor lacks direct evidence of decreased performance, try to meet with someone who has witnessed the change in behavior or work results firsthand.

2. Ask about the onset and frequency of the undesirable behavior or results.

3. Confirm that the person has been told what was observed, what the observer's conclusions were, and what the consequences will be if the behavior does not change or the results do not improve.

4. Find out if other efforts have been made to coach, train, or counsel the employee.

5. If the employee's performance has met expectations in the past, facilitate a discussion with the supervisor and other appropriate parties about what the organization is willing and is not willing to do.

6. If there is concern over a health problem, work with HR to understand the client's policies about requiring medical examinations.

FIELD NOTES: THE EFFECTS OF DIABETES

Kelly, who worked at the insurance company, was asked to find out what was wrong with Mary, who worked in one of the corporate offices. One manager thought Mary should be fired. Kelly found out that Mary had been a consistent performer for years. Nothing had changed about her job. She had had the same boss and coworkers for over five years. What was different was that Mary would disappear. One day a coworker found her asleep in the ladies' rest room. She was even found leaning against a filing cabinet, asleep. When she was asked if anything was wrong, Mary just complained of being tired. Kelly met with Mary and a representative from HR. They told Mary that a record of sleeping-on-the-job incidents would be put in her file and that if she didn't get a physical, HR would start the process of terminating her. She was given thirty days to bring in a doctor's statement attesting that she was able to work. Mary finally agreed to get a physical. She learned that she had diabetes. Once it was under control, her performance returned to what it had been in the past.

ORGANIZATIONS AS SOCIAL SYSTEMS: MANAGING GROUP NORMS

The second model I draw on in assessing how environment affects performance is that of organizations as social systems. This model helps me better understand what influences group norms. I use this model when a group's behavior and attitude is not what the organization wants.

The term *behavior* includes both people's interactions (their exchanges of ideas and information) and their activities (everything else they do). A group's behaviors and attitudes are often called its norms. Just as in the first model, the elements are interdependent; that is, a change in any one element can cause a corresponding change in the others. Figure 5.4 illustrates the different elements.

In the center is the nucleus. It is a combination of (1) what the organization requires or expects in terms of behavior and results and (2) the actual behaviors and attitudes that emerge (called the group's norms) and the results they deliver. When both components of the nucleus are in harmony, everyone is happy. When they separate and become at odds with each other, however, problems occur. The nucleus is surrounded by those elements that the larger organization can more immediately control, such as

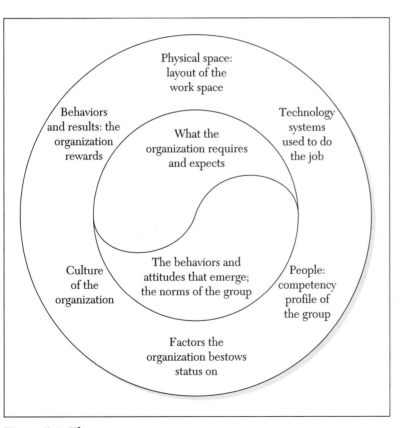

Figure 5.4. Elements of a Social System

- The technology and equipment the people use to do the job

- The physical space where the job is performed (how it is arranged and designed)

- The factors that lead to higher status within the organization

- The behaviors and results the organization chooses to reward

- The culture of the larger organization

- The competency profile of the group

This visual model helps me see the relationships among the various elements and reminds me what the organization can more readily control. Here are some postulates I try to remember:

1. *People adopt behaviors and attitudes for a number of reasons.* For example, people develop new behaviors to compensate for deficiencies in their organization or in how their job is designed.

2. *What is dysfunctional in one context may be functional in another.* People have beliefs or ideas about the world and how it operates, and they tend to act in ways that confirm their beliefs. Sometimes employees' beliefs lead to behaviors that their organization considers dysfunctional.

3. *Norms are what a group's members decide are the appropriate behaviors.* Some norms continue to be reinforced even when they are no longer useful. Because norms are usually unwritten, the best way to find out what they are is to observe the behaviors of people who are considered outcasts or non-team-players by the group. People who consistently violate norms will be ignored or considered outcasts. People are more likely to conform if the group's norms are close to their own beliefs about the world.

4. *People's competencies affect their ability to deal with the world, and competencies influence the number and types of goals people set for themselves.*

5. *People choose behaviors that are consistent with their goals, competencies, beliefs, and values, even if those choices appear illogical to others.* The behaviors most likely to occur in a given situation are those that best reflect a person's self-concept and worldview.

6. *The higher a person's status outside a group, the higher his or her initial position or rank will be within it.*

FIELD TECHNIQUES: IDENTIFYING HOW NORMS AFFECT PERFORMANCE

Here are some guidelines you can use when you want to find out why a group's norms do not support what the group's organization wants, and what to do about it. If there is a performance problem, find out if the problem is unique to an individual or group. If the problem is unique to a group and you think the group's norms play a role, try to find out what happened that caused the group's norms to get out of sync with what the organization wants. For example:

1. If the technology changed, ask
   - How the change affected people's activities and interactions.
   - How the change affected the number of people needed, when they must be in certain places, how much latitude they have, the amount of variation in their work methods, and the level of personal judgement that is required or accepted.
   - How the group feels about the change.
   - What kinds of interactions the change has made easier or more difficult.
   - What kind of expertise the new technology requires and whether it has affected who can be a member of the group, how often group members see one another, and the degree to which they are supervised.

2. If there has been a change in how the organization bestows status on people, find out how that has affected internal relationships within the group. Find out if valuable members of the group are being ignored because they now lack external status and if some people now have more influence than their actual contribution merits.

3. If the level of competence required to do the job has changed, find out if different levels of competence among group members can be tolerated if the work requires everyone to have the same level of expertise.

What to Do

To change a group's norms because they do not support what the organization wants, recommend changing those elements over which the larger organization has the most control, such as

- *The job itself.* It could be that group norms are accommodating a poorly designed job or inappropriate expectations, nonperformance by other groups, inadequate technology, and so on.
- *The physical layout of the work area.* Inadequate space and poorly laid out work areas encourage people to take shortcuts and lead to inefficiency.

- *What gets rewarded.* A reward is more than what an organization does to recognize people performance; sometimes it's what it *doesn't* do. For example, there may be no consequences for inappropriate behavior.
- *The technology used to do the work.* It could be that the procedures or work processes are inefficient or can no longer support the work volume.
- *The culture of the larger organization.* If the larger organization celebrates people who bend the rules or people who focus only on short-term results, the norms of its groups may be similar.

If these strategies do not work or if still more change is desired, then recommend

- Changing the competency profile of the group by adding or switching members
- Increasing or decreasing the amount of status afforded certain members, by recognizing only those people whose behavior and accomplishments support the organization's goals and withholding recognition from those whose behavior and accomplishments do not
- Replacing group members with people whose beliefs are more like those of the organization (or at least are not in conflict with them)

The last thing you want to do is to attack the group's norms directly, because this is usually the least effective course of action.

FIELD NOTES: NEW TECHNOLOGY AND LOWER PERFORMANCE

Deborah's company asked her to find out why the average call-handling time was up at one of the company's customer service centers. She started out by asking what had changed. She found out that the center had put in new computer terminals at about a fourth of its workstations. The terminals ran on new software that required different keystrokes. The new software also gave the CSRs more information about callers, such as their credit history and what equipment they owned. This extra information enabled the CSR to extend credit, arrange payment plans, and decide if a customer could receive a different level of service. In the past only the most senior CSRs had been allowed to do these things.

Deborah learned that the new terminals had been assigned by lottery and were located in the larger, more attractive workstations. In the past CSRs had been assigned stations based on seniority. Deborah also learned that the more senior CSRs used to take their breaks together. Now the CSRs' breaks were scheduled by a shift coordinator, who tended to give the high performers the preferred break times. As a result, the senior CSRs, whether they were assigned to a new terminal or not, increased their average call-handling times so that they could take their breaks together.

Deborah concluded that the new terminals and how they had been assigned had disrupted the norms of the group. The lottery had violated how the organization had historically afforded status to its employees (seniority). The terminals had also introduced a new technology that allowed people who had previously been of lower status greater autonomy in their work. Deborah met with the center managers to confirm what they wanted to change about the group's behavior. She recommended that breaks be assigned on seniority, as in the past. She suggested a plan that would eventually allow everyone to work on a new terminal over the next six months. After that time, the new terminals would be assigned based on a combination of seniority and performance.

Mike was asked to coach Tim on how to get his U.S. product managers to reduce their travel and entertainment expenses. About six months before, Tim had sent out a memo and made an announcement at a staff meeting that some people's expenses had been getting out of hand. No names were mentioned, and no one knew how his or her expenses compared to everyone else's. No one had ever been held accountable for expenses. The only person who knew what each person's expenses were was Tim. Mike suggested that Tim simply publish everyone's expense record—names included—every month on a single spreadsheet, ranked from the highest to the lowest so people could see where they stood. He suggested that the spreadsheet break out everyone's expenses so it would become public how they were spending the company's money. He also instructed Tim to not mention the subject of expenses for the next six months. Within six months the people whose expenses had been way above the group's average dropped. The overall average of the group went down, and the variance was narrower.

EXPERIENCES FROM THE FIELD: ABOUT BEING DIFFERENT

Whether you are an independent, external consultant or an internal consultant, your success will be influenced by the amount of resources your clients are willing to contribute to support your development and processes. Both external and internal consultants are limited by their clients' ability and willingness to dedicate time, people, technology, and space to identifying barriers to performance and developing solutions. External and internal consultants are also influenced by the attitudes of their peers and colleagues. Sometimes when you want to step out of the crowd, take on a new responsibility, or try innovative approaches, you won't get the support you are looking for.

I learned one of the more difficult lessons of my career when I decided to become an independent consultant. My friends all supported the move—until I actually made it. It was as if having the courage to actualize a dream was wrong. The same thing can happen with people who want to become internal consultants. Being a trainer or a facilitator is safe. You work hard, and people know what you do. Being a performance consultant is not safe. You must question business practices, work to get the facts, and recommend actions that will produce results. What I've learned is that I have to be my own conscience and my own steward. It's not that my friends are bad; it's just that I didn't follow their norms.

FIELD TECHNIQUES: LOOKING AT YOUR OWN ENVIRONMENT AND SOCIAL SYSTEMS

Whether you are an internal or an external consultant, step back and begin to study your work environment:

1. What is the larger organization (your employer, department, or client) willing to invest in your development? Will it acknowledge that part of the package in hiring a consultant is to learn about consultants and how they operate?

2. What resources are available to you?

3. Identify the group you are most closely affiliated with. Who is in it? What are its norms? How will it see your roles of developing processes, setting standards for yourself, and measuring your own performance?

4. Go back to the recipe for building credibility and influence. Will the group support your efforts to develop those skills?

FIELD NOTES: DESCRIBING THE JOB OF A PERFORMANCE CONSULTANT

When Deborah and her team first changed their mission, expanded their services to include performance consulting, and learned how to market their new services, their work seemed exciting. It wasn't until a few months had passed that some of Deborah's staff realized that the job had changed. Some still tried to hold on to old behaviors and activities. The result was seventy-hour work weeks. Others tried to let go of the old behaviors and activities so that they could do the new things. But they, too, found the change difficult. Deborah's staff were all longtime employees. They had grown up in the business. They had been promoted because they were conscientious and hardworking. They had gravitated to training because they liked people and knew the content. In the past, they had operated very independently, interacting only with instructors. Now they were being asked to interact with the call center managers. They were put on cross-functional teams to design new technology. They were being asked to track their time and document their processes. It all felt very uncomfortable and even a little scary. They liked operating independently. They liked delivering training. They liked coaching instructors. Now they were in meetings. Now they had to manage budgets and track expenses.

Deborah decided to develop a new job description for the position. She wanted her staff to apply for their own jobs. Her goal was to help them decide for themselves if this was the role they really wanted to play. If they didn't, she was prepared to help them find other positions in the company. Figure 5.5 shows the job description she came up with. Note that it combines some of the attributes of an operational definition with some of the attributes of a contextual job description.

Figure 5.5. Deborah's Job Description

Title: Performance Consultant

Primary customers: Call center managers, instructors, instructional designers, independent contractors, electronic systems support team, methods department, human resources, finance

Purpose: Performance consultants are responsible for assessing the training and performance needs of their centers, ensuring that qualified resources are available to meet those needs, coaching center management, and providing data so the division's products, people, and initiatives can be measured. They may deliver soft skill training courses. They may supervise clerical staff and coordinate instructor schedules companywide.

Why: So centers get the training and services they need and the division's products and services support improved performance and achieve a positive return on investment.

How: Performance consultants consult to and work with call center managers, staff in the methods department, human resources, finance, information systems, and the team assigned to develop an electronic support system. They participate on major teams, serve as experts in performance improvement, provide data to the financial analyst, and negotiate for resources. They may hire contract services.

Structure: They report to the director of performance improvement. They may supervise instructional designers, media developers, and contract personnel. They are members of cross-functional teams.

Givens:
- Performance consultants must acknowledge inherited relationships with call center management.
- Real differences exist between call center managers and their VPs in terms of goals, values, and business practices.
- Call center managers get mixed and contradictory messages from senior management.
- Consultants report to people at remote locations, so there is little opportunity for direct interaction with other consultants.
- Procedures for handling exceptional circumstances are missing or unclear.
- Goals of other home office departments are mixed and contradictory.
- No process exists to keep up-to-date.
- Procedures for deploying new initiatives are missing or unclear.
- Multiple initiatives are always under way, and those initiatives compete for resources.

Knowledge: Performance consultants need to know and understand
- The goals of the division
- The goals and operating style of the other home office departments
- The goals of the centers and their local geography, business protocols, market, and so on
- Instructional design principles and what learning outcomes are
- How people learn; principles of knowledge transfer
- What contributes to or interferes with optimum performance

**Figure 5.5. Deborah's
Job Description,** *cont'd.*

- Each customer's business drivers and current initiatives
- How to appropriately use or apply standardization
- How to get required resources
- How to manage resources within budget
- How to measure performance and return on investment

Skills: Consultants must be skilled in

- Managing staff and other resources
- Establishing credible relationships with other home office personnel
- Facilitating and coaching
- Confronting and negotiating
- Controlling group dynamics
- Conducting feasibility studies
- Assessing and evaluating individuals, processes, and programs
- Measuring results
- Estimating costs
- Communicating vision with clarity and conviction
- Transferring knowledge
- Working within budget

Typical tasks:

- Assessing developmental needs and performance requirements of centers
- Establishing working relationships with other home office personnel
- Assessing the performance of the division's initiatives
- Coordinating the design, development, and delivery of training
- Assessing home office needs
- Maintaining communication with contract services
- Preparing personal development plans
- Maintaining skills and knowledge
- Participating in cross-functional teams and work on special initiatives

Outputs or deliverables: Productivity measures include

- Number of services delivered
- Number of new courses developed
- Number of modifications to current courses
- Number of cross-functional teams supported
- Number of technical innovations adopted

Outcomes: Performance and return on investment measures include

- The time it takes for call center staff and instructors to achieve proficiency
- Positive return on investment for the division's initiatives
- Higher retention and compliance by field personnel
- The division's ability to deliver quality products and services
- The confidence level of call center managers and other home office directors

For the first time, Deborah's staff would be held accountable for and measured against outputs and outcomes. The job description also made it clear that some of them would have to return to school to learn more about technology, the transfer of learning, and organizational behavior. They would have to learn more about business economics, project management, and much more. Some of her staff elected to seek other positions in the company.

SUMMARY

Training focuses its efforts on helping individuals develop the skills and knowledge they need to do their job. But it is important to remember that the work environment significantly shapes performance. If the bank described at the beginning of this chapter had better understood how its culture and norms suppressed critical dialogue, it might have avoided public embarrassment and questionable financial practices.

Organizations are very complex systems. They require us to work in partnership and draw on one another's expertise and support. We also have to be willing to challenge our own beliefs about the world and recognize that they can limit our ability to see new possibilities and approaches.

WHERE TO LEARN MORE

Boyatzis, R., *The Competent Manager: A Model for Effective Performance* (New York: Wiley, 1982). This book is very difficult to read; however, chapters 1 and 2 explain the variables that contribute to competent performance.

To learn more about social systems check out the writings of Adler, Lawler, Nadler, and Argyris. Pay attention to the seminal research they reference if you want to investigate how the study of social systems came about and the ideas it has contributed to performance consulting.

Chapter 6

Needs Assessment

*M*any organizations that experience poor results either resort to blaming people or invest in a single, sometimes simplistic, solution. They do not always take the time to find out what, if anything, has changed in the work environment, the job, or the people in question. It's almost as if they think that blaming people and spending money can solve all their problems.

FIELD NOTES: SOLVING THE WRONG PROBLEM

Lisa, an independent consultant, was hired by a large community bank to develop a training program for its managers. The bank president told her he was disappointed that some of his top performers were no longer meeting his expectations. During Lisa's first meeting with the management team and the president, one of the managers challenged the bank's lending policies. The manager commented that the bank had been founded on the ideal of developmental banking (lending money to revitalize inner cities) but that its current loans were no different from those made by traditional banks. Another manager wanted to know why the bank was expanding internationally. The bank's mission was about helping community business expand, not about expanding itself.

Later Lisa attended a meeting with twenty-five managers and their immediate subordinates, including both professional and clerical staff. Lisa wanted to use this opportunity to get a better understanding of the managers' role in the bank. Lisa asked the professional staff who they reported to—that is, who they went to for assignments, to get approval for a day off, and for guidance on how to handle exceptions (loans, check cashing, and so on). She asked the clerical staff a similar question. Much to Lisa's dismay, everyone gave her the same answer. They all went directly to the executive vice president (EVP) of the bank. No one mentioned his or her supervisor. It seemed as though everyone in the bank reported to the same person for everything. Lisa began to wonder how a training program could help improve the managers' performance, since they apparently didn't do any managing, at least not of people.

This situation illustrates why consultants, both internal and external, need a way to discover and verify performance expectations and determine what is preventing employees from meeting them. Without the facts, you are faced with accepting any solution. It is easier to improve or sustain high performance when you have a clear picture of what is expected and what the barriers to performance are.

A PROCESS FOR IDENTIFYING NEEDS

A needs assessment is a process for discovering and verifying what supports or prevents optimum performance. At a minimum the process should discriminate between environmental factors and people factors. Most needs assessments are done because of a known performance problem. In these situations the client typically starts with a premise, such as

- People in the job lack the required skills or knowledge.
- Processes are poorly designed.
- Expectations are unclear or conflicting.
- The wrong behaviors are being rewarded.

Sometimes needs assessments are done in anticipation of a change, such as rolling out a newly designed work process, replacing old technology, or adding a new product line. In these situations the client starts with the premise that people lack the ability to support the change. In both of these situations the premise might be right, partially right, or wrong. What I've learned is that when you limit the focus of your investigation to a preconceived premise, you reduce your chances of uncovering critical variables that are causing the problem.

What you need is a process that will help you find out which performance problems are worthy of attention and what is really obstructing performance. The process should remind you to consider the organization's goals, the work environment, the way the job is designed, and people's ability to do the job. It should help you find out what is really needed to support a major change. At the same time, I understand that it is not always feasible to consider every variable. Therefore, the ideal process is one that you can expand or contract, depending on the evidence you have and the severity of the consequences if you are wrong. I use two tools for this process. I call them

- *The scorecard.* This tool helps me determine what is worthy of examination and what will be used to measure success or improvement.
- *The hierarchy.* This tool helps me discover what is currently obstructing performance and what might obstruct it in the future.

**FIELD
TOOLS:
THE SCORECARD**

I have found the scorecard to be a very powerful tool. I use it to facilitate discussions with my clients about what is important to them, what gets their attention, and what they take as evidence that things are bad, good, or improving. The scorecard I'm referring to is not the same as the "balanced scorecard" you may have read about in the *Harvard Business Review.* The term *balanced scorecard* refers to the importance of focusing on more than one initiative. Organizations usually combine initiatives, like customer satisfaction, financial return, market share, process improvement, people development, and product excellence initiatives. They have learned that when they focus on only one initiative, they limit their ability to compete. When I introduce the scorecard I explain that I use it to help me

- Identify the costs of poor performance
- Quickly identify performance gaps that need further investigation
- Identify the criteria and metrics for measuring both the gap and future improvement
- Link programs like training to the needs of the organization

Two forms of the scorecard are presented here: the job aid, which has examples (see Figure 6.1), and the worksheet, which is blank and is for you and your client to fill in (see Figure 6.2). Which one you use depends on your situation.

The job aid version of the scorecard helps me break the ice with clients. I also use it when a client wants to implement a major program that requires a big investment, such as a certification program or a multimedia training program. It helps clients begin to understand how to build a business case for their program and why they need to build one. The job aid has examples of common organizational initiatives, how companies measure the performance of such initiatives, different performance gap sizes, how to identify the cause of performance gaps, and the kinds of things organizations accept as evidence of improvement. In using the job aid with clients, I ask which examples are or are not relevant to them and how they would change the scorecard to make it work for them; their answers give me a much better understanding of what is important to them. The worksheet version is the same, but you fill in the information relevant to your situation. Here is an explanation of what goes in each column:

- *Column 1: Key initiatives.* These are frequently stated as objectives or strategies, like "increase market share," "reduce turnover," "reduce costs," or "increase sales." They are what the organization pays attention to, whether it is a major business unit, a department, a small work unit, or a task force.

Objective: to model how initiatives can be linked to business measures. This job aid will help you communicate what information does or does not exist, what the organization does or does not track, and where a deeper analysis might add value. You can also use it to facilitate discussions about evidence—what it is and how to get it.

1. Key initiatives, strategies, or objectives: what the client pays attention to and values	2. Measures: what the client tracks to measure performance	3. Standards or goals versus actual performance: what the client wants versus what is real; the gap	4. Assessment: how to get data that will identify the cause of the performance gap	5. Measured results: what has to change for the intervention to be a success and be worth it
Customer satisfaction, employee satisfaction	Ratings (five-point scale), number of complaints and grievances	Goal 4.2, actual 3.7	Survey data, focus groups, interviews	Higher ratings, less complaints
Market share	Percentage compared to potential	Gap over competition	Market research	Increased share
People performance: time, quantity, frequency, rework and waste	Process time, cycle time, number of calls or visits per time period	Non-value-added less than x percent, ratio of x percent, number per time period, waste of less than x percent or x dollars	Time sheets, interviews, industry indices, worksheets, observations	Improved performance of products, people, and processes; less waste
Financial performance: cost, cost benefit, sales revenue, cash flow	Fixed to variable costs, ROI, return on assets, return on capital employed, contribution margin, percent of growth	Cents or dollars per unit, sales call, or proposal; cost of sales less than x dollars or x percent; incremental sales of x percent; growth at x percent	Daily reports, actual dollars versus budgeted dollars, sales analyses	Improved ratios, lower costs, higher margins, higher revenues, increased cash flow
Product performance: accuracy, consistency, compliance	Variance, percent yield, unscheduled service, formal filings	Zero defects, less than x percent variance, ratio of unscheduled to scheduled service	Statistical process control data, quality control reports, complaint calls and citations	Less variance, higher yields, better ratios, fewer reportables

**Figure 6.1.
Scorecard Job Aid**

- *Column 2: Key measures.* These are the data the organization tracks and takes as evidence that what it is doing to support the initiative is achieving the goal or purpose. Sometimes these measures are well documented and understood; other times they are chosen intuitively by management. However they've been selected, you need to find out what they are.

- *Column 3: Standards or goals versus actual performance.* This refers to the performance gap: the difference between where the organization is today and where it wants to be. Some organizations have sophisticated systems in place for tracking their performance against their goals. Other or-

Objective: To serve as a worksheet to capture what is important to your client's organization. The worksheet can be used to facilitate discussions about what you and your client expect of each other.

1. Key initiatives, strategies, or objectives: what the client pays attention to and values	2. Measures: what the client tracks to measure performance	3. Standards or goals versus actual performance: what the client wants versus what is real; the gap	4. Assessment: how to get data that will identify the cause of the performance gap	5. Measured results: what has to change for the intervention to be a success and be worth it

Figure 6.2. Scorecard Worksheet

ganizations do not. You need to know if the organization you are working for has the capability to measure performance and, if it does, how its performance stacks up to its goals. If the organization does not have systems in place to measure performance, then it is making decisions based on incomplete data—and you need to know this, too.

- *Column 4: Assessment.* This is how the organization plans to get data that will identify the cause of the gap and measure its extent. Use this column to identify what data is already being captured, where and by whom it is being captured, what other data would be helpful, and how to get it. What you learn as a result of analyzing the data will help you identify the appropriate interventions.

- *Column 5: Measured results.* This column is used both before and after an implementation is carried out. Use it to specify what has to change for the client to consider the intervention a success and worth the cost. This is where you begin the discussion about how much benefit the client must gain to offset the costs of taking corrective action. After an intervention has been implemented you can go back and put in what actually changed, how much it changed, and how much it cost.

Sometimes the information you need for the scorecard job aid will not all be available. The scorecard brings to light what the organization really knows and where it has to do a better job of defining its expectations, its current performance, and its deficiencies.

FIELD TECHNIQUES: FOCUSING YOUR INVESTIGATION

Depending on your relationship with your client and what you already know about the client, you may or may not want to use the job aid version of the scorecard. I always keep a copy of the job aid in my briefcase, however, should a client need help coming up with ideas about what to focus on or how to measure performance. Throughout the process you will be working in partnership with your client. At one moment you might participate by contributing ideas and suggestions; at other moments you might facilitate discussion between members of your client's group. Whatever role you play, you want to keep your clients' attention focused on identifying where performance problems exist, which ones they need to address, where to get better data, and how to measure success. Here are some guidelines on how to proceed:

1. Meet with your client. If appropriate, show your client the scorecard job aid and discuss a few of the examples.

2. Explain that the scorecard can be used either to find out where there are opportunities for improvement or to target those areas with the bigger performance gaps for a needs assessment.

3. If you are unsure about what is important to your client, ask about the client's major initiatives, objectives, or strategies. Record the client's answers on the worksheet version of the scorecard.

4. Ask how the client measures those objectives now. Ask what kind of data the client uses to measure performance.

5. To identify which performance gaps to work on, explain that you want to confirm

   - Where there are gaps in performance
   - What costs are associated with those gaps

- Which gaps are worth examining to find out the cause

  - How much an intervention would have to reduce the gap to be considered a success or worth the cost

6. Next, help the client identify those gaps for which a more thorough analysis would be beneficial.

7. If the client cannot provide all of the information or is unsure about what gets measured, why it gets measured, or how big a particular performance gap is, help the client decide how and where to get the missing information.

8. Once you get the missing information, return to the scorecard and, together with your client, decide which interventions are more likely to reduce or eliminate the performance deficiency.

9. Work with the client to pinpoint which aspects of performance the interventions will positively impact and what data the client will use to measure improvement.

10. Together, estimate how much change the intervention will produce and if it will be enough to outweigh what you estimate its cost will be.

FIELD NOTES: USING THE SCORECARD
TO IDENTIFY MEASURES OF PERFORMANCE

Deborah's company asked her to help the VP of sales improve sales performance at the company's call centers. The president of the company had recently announced that management would soon begin evaluating the call centers based on their sales performance. This was a significant shift. In the past the company had evaluated the call centers based only on average call-handling time.

Deborah began her meeting with the VP of sales by asking about how sales were currently measured, what type of sales were going to be tracked, and to what degree the centers were meeting their sales goals now. During their meeting Deborah used the scorecard job aid to illustrate the types of things other organizations focus on when they want to improve sales performance. She believed that stressing sales volume alone would not lead to optimum sales performance. She wanted the VP to consider how to reduce the cost of sales.

As a result of their conversation Deborah identified what her department could do to support overall sales performance: rapidly improve CSRs' product knowledge and selling skills, develop systems to improve order accuracy, and provide guidelines to qualify customers' creditworthiness. Errors in orders increased costs, because someone else had to spend time correcting the order. Selling to customers with poor credit also potentially increased costs, because such customers were more likely to require special payment plans.

Russ, the HRD manager at a medical supply manufacturer, was asked to lead a team charged with making a new product line successful. One of the company's divisions had announced that its goal was to become the world leader in diagnostic equipment. The company currently had 40 percent of the market worldwide. One strategy for increasing the company's market share was to promote a new line of equipment acquired from another manufacturer. Russ suggested that the team develop a scorecard to make sure they hadn't overlooked any factors that could significantly jeopardize this product's success. He handed out the scorecard job aid to illustrate what theirs might look like once they had completed it. He talked about the types of initiatives other companies focus on. The team was able to agree on the following initiatives:

- *Improving product performance.* The number of service calls due to product failures was higher than the team had expected. They decided that they could track service calls now, determine their costs, and measure improvement in equipment performance by the number of service calls received in the future.
- *Improving customer satisfaction.* Survey data indicated that customers had doubts about the capability of the company's field technicians. The team decided to continue to use surveys to measure if customer satisfaction improved.
- *Improving field technician performance.* The company's field technicians reported that they felt unprepared to support the new product line. In particular, they felt inadequate in the area of diagnosing equipment failures. The team decided to survey the technicians periodically to see if their training and performance aids had increased the technicians' confidence level.

Now the team could focus on finding out what caused equipment failures and what the technicians needed in terms of skills, knowledge, and performance aids to increase their ability to service the new line of equipment.

PERFORMANCE CRITERIA FOR THE NEEDS ASSESSMENT PROCESS

Once you know what to focus on you can begin the process of finding out why performance is not at the level the organization wants. When I first began to learn about needs assessment, I heard an expression that went something like "put a competent person in a bad system, and the system wins every time." At national conferences I heard a lot about how training was the most expensive and sometimes the least effective solution to performance problems. With this in mind I went about developing a process for discovering and verifying what supports performance in an organization and what interferes with it. I began by setting some criteria for my process:

1. It must be based on the idea that the work environment, the design of the job, and the capability of the people involved all contribute to performance. Therefore it must help me and my clients distinguish between these elements.

2. It must not be biased in favor of a particular solution. If the problem is a lack of skills or knowledge, I want to know that; but if it is something else, I want to know that, too.

3. It must be designed to help me get facts and corroborating evidence. Hearsay and folklore are stories people tell to rationalize their behavior. They are not facts. One source of information is not enough.

4. It must help me work with my client as a partner but also position me as an expert in assessment and measurement. It should help me contribute expertise as appropriate, yet it should also facilitate the client's retaining ownership of the problem and the solution.

5. It must work for organizational units of all sizes. I wanted a process I could apply to

   • Work groups assigned to specific jobs (such as the CSRs Deborah had to support)

   • Teams working on key initiatives, projects, and programs (such as Russ's team assigned to improve equipment performance)

   • Departments (such as Mike's, Kelly's, and Deborah's departments, which all wanted to move toward performance consulting)

   • Functions or larger divisions in the organization (such as the call centers where Deborah had to improve sales performance)

6. It must provide me with a way to organize my approach to identifying the major causes of performance problems.

FIELD TOOLS: THE HIERARCHY

The result was the hierarchy (see Figure 6.3). I call it that because problems at one level cannot be fixed by interventions aimed at a lower level. For example, investing in training and facilities will reap fewer benefits if management is not in agreement on where the organization is going or if processes are inefficient. I use the hierarchy to identify what is causing poor performance (that is, lack of congruency, inefficiency, or lack of investment in environmental, job, or people resources) and to confirm that people are prepared to support a change.

Congruency and Clarity:

1. Vision and mission
2. Goals and objectives
3. Values, incentives, rewards, and policies

Efficiency:

4. Organizational and job structures
5. Work processes, procedures, and practices
6. Documentation and standards
7. Job aids, signage, and labels

Resiliency and Capability:

8. Physical facilities and space
9. Training and development
10. Resource capacity and sufficiency

Figure 6.3.
The Hierarchy

The Need for Skepticism

To use the hierarchy successfully you have to be skeptical. You cannot just believe a single source of information; you must look for corroborating evidence. Wherever possible, try to obtain direct evidence—that is, see it, read it, or hear it firsthand. Don't accept hearsay or folklore as proof. Hearsay and folklore do not provide credible evidence of what customers expect, how work gets done, or what adds unnecessary costs. Look for ways to get other evidence that supports or refutes your original source.

I found it helpful to divide the hierarchy into three sections, simply because it is easier to remember three variables instead of ten. Also, the order of the elements under each section is less important. What is important, however, is that there has to be congruency and clarity (the first subheading) before you can fully benefit from addressing the other issues.

Congruency and Clarity

Considering the first three elements in the hierarchy will help you identify problems with how the organization has defined itself. If there is incongruence between the organization's vision and mission, between its goals and objectives, or among its values, incentives, rewards, and policies, then the organization's identity is unclear. Investigating these issues will help you validate whether or not people are clear and share an understanding of what they are doing and why. When people are unclear about their roles, when the leadership is not in agreement, or when people get mixed signals, resources are wasted and performance suffers.

Efficiency

Investigating the next four elements will help you identify operating inefficiencies, waste, and unnecessary costs.

Resiliency and Capability

Considering the last three elements will help you validate whether or not the organization is making appropriate investments in its physical and human resources.

Depending on what you know about the particular situation, your investigation may be limited to one or more of the three areas (that is, congruency, efficiency, or resiliency).

FIELD TOOLS: THE HIERARCHY JOB AID

The hierarchy, like the scorecard, is both a job aid and a worksheet (Figure 6.4 is the job aid and Figure 6.5 the worksheet). As a job aid it helps me remember all the variables I want to look at. I use the hierarchy in the same way as I use the scorecard, to work with my clients in designing needs assessment studies, to drive conversations about what is really known and what is hearsay or folklore, and to determine how we might get the information we need. Column 1 has sample questions for each of the ten elements in the hierarchy. Column 2 has examples of operating hypotheses. Column 3 lists the types of data you might want to get, and Column 4 suggests ways to get the data.

FIELD TECHNIQUES: GETTING EVIDENCE OF CONGRUENCY

The first three elements in the hierarchy are about congruency. Your goal should be to find corroborating evidence that confirms that where people are going, what they are focusing their energy on, and what they get rewarded for are aligned and not in conflict.

Vision and Mission

You need to examine vision and mission first, because you want to verify that there is agreement on what each program, team, or initiative is supposed to accomplish. The vision tells you where people want to go; the mission tells you what people are about or what business they are in. *Fulfilling the mission should bring people closer to their vision.* The organization's guiding principles should also move the organization closer to its vision. Without a vision, an organization cannot move forward; it will have no basis for building a long-range plan or road map for the future. Confirm that the organization's guiding principles are in alignment with the stated purpose and vision of the program, team, or initiative. Again, be skeptical; your hypothesis or operating assumption should be that the vision and mission (or the people) are *not* in agreement. Then look for evidence that people in the organization have a vision, know what the mission is, and have the same understanding of the vision and mission as their leadership. Seek to prove your hypothesis incorrect. It is not enough to ask people if they have a vision statement or team charter; instead, ask each person in a group separately to tell you what it is and what they think it means. You can then compare their answers with what the organization says about itself. Find out if the organization has devoted adequate resources to programs that directly support the mission.

Goals and Objectives

Next you want to confirm that the goals and objectives they are working toward support the vision and are not in conflict with the stated mission. Your hypothesis should be that they are *not* in harmony and are probably in conflict.

1. Hierarchy model and questions	2. Hypotheses: what to confirm	3. Data to collect	4. How to get data
Congruency and Clarity:			

1. *Vision and mission*
  A. Are there vision and mission statements?
  B. Does the mission reflect the organization's current requirements and desires and the environment in which it operates?
  C. Is there consensus on what the vision and mission are?
  D. Does the mission support the vision?
  E. Does the company's long-range plan support the vision and mission?
	• What is the mission?
	• Is there consensus on the mission among all work groups?
	• Who are the customers?
	• How is the mission communicated?
	• Is there a long-range plan?
	• Does the company realize it needs to change?
		• Mission statement
		• What people say the mission is
		• What people say the mission means to them
		• What customers need and how the business responds
			• Written mission statement
			• Written communications to staff
			• Customer satisfaction surveys
			• Market research
			• Stratified random survey of employees
			• Interviews

2. *Goals and objectives*
  A. Are the goals congruent with the mission?
  B. Do they reflect the resources and operating specifics required to progress as a whole?
  C. Do they exist for each operating unit?
  D. Do people know what they are?
  E. Do they follow them?
	• Do the goals and objectives of each department support the mission?
	• Do they agree with one another?
		• Department goals and objectives
		• What people say their objectives are
		• How well resources match objectives
			• Nominal groups
			• Business plans
			• Managers' objectives

3. *Values, incentives, rewards, and policies*
  A. What are the leader's values?
  B. Are those values known and shared?
  C. What is the organization's culture, and what specific behaviors does it support?
  D. Are those behaviors really rewarded?
  E. What are the rites and rituals?
  F. Do conditions support what the organization says it values (such as commitment, innovation, compliance, teamwork, individualism, entrepreneurship)?
  G. Do the company's policies support its values, mission, and vision?
	• What's important?
	• How are the values prioritized?
	• Are the values and rewards congruent with each other and with the company's mission, goals, and objectives?
	• What are the consequences of nonperformance?
		• What does success look like?
		• What does the company measure?
		• What is a "good person" like?
		• What is rewarded?
		• How are people promoted?
		• Who are the heroes?
			• Values statements
			• Customer satisfaction surveys
			• Sociograms
			• Reward and recognition programs:
			  – documentation
			  – awards
			  – recipients
			• Focus groups

Figure 6.4. The Hierarchy Job Aid

1. Hierarchy model and questions	2. Hypotheses: what to confirm	3. Data to collect	4. How to get data
Efficiency			

4. *Organizational and job structures*
  A. Are jobs clearly defined?
  B. Are jobs given needed responsibility?
  C. Are positions, responsibilities, and reporting effective and efficient?
  D. Does structure aid communication, decision making, and accountability?
  E. Are tasks grouped efficiently?
  F. Is the span of control effective?
  G. Is each unit of command appropriate?
	• What is the formal organizational structure?
	• What are the formal job descriptions and responsibilities?
	• What are people's concepts of the organizational structure and their own job?
	• Who has what authority to make what decisions?
	• Does the organization's structure match the market? Does it match the mission?
		• Organizational charts
		• Job descriptions
		• People's percep-tions of the orga-nization and their job
		• Decision referral up the chain
		• Location map and location decision-making process
		• Organizational charts
			• Job descriptions
			• Focus groups
			• By asking people to
			  – draw the organization
			  – define their job responsibilities
			  – describe who can make what decisions
			• By listening in on phone calls to see how customer problems are resolved
			• Site selection criteria and processes

5. *Work processes, procedures, and practices*
  A. Could tasks or processes be automated?
  B. Are processes well designed?
  C. Are duties assigned in ways that are effective and efficient?
  D. Do procedures exist, and are they followed consistently?
  E. Are resources used wisely?
  F. Do management practices support development, innovation, commitment?
  G. Do people get feedback and information they need when they need it?
  H. Does nonperformance have consequences?
  I. Are those consequences carried out?
	• What are the formal processes and procedures for
	  – getting work done?
	  – handling customer complaints?
	• How is the work actually done?
	• What information is available at what points in the work process?
	• What are the consequences for not following the formal process?
	• How do customers react to the processes and procedures?
		• Formal processes and procedures
		• Actual processes and procedures
		• Information flow
		• Feedback, discipline, reward actions
		• Customer praise and complaints
			• Policies and procedures handbook
			• Observations of performers in all job functions
			• "Silent shopping"
			• Forms
			• Customer complaint letters and log

Figure 6.4. The Hierarchy Job Aid, *cont'd.*

1. Hierarchy model and questions	2. Hypotheses: what to confirm	3. Data to collect	4. How to get data

6. *Documentation and standards*
  A. Are procedures and practices documented?
  B. Are they accessible and usable?
  C. Do they reflect desired practice?
  D. Are there standards?
  E. Does standardization support innovation, compliance, commitment?
	• Do the documents and standards match the work processes and procedures?
	• Do the same standards work for each location?
	• Are the standards used?
	• Can the standards be changed?
		• Documents from multiple locations
		• Employee use of standards documents
			• Documents
			• Observation
			• "Silent shopping"
			• Interviews

7. *Job aids, signage, and labels*
  A. Do job aids, signs, and labels exist?
  B. Are they used?
  C. Is intelligent, exemplar performance captured in a usable form?
  D. Do job aids, signs, and labeling support the desired and required performance?
	• Are there job aids?
	• Are they used?
	• Are there any that are needed that are not there?
		• Job aids from multiple locations
		• Employee use of job aids
			• Job aids
			• Observation
			• "Silent shopping"
			• Interviews

Resiliency and Capability:			

8. *Physical facilities and space*
  A. Is space adequate and well-used?
  B. Does the space and layout facilitate work flow?
  C. Does the space and layout aid communication?
  D. Do the technology and systems support the required work processes?
  E. Are work conditions safe?
  F. Do environmental conditions (temperature, light, noise) support the required work processes?
  G. Do environmental conditions support health?
	• How does the computer system support desired processes and procedures?	• Computer system capabilities and use	• Documentation
			• Observation
			• Interviews

Figure 6.4. The Hierarchy Job Aid, *cont'd.*

1. Hierarchy model and questions	2. Hypotheses: what to confirm	3. Data to collect	4. How to get data
9. *Training and development* A. Are skills maintained? B. Are skills developed? C. Are skills and knowledge adequate for required and desired processes? D. Are innovation and self-empowerment supported? E. What methods are used for development (coaching, cross-training, and so on), and do those methods support the desired and required performance?	• What skills do people in each job – have upon hiring? – get from initial training? – get from coaching and feedback? – get from follow-up/advanced training? • Do skills match job descriptions and work processes?	• Training curriculum and courses for all employees • Employee evaluation reports and development plans	• Documents
10. *Resource capacity and sufficiency* A. Do people have the emotional, physical, intellectual, and economic capacity to achieve the desired and required performance? B. Are there support systems and processes in place to either offset, reduce, or remove deficiencies in capacity? C. Are support systems sufficient for the desired and required performance? D. Do values conflict with requirements of the job or the desired outcomes?	• Whether or not they've done capacity studies • How turnover, absenteeism, injuries compare to industry standards	• Workers' comp claims • Absenteeism • Turnover • Employee complaints	• Exit interviews • Insurance records • Turnover, absenteeism records

Figure 6.4. The Hierarchy Job Aid, *cont'd.*

Look for evidence to prove yourself wrong. For example, it is not unusual for short-term objectives to be so demanding that no resources are left to work on longer-range goals. Examining the congruence between goals and objectives is similar to confirming congruence between vision and mission. Ask people what their goals and objectives are, how those goals and objectives relate to the company's vision or mission, and what they are currently working on. Then compare their answers. Another hypothesis to test is that the goals most closely aligned with the vision and mission are not funded or have very limited funding. Find out what programs are actually budgeted and which ones directly support the goals and objectives.

1. Hierarchy model and questions	2. Hypotheses: what to confirm	3. Data to collect	4. How to get data
Congruency and Clarity:			
1. *Vision and mission*			
2. *Goals and objectives*			
3. *Values, incentives, rewards, and policies*			
Efficiency:			
4. *Organizational and job structures*			
5. *Work processes, procedures, and practices*			

Figure 6.5.
The Hierarchy Worksheet

1. Hierarchy model and questions	2. Hypotheses: what to confirm	3. Data to collect	4. How to get data
6. *Documentation and standards*			
7. *Job aids, signage, and labels*			
Resiliency and Capability:			
8. *Physical facilities and space*			
9. *Training and development*			
10. *Resource capacity and sufficiency*			

Figure 6.5.
The Hierarchy Worksheet, *cont'd.*

Values, Incentives, Rewards, and Policies

The next step is to look for evidence that the accomplishments and behaviors that actually get rewarded are what people have been told will be rewarded and that they support the stated goals and objectives. Again, your hypothesis should be that what actually gets celebrated and recognized does *not* support the goals and objectives. Find out what the criteria are for merit raises, how people get selected for coveted assignments, who gets access to the leadership, and who gets special mention in the company newsletter. These may in fact be people whose results and behaviors conflict with the goals and guiding principles of the organization: people whose behaviors are just the opposite of what the organization says it wants. Find out when awards are announced, who won in the last round, and what the criteria were for winning. Check who has been featured in the company newsletter. Investigate whether the company's HR policies support what the organization says it values, where it says it is going, and how it says it is going to get there. Look for congruency between the first three elements in the hierarchy.

FIELD NOTES: AGREEING ON GOALS

The call centers are Deborah's main customers. She and her department are responsible for helping call center managers get what they need to be successful. Deborah was unclear about how the call centers' performance would be evaluated in the coming year. She used the hierarchy to guide her in finding out if senior management had clearly stated their goals for the centers and if they were in agreement over those goals. Her hypothesis was that they were not in agreement and were probably not even clear about what they expected. She decided to interview each VP separately. She thought this would allow them to speak more freely, and it would give her an opportunity to compare their responses and check her hypothesis.

She met with the VP of sales first. She asked what his goals were for the call centers in the coming year. He answered, "The big change is that every call center manager will have full profit-and-loss accountability in the coming year, and they will be evaluated in terms of sales. My plan is to have more contests to reward those managers who achieve their sales goals."

He also mentioned that two call center managers had been promoted and that he wanted more call center managers like them. In her effort to get corroborating evidence that senior management was in agreement with these goals, she asked the VP of operations what he understood the call centers' goals would be in the coming year and what criteria the company had used in promoting the two managers. He answered, "I'm not sure why they were promoted. The turnover rate at one of their centers was at least 30 percent. One goal is to implement an electronic support system for customer service representatives in every center. Our major goal is customer service; we want to be number one in the customers' eyes when it comes to service."

Deborah then interviewed the senior VP of finance and asked what initiatives had been budgeted or funded to support call center performance in the coming year. He answered, "The only initiative under consideration is the electronic support system for customer service reps. I want to know what the costs will be to maintain the system, however, and how the return on investment will be determined. Without a clear business case that shows the return on investment, funding will not be approved."

She also asked about call center managers' having profit-and-loss accountability. He answered, "That's not going to happen. We can't track costs by center. We can't even link revenue to a particular center. We don't have the systems to support something like that. The subject hasn't even been brought up for discussion, and it won't be."

Deborah began to suspect that the VPs were not in agreement about the company's goals for the call centers. She also suspected that their lack of agreement had resulted in mixed signals to the call center managers. Her next step was to interview the call center managers to get their understanding about what the goals were and how their performance would be measured.

FIELD TECHNIQUES: GETTING EVIDENCE OF EFFICIENCY

Once you have evidence of congruency, you can shift your focus to efficiency. In fact, you might want to extend your investigation to efficiency issues even if you do find evidence of a lack of congruency, if only to find out if the lack of congruency is negatively impacting efficiency.

Organizational and Job Structures

While you are finding out if there is congruency in the first three elements in the hierarchy, you can also get people to describe how the business or unit is organized, including who reports to whom, who is responsible for what, and why work is structured the way it is. Ask people to describe how customer calls get routed, who makes the final decision, who has sign-off authority, and so on. Your hypothesis should be that people are unclear, unsure, or do not agree on the answers and that the existing structure hides redundancy and lack of accountability. Ask enough questions to determine

- The functions, roles, and responsibilities of each department, unit, and so on

- The customers of each function, division, and so on

- The outputs (deliverables, or products) of each function, division, and so on

Just as you did for the first three elements, compare everyone's answers. Again, look for evidence that there is a shared understanding of the organization's structure and how the organizational units relate to one another.

Work Processes, Procedures, and Practices

This element addresses work processes, procedures, and practices (also called work rules), whether for a discrete task or a job. Your hypothesis should be that processes are poorly designed, resulting in waste and unnecessary costs. Ask people to tell you how they do their work, and then watch them to confirm how many resources they actually require, if and where technology plays a role, how many interactions they have with others, how many approvals they have to get, and at what points in the process they have to get them. Check work records (job tickets, time sheets, and so on) to find out how long each task took and where cycle times were significantly longer than actual times at task. Look for evidence that work processes are well designed, do not result in rework, and use resources wisely.

Documentation and Standards

Easily accessible, user-friendly, accurate documentation contributes to efficiency. Standards improve interfaces, allow for an appropriate type of flexibility, and result in lower costs because they permit economies of scale. Watch work being performed and note what documents are used, when they are used, and by whom. Ask where documents and work records are kept; those that are not readily accessible are probably not used. Notice if documents are well-worn and personalized (with bent corners, for example). Again, be skeptical. Do not believe documents exist or are useful until you see them and have corroborating evidence to that effect.

Job Aids, Signage, and Labels

Check to see if there are visual and auditory cues to help people perform complex, infrequent, or critical procedures accurately. Notice if job aids, signs, and labels are well placed and designed in a way that helps people work quickly and smartly. Look for evidence that cues support efficiency by keeping people on task and on the right task. Your hypotheses should be that cues are lacking, unintelligible, or inconsistent and that as a result there are errors, rework, and added costs.

FIELD NOTES: THE SEARCH
FOR OPERATING INEFFICIENCIES

Russ was asked to identify the training needs of the company's CSRs. It seemed that the number of callbacks (customers who call a second or third time because they get the wrong information the first time) was too high.

Russ knew that the customer service reps handled all customer requests for information about how to operate, repair, and install the company's products. They also answered questions about delivery status, part status, and billing. The company had manufactured four product lines for over sixty years, plus it had recently acquired a new line of diagnostic equipment. Customers (medical technicians who worked in hospitals, laboratories, and medical clinics) who needed information called an 800 number that appeared on the equipment. The CSR who answered knew what product line the customer was calling about from the 800 number that was dialed. The CSR was expected to confirm that the customer was capable of safely dismantling the equipment and removing parts, no matter which product.

Russ's operating hypotheses were that the design of the CSRs' job (having to handle all product lines, all models, and all types of requests) resulted in inefficiencies and waste, that the equipment manuals the CSRs used did not support their need for fast and accurate information, and that there were no consequences for giving out incorrect information. Russ asked to observe the CSRs taking calls and to interview a few of them. He asked how the CSRs were evaluated and learned that

- They were evaluated based on call volume and average call time
- Large digital clocks positioned around the room displayed the average call time for the center
- The CSRs had to be familiar with four different product lines, as well as multiple generations (models) of each line (sixty years' worth).

Russ asked some of the CSRs how they get the information they need about older models. He was shown where the manuals were kept for every model of every line. He noticed that

- The manuals were at the far end of a large room.
- It took at least one minute to get there.
- There were hundreds of manuals, all with the same white covers. The year was printed in small blue print on the spine.
- The CSRs were not allowed to remove the manuals from the area. They had to look up the information there, then return to their desk and resume their conversation with the customer.

Russ began to suspect that the punishment for giving customers the wrong information (or making it up) was less painful than for exceeding the center's average call-handling time.

The last three elements in the hierarchy are about investment. You need to find out if the organization invests in its people, facilities, systems, and technology so that it can handle rapid change, growth, and market challenges. Not investing just delays costs and limits the organization's ability to respond to changes in the marketplace or advances in technology. It can also erode employee and customer loyalty and relations.

Physical Facilities and Space

Shift your attention to how the design and maintenance of the company's buildings and equipment support performance. Be skeptical, just as you were when investigating the other elements. Pay attention to buildings, parking lots, bathrooms, cafeterias, closets and lockers, and so on. Look for dirt, disrepair, ill-lit rooms, and graffiti. Confirm that the physical environment has adequate lighting, noise control, air quality, water, electricity, temperature control, and space to support the work that is done there. Pay attention to how the work space is arranged: does it allow for easy access, noise control, and adequate room to support the required tasks and interactions? Check preventive maintenance records, OSHA reportables, and EPA reportables. Remember that an organization's physical space communicates at lot about what it values.

Training and Development

Look for evidence that people's skills and knowledge are maintained, and find out who is eligible for training. Your hypotheses should be that few, if any, employees get training, that it is hard to get training, and that training is not linked to any business initiative. Assume that there is no strategy for keeping people current. Ask to see the training budget, how many people have development plans, and how many people have had development discussions with their supervisors. Find out how developmental needs are identified, if training records are kept, and how training programs are evaluated. At the same time, look for evidence that what was planned actually happened, that training and development are linked to the organization's business strategy, and that the training department can substantiate the value it adds.

Resource Capacity and Sufficiency

The last element in the hierarchy is about verifying that there are enough resources and that what resources there are have the capacity (emotionally, physically, and intellectually) to perform well. Find out if there are excess resources and, if there are, to what degree they increase fixed costs. Your hypothesis should be that when it comes to resources, there are either not enough or too many. You want to verify that the right amount of resources (systems, space, people, and equipment) exist to do the required tasks and that those resources have the capability to do the task. Look for and ask about what is not getting done (and whether it matters), how much work is outsourced (and whether it matters), how people compensate for a lack of resources, what they put at risk to do so (human or physical assets, customer service, and so on), and how much time is spent on task.

Clues that indicate resources are insufficient include things like the following: preventive maintenance does not get done because production lines are operating around the clock; people do not receive training because there is no one qualified to fill in for them while they train; vacation time goes unused, but the trend in sick leave is up; exit interviews show an increase in the number of people leaving because they felt overworked or abused. Again, look, ask questions, and check records.

FIELD NOTES: THE SEARCH FOR A DEFICIENT INVESTMENT IN RESOURCES

Mike, who is in charge of performance consulting for his company, worked at corporate headquarters. Mike's department supported the company's product managers, who were responsible for developing the supply chains for the system worldwide. A long-term supplier was in financial trouble, and the supply company's president was asking Mike's company for interim financing until he could turn his company around. Mike was asked to find out more about what was really happening. The supply company's president told Mike that morale was low, productivity was down, and employee theft was up. Mike suspected that if these statements were true, then something in the supply company's environment must have changed, because in the past the company had been known for being efficient and for having a conscientious workforce. Mike asked to visit the supplier's facility to get a better understanding of the problem.

When he pulled into the employee parking lot, Mike noticed that the grounds were covered with litter, the curbs in the parking lot were crumbling, the lawn had bare spots, and the employee entrance door was filthy. While in the building he went to the restroom, which was foul-smelling, had a broken toilet, and lacked paper towels. Mike suggested that he and the facility manager have lunch in the employee cafeteria, but he was told that the professional staff never ate there. He asked to visit the plant floor, and while he was there he noticed that some of the forklift drivers did not wear safety belts, the aisles were dirty, one production line was not running, and a number of light bulbs were burned out. Mike began to formulate some hypotheses: that the president had not reinvested earnings back into the business; that this had resulted in increases in the cost of operations, which had eroded profits; and that there were no incentives to reinvest.

Mike then began his search for corroborating evidence. He reviewed the plant's operating budget and the plant manager's bonus plan. Later he compared the budget and bonus plan to industry standards for similar plants. Mike began to suspect that because the president had not invested in the firm for some time, it could no longer operate cost-effectively.

Kelly's company asked her to find out why employee turnover was high. She asked if the problem was across all jobs and departments or somehow isolated. HR told Kelly that the highest turnover rate was among nonexempt staff companywide and among professional staff in information systems (IS). Kelly asked to see any exit interview data HR had on file. A summary of the exit interview data indicated that a lack of training and a lack of advancement opportunities were both frequently mentioned.

Kelly began to hypothesize that the lack of training contributed significantly to the turnover problem and that the money saved by not supporting training was outweighed by the costs that were shifted to other areas, such as recruitment and training for new hires. She reviewed the training budget and discovered that there was no budget for nonexempt employees, because they were not eligible for training. She also discovered that very little was budgeted for IS. When she interviewed some of the IS staff she was told that they couldn't afford to stay with the company, that their skills would soon be out of date because of the lack of training. If they stayed on too long, they felt, they could never compete on the outside. Kelly decided to continue her investigation of the implications of not investing in human resources, particularly the costs of turnover, recruitment, and training new hires.

FIELD TECHNIQUES: GROWING YOUR CLIENT'S SKILLS IN ASSESSMENT

Needs assessments are difficult, which is why I want my clients involved in them. Clients bring a deeper understanding of the organization. I bring discipline, objectivity, and a fresh perspective. Together we do a better job. I use the job aid version of the hierarchy as a way to coach the client, particularly in working with me at creating hypotheses and getting data. I use the worksheet to document what we want to find out, our hypotheses, what data we want to get, and how we will get the data. Documenting the process helps me measure and improve my efficiency. It helps the client participate, explain the process to others, get cooperation, and build a case for change. It also gives the client a model for future projects. Here are some guidelines for working with your client to assess the client's needs:

1. Show the hierarchy (Figure 6.3) to your client.

2. Explain each element and what the concept of the hierarchy is designed to accomplish.

3. If you want to join with your client in designing a needs assessment, use the job aid (Figure 6.4) to get ideas about what to ask, possible hypotheses, and how to get the data.

4. Come up with some working hypotheses concerning why a performance gap exists or where gaps might exist.

5. Come up with a list of methods to prove your hypotheses right or wrong.

6. Decide how you will get the evidence.

7. Decide who will be involved in the process, how they will be involved, and when.

STAYING DISCIPLINED AND SETTING YOUR OWN STANDARDS

The hierarchy is only a tool to help you take a disciplined approach to needs assessments. It is not a performance checklist on which you sign off after checking each element in sequence. In practice, you might come across information about facilities before you learn anything about the direction of the work unit, simply because you have to walk through the work area. Or your client might direct to improve processes already identified as inefficient or to provide training because of errors due to lack of skills. But just because you start with what you discover first or where the client directs you to begin doesn't mean you should overlook the importance of confirming congruency between the company's vision, mission, goals, and rewards. You can't improve processes unless there is agreement about what those processes are expected to accomplish and the company awards people for being efficient. Job skills training will not compensate for conflicting directions from management or inefficient work procedures.

The hierarchy is designed to help you consider all the variables that support performance and all that impedes it. When you find corroborating evidence, you get the information you need to develop your business case for doing what it will take to improve performance. Your recommendation may be for management to define and agree on where they are going, to start rewarding the behaviors and results that support their vision, to redesign work processes so they do not add unnecessary costs, or to invest in the resources required to accomplish the vision.

Decide in the beginning how rigorous you need to be in your process. Rigor, in this case, means defining your questions up front, carefully recording responses, and consistently engaging people in the same way. You might even pilot test your data-gathering methods to confirm that they work the way you expect them to. How rigorous you need to be depends on

- The degree of confidence you have in your information (and the degree of confidence you need in order to defend your findings before management)

- The kind and amount of risk associated with acting prematurely on your conclusions

- The extent to which you want to periodically replicate your process to determine the reliability of your findings or evaluate the effectiveness of your interventions

- The extent to which you want to generalize your conclusions (broaden the area of application)

- The extent to which your processes, results, and actions have to withstand outside scrutiny (such as from a regulatory agency or collective bargaining unit)

Here are two standards I follow:

1. *Use more than one method to collect evidence, and get it from more than one source.* You need corroborating evidence from more than one source. If you interview people, also check their work records. If you send out a survey, combine it with direct observation. The reason you need to use more than one method is to control any bias you may have introduced by how you asked questions, how you chose to include people, or how you conducted your study. The primary sources of bias are administrative error, questioning error, and sampling error (see Figure 6.6).

2. *Follow the guidelines in Figure 6.6 to control bias.*

FIELD TECHNIQUES: IDENTIFYING BARRIERS TO BECOMING A PERFORMANCE CONSULTANT

To increase your understanding of and proficiency in the process of identifying barriers to performance, practice on yourself. For example, think of your transition to performance consulting as an intervention, and use the scorecard to link your contemplated services to your client's needs. Follow these steps:

1. Meet with your colleagues, team, supervisor, and key clients. Build a scorecard to identify how adding performance consulting to your repertoire of services will benefit the organization.

2. Identify the initiatives and performance gaps that your becoming proficient at performance consulting will affect.

3. Assess how much success you will have to demonstrate to justify your investment (in time and dollars) in becoming a performance consultant.

4. Next, apply the hierarchy to identify barriers to and opportunities for adding performance consulting to your services. Confirm that you, your colleagues, your supervisor, and key clients have the same understanding of what performance consulting is. Then follow these steps:

- Develop your hypotheses concerning what the barriers and opportunities are. For example, is one barrier a lack of understanding of performance consulting or of something else? Is one barrier an unwillingness to reward or reinforce the behaviors of following a consulting process, measuring your own effectiveness, developing processes for identifying causes of poor performance, and so on? Do your colleagues, supervisor, and key clients agree on what performance consulting is or even have a similar understanding of what it can contribute? What do they think you will do differently from what you do now? Do you think the behaviors of a performance consultant will be rewarded? How about your results?

- Share the model consulting process, the suggested measures of efficiency and effectiveness, your vision and mission, your list of products and services, and the model operational definition from Chapters One and Two and ask them what they think these mean.

- Ask them which behaviors they think will be rewarded.

- If possible, get corroborating evidence that either supports or refutes your hypotheses about what you think will be the barriers and opportunities.

- If you discover that the group does not share the same understanding, help everyone come to a shared understanding of what performance consulting is and what it can contribute.

5. Confirm that the way your department or work group is structured, the processes you use, your documentation and standards, and your job aids support your being efficient:

   - You will now have a model consulting process, a model needs assessment process, and job aids for evaluating your processes and doing performance consulting. Again, develop your hypotheses concerning the adequacy of these processes and the need for other processes, documentation, and so on.

   - Decide how you will get the data you need to measure how efficient you are today and what interferes with or supports your being efficient? You can begin to measure your efficiency and see if it improves over time.

6. Confirm how much of an investment you have already made or plan to make in your professional development and in the development of your processes, standards, and performance aids to support this new role.

   - Develop your hypotheses concerning how much agreement there is about the amount invested to date and the amount needed in the future.

   - Decide how you will get the data you need to find out what the investment has been to date and what it will be in the future.

Source of bias

1. Administrative error

Administrative error happens when

- You do not ask people the same questions.
- You ask the questions in a different sequence.
- You give people different amounts of time to answer.
- Your preamble to your questions is emotionally laden.
- Your recording of answers (or observations) is incomplete or inaccurate.

How to control it

- Write out what you are going to say to introduce an interview, to explain the purpose behind the study, and to explain how people were selected to participate.
- Stick with the script. This does not mean you have to memorize it. It does mean you must strive to be experienced in the same way by everyone.
- Prepare your forms for collecting data in advance. Record your findings as soon as possible. Preferably, record the data as you are getting it.
- Give yourself a trial run. Practice explaining the reason for the study and your procedures.

2. Questioning error

This happens when the questions you ask

- Are unclear or misleading
- Are not relevant to the topic
- Fail to adequately cover the subject
- Focus on inconsequential or irrelevant aspects of the topic

- Ask simple questions. Limit each question to a single topic. Avoid compound questions, such as "do you like ham and eggs?"
- Avoid double negatives.
- Avoid indicating what other people said or thought before letting the person you are interviewing answer.
- If you are concerned that people will censor their answers, interview them individually and in private.
- Do a trial run to find out if your questions elicit the quality of responses that you are looking for.

Figure 6.6. How to Control Bias

- Decide how will you get the data you need to confirm what the groups will accept as evidence that you are capable of providing performance consulting.

7. Now, plan how you will use the scorecard and hierarchy on a client's project.

8. To practice developing hypotheses, think of some organizational unit, like a work group, team, or department, and ask yourself the following questions:

- What are your assumptions about how clear the unit's vision, mission, and goals are and to what degree its people are in agreement? How does this clarity (or the lack of it) affect performance?
- What behaviors and results do you think get rewarded? How does what gets rewarded affect performance?
- What do you know about the unit's work processes? Are they well designed? How do they affect performance?

3. *Sampling error*

This happens when you

- Rely too much on one voice (audience)
- Fail to include other legitimately vested voices
- Do not adequately sample
  - the people
  - the documents
  - the work records
  - the product or outputs of the task

- Make sure you include all the relevant voices or populations. There are four categories of people whose voices should be included:
  - The people who are the subject of the investigation, usually called the target audience
  - The targets' bosses (the people who give the target audience direction and evaluate their performance)
  - The targets' customers or clients (the people who receive the targets' output or benefit from their performance)
  - The targets' suppliers (the people, processes, information, and systems that the target audience relies on to perform their work)
- Sample all of your populations. You can pick everyone in a population (a 100 percent sample) or select a smaller number. If you sample, you can handpick people or choose them randomly.
- Whether you pick the targets or they are nominated by someone else, they should be
  - Knowledgeable (that is, able to give you the information you want)
  - Credible (that is, perceived as believable)
  - Capable (that is, able to present a perspective that you can use to test the reliability of data gathered from other sources and in other ways)
- If there is variability in the target population, you can pick a stratified random sample.
- Remember that sampling applies to more than people. You can pick places, situations, locations, documents, and types of things to investigate. The objectives for assessment and guidelines for selecting the sample apply no matter what you are sampling.

Figure 6.6. How to Control Bias, *cont'd.*

- Are there standards? Is the documentation accurate and accessible? How do these affect performance?
- Do job aids exist? Do people use them? Do they create their own? How does the adequacy (or inadequacy) of the job aids affect performance?
- What do you know about the facilities? Is the space really designed to support the work the people do?
- Who gets trained, and why? Who doesn't get trained, and why?
- Do people have to fill time by looking busy? Are people overworked? Do people have what they need to be effective?

These questions should help you to realize that you already know a lot about your client. Developing hypotheses is not that hard. Once you have some idea about what it is you want to confirm, you and your client can decide how to get the data you need about what is or is not true and the effect on performance.

SUMMARY

Performing needs assessments should become a natural part of your doing business. You are always in a position to question, confirm, and reconfirm that people share the same vision and goals, that job procedures support efficiency, and that people have the skills and knowledge they require. There is always time to find out why accidents, errors, and waste are increasing, rather than assuming that you know the answers. There is always time to find out if the people and the organization can support a new structure. Jumping to conclusions wastes time and resources.

If Lisa had used the hierarchy she would have known to confirm whether or not the bank president and his management team were clear on and in agreement with the bank's vision, mission, and goals. Her hypotheses would have been that they were not in agreement on their vision, that they were unclear about their goals, and that the behaviors they rewarded did not support accountability or performance. Another hypothesis might have been that the president's goals for the bank had changed and were no longer aligned with the bank's publicized vision and mission statements, or that the president was unable to explain how the bank's new practices aligned with its vision and mission. She could have interviewed the president privately to learn more about his expansion goals and to find out if the bank's lending practices had really changed or if only a few loans had fallen outside its stated goals.

What Lisa discovered when she asked people to describe the organizational structure of the bank should have led her to still another set of hypotheses: that changes in the bank had disrupted old reporting relationships; that managers were being undermined by the EVP, and as a result they really did not have a managerial job under this structure; and that the managers were comfortable with the arrangement, because it meant they were not accountable for anyone's performance, including their own. She could then have found out how managers were chosen for the job, how their performance was evaluated, and whether or not there were any consequences for poor performance. In her process of creating a training program she could have begun to get the president to better understand his responsibility for supporting performance.

WHERE TO LEARN MORE

Hale, J., *Standards for the Training Function* (Washington, DC: International Society for Performance Improvement, 1996). Accompanying these standards are checklists and surveys for evaluating the adequacy of processes used to identify client needs, demonstrate leadership, manage capital assets, and measure results.

Mager, R., *Goal Analysis*, 3rd ed. (Belmont, CA: Fearon, 1972).

Mager, R., and Pipe, P., *Analyzing Performance Problems* (Belmont, MA: Fearon, 1977).

Rummler, G. A., and Brache, A. P., *Improving Performance: How to Manage the White Space on the Organization Chart*, 2nd ed. (San Francisco: Jossey-Bass, 1995).

Chapter 7

Interventions

..........................*I*n this fieldbook the term *intervention* is all-encompassing. It refers to any change, program, or event intended to improve organizational or people performance. Organizations implement changes and adopt programs in the hope of improving productivity and performance. Those changes and programs frequently require a major investment in time and dollars. The changes companies implement and the programs they fund redefine work and work relationships. They affect people's lives. Consider the following situations.

FIELD NOTES: EXAMPLES OF INTERVENTIONS

A bank opened an elementary school (grades K–8) on-site. An insurance company installed an expert system for claims handling. A direct sales merchandiser decided to certify its product trainers. A multinational company installed an Intranet so all of its sites could more efficiently communicate with one another. A manufacturer organized its production line employees into self-managed teams. A field office sent everyone to attend a sexual harassment class. A retailer met with its distributor and paper bag manufacturer to standardized packaging sizes. A restaurant chain set criteria for determining the salary level of key jobs.

What these situations have in common is that each organization did something to solve a business problem. It is unclear, however, what the chosen solution was expected to fix, change, or improve. The goal may have been to reduce costs, to shorten cycle times, to retain employees, to avoid paying fines, or to improve customer confidence. Whatever the reason, these companies' actions were not arbitrary. They planned their actions and committed resources. What they may or may not have had was a process that helped them fully understand the consequences of their actions and measure the results.

A LITTLE HISTORY ON INTERVENTIONS

The term *intervention* has traditionally been used by professional counselors, to mean a purposeful confrontation intended to get individuals to accept responsibility for their actions and change their behavior. The term was first adopted by training and development professionals after Barry Booth and Odin Westgaard used it at a national conference in 1979. The term soon began appearing in professional journals in reference to solutions other than training (specifically, job aids) that were aimed at improving performance.

The term is still a performance consultant's word; it's not part of the language of our clients. Clients do not talk about interventions. They talk about initiatives, programs, and strategies to solve problems, increase productivity, and reduce costs. Clients want to accomplish a goal, such as

- Increase stockholder returns
- Improve market position or share
- Increase productivity
- Improve product performance
- Improve people performance
- Improve financial performance
- Achieve regulatory compliance

About ten years ago I conducted a research project to identify what companies were doing to improve performance. It was this research that got me to think less about specific interventions and more about what stimulated or triggered the need for change, and thus the intent behind interventions. I learned that companies implement changes in response to a combination of factors: business needs, poor productivity, poor employee morale, the availability of new technology, and social pressure. Another thing I noticed was the role that the popular press, and later the mass media, played in influencing the types of interventions management sponsored.

That research has been helpful to me in a number of ways. I discovered that most interventions are initiated in response to a major event or real need, and some are implemented because of the influence of a strong, popular personality. Therefore when I'm hired after a client has already decided on an intervention, I still want to go back and identify what drove the decision. Was it the results of a needs assessment? Was it the desire to take advantage of a new technology? Or did someone just want to follow the managerial fad of the day? I can't measure the effectiveness of a program unless I know the stimulus and intent behind the particular solution. If my client has not already decided on a course of action, I want to understand the problem well enough to recommend the appropriate solution.

Here is a very brief overview of some significant events and people that have influenced the business world's ideas about how to improve managerial and organizational effectiveness. My intent is to encourage all of us to question what affects performance and to investigate how best to improve it. Understanding why organizations chose certain interventions in the past will put us in a better position to recommend the same or a more appropriate intervention in the future.

Big business as we know it today was born during the first part of the 1900s. The manufacturing, retail, mining, banking, and other industries of the day had two problems: very high turnover and the need to coordinate the efforts of more people than they had ever had to deal with in the past. Organizations turned to the leading thinkers of the day. Managers were impressed with the work of Frederick Taylor, a mechanical engineer who later became known as the father of scientific management. Taylor, along with Frank Gilbreth (who refined the use of time and motion studies) and his wife, Lillian (who earned a doctorate in psychology from Brown University), was actively engaged in studying how jobs and tasks are designed. Rather than focusing on how to reduce turnover, they used time and motion studies to reduce jobs to a few discrete tasks, so people could be trained in them in hours instead of days. (Task and job redesign remains a popular intervention today; however, the goal has gone beyond that of reducing training time, to improving efficiency.) At about the same time, management theorists began to define the job of the supervisor versus that of the worker.

Organizational theorists also began to propose ideas about how to structure, or organize, large businesses. The concepts of vertical and horizontal integration were introduced, and they are still debated today. Vertical integration occurs when a company owns or controls everything in a supply chain (from producing the raw materials to manufacturing, marketing, and distributing the finished product). For example, think of a cardboard box company that owns the forests, the lumberyard, the paper mills, the plant that manufactures the boxes, and the stores that sell them. Horizontal integration occurs when a company owns or controls the entire market in one segment of a supply chain (by owning every forest or every paper mill, for example).

The result of vertical and horizontal integration in the early decades of the twentieth century was the emergence of monopolies. Today we see organizations creating holding companies, franchises, and joint ventures as ways of controlling markets. The point is that organizations still wrestle with the problem of finding the optimum structure and size. Restructuring, or reorganizing, is still a common intervention used to solve business problems.

It was at about the time of the stock market crash of 1929 that organizations began to shift their attention to what motivates workers. There were riots in Washington, D.C., in 1932 and sit-down strikes in Detroit in 1937, and unemployment ranged from 12 to 15 percent during the Depression. Elton Mayo conducted a landmark study from 1927 to 1932 at the Western Electric Company. He concluded that workers respond to the total work situation and that their attitude toward work and their social relations were important.

There was also increasing attention on the role of managers. Dale Carnegie's book *How to Win Friends and Influence People* was published in 1936 and was outsold only by the Bible. Chester Barnard, an executive with the American Telephone & Telegraph Company, wrote *The Functions of the Executive*—a leading book in 1938—on the role of management. He was the first to distinguish between effectiveness (accomplishing goals) and efficiency (doing so without harmful consequences). He also stressed the role of management as a vehicle for communication, a conduit for ideas and information. The Hawthorne studies, done between 1927 and 1931, were published in 1939, the same year that the plight of the migrant farmworker was popularized in Steinbeck's *The Grapes of Wrath.*

The threat of war in 1941 accelerated the search for better ways to increase productivity. The U.S. government, together with big business, launched the "training within industry" program. This program, although created in anticipation of the United States' entering World War II, was also intended to address growing labor unrest around the nation by training supervisors in what was called pragmatic human relations. It was also designed to train civilian and military supervisors in how to lead and motivate. The program was framed around two assumptions: it takes a strong leader to motivate workers, and the most important skill needed is the ability to persuade. One hundred speech teachers were trained at Harvard University to teach the program. The primary text they used to train both military officers and civilians was Monroe's *Principles of Speech,* which was first published in 1935. This book was the primary text used to train military leaders until the mid-1950s. Every officer was subjected to Monroe's "motivational sequence," which combined traditional rhetoric with modern psychology. The belief that communication skills are key to leadership persists today.

Technologies that were by-products of the war (such as mainframe computers in 1944 and transistors in 1948) would later alter how and where work was done. The introduction of direct-dialed phone calls in 1951 changed the way organizations communicated. At the same time, another technology was evolving that would shape the workplace of the future. This technology grew out of a search for ways to change the physical workplace to improve productivity. The Eames brothers began their experiments with molded plywood in 1941. Synthetic fabrics, furniture, and flooring were developed in the 1940s and 1950s. Molded plywood and synthetics resulted in stackable modular furniture. The concept of the "office house" premiered in 1943. Furniture systems and suspended ceilings were introduced in the 1950s. The rising cost of health care and new work-related injuries and illnesses such as carpal tunnel syndrome, lower-back injuries, and breathing disorders continue to force companies to experiment with new ways to design work space and equipment. The American Disabilities Act of 1992 forced organizations to redesign their facilities to allow greater access to all people. In 1997 the American Society of Interior Designers published a major study on how to improve productivity through better lighting, layouts, furniture design, and carpeting. Today organizations invest significant resources in designing work spaces and equipment in the hopes of reducing costs and improving performance.

The idea of lifelong learning began in the mid-1960s, when junior colleges started to offer adult continuing education programs. The civil rights movement and the protests of the 1970s fueled more aggressive investment in management training and triggered the introduction of coaching and counseling in the workplace. The economic downturn in the early 1970s brought the realization that lifelong employment might not be possible, however. Companies introduced the first career counseling and preretirement planning programs in the early 1970s, signaling a shift in responsibility for job security from the organization to the individual. The 1980s and 1990s continued to see health and fitness programs moving into the workplace, along with employee assistance programs.

The space race started in the 1950s, and when NASA announced on nationwide television that it had adopted zero defects as its standard, the business world began to pay more attention to standards. Japan began to establish itself as a dominant force in the automobile and electronics industry in the 1960s. The Baldrige Award was created in 1986 by President Reagan, and the ISO 9000 Standards were published that same year. Soon popular books about total quality management and reengineering increased our understanding of how standards, well-designed processes, measurement, teams, and leadership could affect performance.

Companies still experiment with many of these same ideas to improve performance. Especially with globalization increasing, companies are still interested in changing their structures, reengineering their processes, using new technologies to redefine how work is done, introducing programs and incentives to motivate workers, redesigning the workplace, and experimenting with theories about management and leadership.

The programs organizations adopt to improve performance are implemented at many different levels. Figure 7.1 lists examples of what organizations do at the individual, work group, department, and division levels to improve performance.

Interventions designed to improve individual performance:

- Redesigning a job or workstation to accommodate physical limitations
- Allowing flextime work schedules
- Permitting job sharing
- Providing personal financial or family counseling through an employee assistance program
- Installing electronic performance support systems

Interventions designed to shape or improve work group and team performance:

- Adopting agile manufacturing practices
- Making cross-training available
- Implementing self-directed work teams
- Offering diversity training
- Holding competitions
- Building identity through departmental slogans or uniforms

Interventions designed to improve the performance of whole departments and divisions:

- Adopting uniform standards
- Replacing traditional compensation structures with job banding
- Creating vision and mission statements
- Installing Intranet and e-mail systems
- Giving business units profit-and-loss accountability

Interventions to improve the performance of major divisions, subsidiaries, and even whole companies:

- Selling off a product line, plant, or division
- Buying or merging with another division or company
- Decentralizing or centralizing staff functions
- Consolidating functions
- Reengineering major cross-functional processes, such as order-to-ship processes
- Adopting a new logo or corporate name

Figure 7.1. Interventions at the Individual, Work Group, Department, and Division Levels

Because performance consultants come out of HRD, OD, training, quality assurance, and other staff functions, they are more likely to get involved in interventions at the individual, work group, team, and department levels. Nevertheless, they may be part of a team working on a major initiative that can affect a whole division or company.

FIELD TOOLS: THE FAMILY OF INTERVENTIONS JOB AID

When I first began thinking about different types of interventions, I found it helpful to classify them into "families." Otherwise, the list of all the interventions an organization could possibly implement would be too long to be manageable. I finally settled on thirteen families, which I later sorted into four groups. Each family of interventions has a unique label (see Figure 7.2).

The label quickly communicates the purpose or reason for the intervention; it tells you what a specific activity or program is supposed to accomplish. It also helps me identify the appropriate action or set of actions to improve performance, stay focused on what I'm trying to accomplish, and not overlook supporting interventions. The labels do something else as well. They help me establish credibility, because I have a method for sorting, comparing, and selecting the most appropriate interventions. I use Figure 7.2 as a job aid and openly share it with clients.

Group	Families (Labels)	Examples
Information-focused	1. Interventions that *define:* Activities that specify or clarify the vision, mission, purpose, process, products, services, market position, roles, relationships, responsibilities, outcomes, expectations, and so on	Holding sessions to create vision statements; confirming market direction and market niche; mutually setting performance goals
	2. Interventions that *inform:* Activities that communicate goals, objectives, expectations, results, discrepancies, and so on	Producing internal newsletters; holding debriefing sessions; giving feedback
	3. Interventions that *document:* Activities that codify information (to preserve it and make it accessible)	Setting up libraries; creating manuals, expert systems, job aids, and decision guides
Consequences-focused	4. Interventions that *reward:* Activities and programs that induce and maintain desired behaviors, eliminate undesirable behaviors, and reward desired outcomes	Holding public ceremonies and annual recognition events; paying for performance
	5. Interventions that *measure:* Activities and systems that provide metrics and benchmarks so people can monitor performance and have a basis to evaluate it	Developing a scorecard; tracking means and variance in performance over time
	6. Interventions that *enforce:* Activities that actualize consequences and achieve compliance	Policing; reviewing; double-checking; suspending; removing; withholding pay
Design-focused	7. Interventions that *organize:* Activities that change the structure of or arrange business units, reporting relationships, work processes, jobs, and tasks	Reengineering processes; merging functions; reorganizing responsibilities
	8. Interventions that *standardize:* Activities that systematize or automate processes and standardize tasks, tools, equipment, materials, components, or measures	Adopting ISO 9000, ANSI standards, and so on; implementing uniform standards
	9. Interventions that *(re)design:* Activities that result in useful, easy-to-use, safe, and ergonomically designed environments, workplaces, equipment, and tools	Building in safety features; designing for ease of installation, service, maintenance, and upgrading
Capacity- and capabilities-focused	10. Interventions that *reframe:* Activities and programs that generate new paradigms so that people can experience new perspectives, find creative solutions, integrate new concepts into their behavior, and manage change	Facilitating challenging assumptions; engaging in dialogue; entering into new alliances; brainstorming; creating alternative futures
	11. Interventions that *counsel:* Activities and programs that help individuals, either singularly or collectively, deal with work, personal, career, family, and financial issues	Offering on-site daycare, preretirement seminars, on-site physical fitness centers, and employee assistance programs
	12. Interventions that *develop:* Activities and programs that expand skills and knowledge	Offering training, coaching, and structured on-the-job experiences
Congruence-focused	13. Interventions that *align:* Activities and programs that work toward congruency between purpose and practice	Setting up cross-functional teams; soliciting customer (internal and external) feedback

**Figure 7.2.
The Families
of Interventions**

FIELD TOOLS: THE INTERVENTIONS IF-THEN TABLES

The interventions if-then tables (Figures 7.3 through 7.7) are meant to be used more with your team than with your client. Use them to decide what to do, as a reminder of what you want to accomplish, and to help you think about what you will accept as evidence of success.

Information-Focused Interventions

The interventions in the first three families focus on information (see Figure 7.3). They are the most important group of interventions, because

- They are valuable in their own right. They are frequently the only things you need to do to improve performance.

- They also support most if not all of the other interventions.

- If they are not done well or are overlooked, it can greatly reduce the effectiveness of the other interventions and even cause them to fail.

These interventions are more likely to draw on your interpersonal and facilitation skills. They require you to be politically savvy, to remain impartial unless you have relevant information to share, to stay focused so the group does not get off track, and to challenge the assumptions of the group. Here are explanations and examples of interventions from the first three families:

Interventions That Define. Interventions in this family are used to gain clarity. They are meant to contribute definition and dimension, to help people find out what they agree or disagree about regarding their sphere of responsibility; where they are going as an individual, a work group, or a company; and what they are about (that is, their mission). Here are some specific examples of this type of intervention:

- Creating vision and mission statements that clarify a group's purpose, goals, and expected deliverables

- Developing team charters that clarify why a team was created, who its customer or sponsor is, what the team is expected to accomplish, and when it is expected to accomplish it

- Developing job descriptions that define responsibilities, roles, accountability, and so on

- Developing documents of understanding with contractors and suppliers to ensure a shared understanding of expectations

Recommend these types of activities when people are unsure, disagree, or have different expectations because of dissimilar experiences, knowledge, or motives.

Family	If you have evidence that	and	then decide
1. *Interventions that define*	People are unclear, disagree, or have different expectations; there are conflicting objectives; or people do not have a shared understanding.	You believe you can help; it would be a benefit for people to better define and come to consensus about what they mean, expect, require, hope to accomplish, and so on; and it is feasible to facilitate a session to arrive at a shared understanding.	• Who needs to be involved in the session • Who will contact the people • Who will present the problem and explain why resolving it is important • Who will facilitate the session • When you will do it • How you will measure success
2. *Interventions that inform*	Information has changed, the people have changed, or the people are uninformed, and the consequence is poor performance; or people don't get the information they need.	There is agreement on what information people should have to perform their jobs; there is agreement on the amount of detail the information should contain; and there is agreement on who needs to know what.	• How to best get them the information they need • Who will do it • Who else should be involved • When it will be done • What resources it will require • How you will measure your success
3. *Interventions that document*	Information is not accessible over time or is too complex; job aids, manuals, help screens, and so forth are lacking or inadequate, inaccurate, or hard to access.	You agree that the variance in behavior is undesirable and can be reduced with accessible information; you agree to document the information in a form that makes it easily accessible and facilitates consistent interpretation or compliance.	• How to best codify the information so it is available in a form people can use • Who else needs to be involved • Who will arrange for their involvement • When others will be involved • How you will measure the effectiveness of the documentation

Figure 7.3. Interventions Job Aid: Information-Focused Interventions

Interventions That Inform. Interventions in this family make sure that the people who need to know do know. It is not enough just to define purpose, responsibilities, and so on; this information has to be communicated as well. Calling staff meetings, broadcasting employee announcements, and sending memos, faxes, and e-mail are examples of activities intended to inform. Recommend these types of activities when either the information has changed or the people have changed.

Interventions That Document. Interventions in this family make information continuously accessible. In many cases it is not enough to communicate information just once; it is important that people be able to retrieve and reference information on an as-needed basis. Job aids, help screens, contracts, process flowcharts, procedural manuals, diagrams, and if-then tables are just a few examples of interventions designed to make information retrievable and accessible. Recommend activities and programs of this type when information is complex and documentation can help reduce variance in performance.

Your consulting and needs assessment processes should enable you to estimate the cost of getting, communicating, and codifying information and to compare that cost to the cost of doing nothing or doing something else. The operational definition worksheet (Figure 1.6), the product portfolio worksheets (Figures 2.3 and 2.4), and the process or task performance worksheet (Figure 3.9) are tools you can use to clarify, gain consensus, and help make information available.

FIELD NOTES: CULTIVATING AGREEMENT

Deborah knew that the VPs were not in agreement on either the goals for the coming year or what they expected of the call center managers. She met with the VP of sales and explained what she had discovered. She suggested that they meet with the VP of operations and the senior VP of finance to discuss everyone's goals and expectations. Deborah offered to facilitate the meeting, since she wanted everyone to have an opportunity to speak without being censored. She wanted them to experience for themselves just how far apart they were.

She planned to share the call center managers' experience during the meeting, to illustrate how the VPs' lack of agreement had affected the performance of the centers. The call center managers could cite examples of false starts and conflicting objectives, and they could put a dollar value on the waste. She could then begin the process of bringing the VPs to agreement. Deborah knew that without clarity there could be no agreement. She knew that gaining consensus on goals was key to coming up with criteria for measuring call center performance.

Consequences-Focused Interventions

The activities and programs that fall within the next three families of interventions deal with consequences. Like the interventions in the information-focused group, these also work together; however, they cannot be implemented effectively without first achieving the outcomes targeted by the first group of families. Consequences-focused interventions also require skill in facilitation, as well as expertise in defining and measuring performance (see Figure 7.4).

Family	If you have evidence that	and	then decide
4. *Interventions that reward*	Current incentives either reinforce the wrong behaviors or ignore the desired behaviors; or there are few incentives for people to do better, more, or differently.	You have identified and agree on what behaviors or outcomes you want the incentives to reinforce; you have identified the appropriate incentives; you agree on the procedures and criteria for receiving the incentive or reward; and you agree to stop incentives that undermine the desired behaviors or send contradictory messages.	• What you want to measure • What metrics you want to use • Who else needs to be involved • Who will arrange for their involvement • When you will do it • How you will measure the effectiveness of the measures
5. *Interventions that measure*	People don't know what criteria are being used to judge productivity, performance, value, and so on, and they could better control their own performance if they knew what the criteria were; measures of good performance are lacking; or measures are inappropriate.	You agree to make public what is being measured, what metrics are being used, and who is doing the measuring; you agree to identify ways people can do their own measuring.	• What you think the consequences should be • Who should be responsible for making the consequences real • Who else needs to be involved • Who will arrange for their involvement • When you will do it • How you will measure the effectiveness of the change
6. *Interventions that enforce*	Consequences for poor performance or unacceptable behavior are hidden or not enforced.	You agree there should be consequences for poor performance; you agree to identify why consequences are not enforced, whose needs are being met by keeping them hidden, who should support their actualization and put in a process for enforcing them.	• What you think the consequences should be • Who should be responsible for making the consequences real • Who else needs to be involved • Who will arrange for their involvement • When you will do it • How you will measure the effectiveness of the change

Figure 7.4.
Interventions
Job Aid: Consequences-
Focused Interventions

Interventions That Reward. The interventions in this family encourage and reward behaviors and results that benefit the organization. Bonuses, merit increases, gifts and gift certificates, award banquets, plaques, tickets to major sporting events, and dinners are examples of incentives designed to reward behaviors and accomplishments the organization values. Recommend these types of activities and programs when current incentives either reinforce the wrong behaviors or ignore desired ones.

Interventions That Measure. Interventions in this family compare actual behaviors or results to some identified standards, criteria, or expectations. Measuring emphasizes the organization's commitment to meeting its expectations and goals. What organizations measure, when they measure, and the measurement criteria they use make public what the organization thinks is important. Measures tell people how the organization will weigh behaviors or results when it makes decisions about money, promotions, and resources. Examples of uses of measures and measuring include

- Signs that display expected call-handling times and flash actual average times
- Reports that show the difference between planned and actual performance in such areas as turnover, cycle times, fixed costs to variable costs, percent of yield, time lost to accidents, and sales

Recommend activities that measure when the information they provide will help people monitor their own performance or assess it against some standard.

Interventions That Enforce. The interventions in this family carry out consequences. It is not enough to reward and measure. Consequences, good and bad, need to be actualized if they are to be effective. Promises and threats produce cynicism when they are not made real. Some examples of this type of intervention are

- Recognizing employees who meet goals, and withholding bonuses from those who do not
- Celebrating supervisors whose crews have worked accident-free, and holding them accountable for time lost to accidents

Recommend that your client always enforce rules and standards, since compliance and achievement reduce costs, increase customer satisfaction, and ensure safety.

Your consulting and needs assessment processes should enable you to determine the cost of interventions that reward, measure, and enforce and compare that cost to the potential gains. You can use the examples of standards and measures (Figures 2.1 and 2.2) and the tools in Chapters Eight and Nine to facilitate discussion of and eventual agreement on what measures are appropriate.

FIELD NOTES: ENFORCING WORTHY MEASURES

Kelly was asked to join a team charged with coming up with better incentives for the company's insurance agents. The agents were selling, even meeting their goals, yet management thought the company's cash flow could be better. Also, an audit of the property and casualty line had shown some major exposures for the company. Kelly and the team met with agents, finance personnel, and sales employees to find out just what the problem was. They discovered that agents' bonuses were based on the dollar volume of policies sold. Extra incentives were given during the fourth quarter of the fiscal year (the fiscal year ended in October). As a result, 60 percent of sales were made during the last quarter, 60 percent of that amount were made during the final month of the quarter, and 60 percent of *that* amount were made during the last week of the last month. This sales pattern had a substantial effect on the company's cash flow. There were other problems as well. Agents that sold property and casualty insurance were encouraged to sell as many policies as possible. This meant they would try to sell to every home on the block and every small business in the mall. This was fine except when major disasters such as tornadoes, fires, floods, and violent storms occurred. Major disasters tend to damage everyone on a block or in a mall, resulting in significant losses for insurers with this type of coverage pattern. Kelly and her team began to suspect that the agents concentrated their efforts on customers whose policies expired during the fourth quarter, and relied heavily on referrals for new business.

Kelly and her team knew that the way the agents were compensated and rewarded partially contributed to the company's cash flow and exposure problems. The team decided to recommend that the company develop an incentives package that would reward agents for bringing in business throughout the year, which would increase cash flow, and for turning down a certain percentage of business, so the company's overall risk level would decline. To accomplish these goals the incentive package could not punish agents if their fourth-quarter sales went down. Because the agents' traditional approach to generating sales depended on a policy's expiration date, this would require either designing policies with nontraditional expiration dates or encouraging the agents to identify potential customers with expiration dates throughout the year. Kelly and the team met with finance to determine the feasibility and cost implications of a package designed to help the agents change their approach so business would be less cyclical. Kelly's solution incorporated defining and getting agreement on the problem and establishing new criteria for the incentives package so it would better support the needs of the company.

Design-Focused Interventions

The interventions in the next three families are concerned with design—specifically, the design of relationships, work, and physical things. Like the interventions that address consequences, these too should be performed after or in conjunction with those that deal with information. These interventions may require you to join with other experts, such as industrial engineers and interior designers; however, your expertise in job and task analysis and in the development of performance checklists will be uniquely valuable. If you do work with other experts, your skill in facilitation and keeping the group focused will come into play. Also, having some external status will help you establish credibility with the other experts. These interventions are summarized in Figure 7.5.

Interventions That Organize. Interventions in this family address the design of organizations, functions, duties, jobs, and tasks. Their goal is to provide a structure or sequence that enhances efficiency without sacrificing due diligence or safety. Examples of interventions that organize include decentralizing functions, reengineering processes, redesigning jobs, and combining tasks. Recommend these types of interventions when the current structure is inefficient, results in redundancy, adds excess cost, overly burdens cycle times, or hides accountability.

Interventions That Standardize. Interventions in this family address the design of equipment, materials, and procedures. Their goal is to achieve consistent performance, allow for interchangeability, or increase product flexibility and longevity. A common example is when manufacturers of different brands adopt industry standards that allow customers to interchange parts; in such cases, standardization allows the consumer to mix and mingle components from different products built at different times. Another example is when standardization allows for automation; in this case procedures and work protocols are standardized so that the same tasks can be automated. Examples of interventions that standardize include

- Requiring all production runs to produce the same volume of product
- Using the same packaging sizes for multiple products
- Requiring production workers to follow the same line setup procedures
- Adopting standard labels and icons
- Designing new technology to work with older technology
- Applying the same formatting rules to documents and training materials
- Using an automated answering system to handle customer calls
- Installing process controllers to monitor and run production lines

Recommend interventions that standardize when deviation adds extra costs, results in lower yields, or causes variance in the quality of work.

Interventions That Redesign. Interventions in this family address the design of physical things, to enhance safety and reduce injury. Physical things include space, equipment, tools, and materials. These interventions call for

Family	If you have evidence that	and	then decide
7. *Interventions that organize*	The current structure is inefficient, results in redundancy, adds excess costs, overly burdens cycle times, and hides accountability.	You agree that the way tasks and jobs are structured adds costs, reduces morale, interferes with service; you agree to either propose a way to restructure work or to create a task force to redesign the way work gets done.	• What changes to the structure you want to make • How you will do it • What process you will use • Who needs to be involved and what they will do • How you will get them involved • Who will be affected by a change in structure, and how • What the new structure will look like • How you will measure the effectiveness of the change
8. *Interventions that standardize*	Deviations in equipment, materials, specifications, procedures, common practices, and so on add extra costs, result in low yields, and cause variance in the quality of work.	You agree the lack of standardization is adding unnecessary costs; you agree to standardize whatever is causing the deviation; or you agree to do a feasibility study or cost-benefit analysis to answer the question of whether standardization is appropriate.	• What should be standardized • What process you will use to develop the standards • Who is in the best position to do it • What kind of a business case you need for the change • Who will prepare the business case • Who will facilitate the development, testing, and implementation of the new standards
9. *Interventions that (re)design*	The current work space, equipment, tools, or materials encumber, result in non-value-adding activity, or put employees' health and safety at risk.	You agree that the way the equipment, materials, tools, or work space are designed adds time, costs, or errors or reduces morale; you agree that a feasibility study or cost-benefit analysis on redesigning the thing or space should be performed.	• How the current equipment, materials, tools, or work space is affecting costs today and in the future • Who needs to be involved • Who will arrange for their involvement • Who will own the project and facilitate changes • How you will measure success

Figure 7.5.
Interventions
Job Aid: Design-Focused
Interventions

changes in lighting, furnishings, fixtures, finishes, and fabrics. They call for the reconfiguration of space, computer screens, and keyboards. Recommend interventions that redesign work space, equipment, tools, and materials when the current design results in non-value-adding activity or endangers people's health and safety.

Again, your processes should enable you to determine the cost of reorganizing, standardizing, and redesigning relationships, tasks, procedures, workplaces, or equipment and compare that cost to the anticipated gain.

FIELD NOTES: REDESIGNING MANUALS AND WORK PROCEDURES

Russ knew there had to be a better way for the CSRs at his medical supply company to get information about the company's different equipment models. He knew that the manuals were located too far away from the CSRs' call stations and that it was too time-consuming to locate the specific information required to answer customers' questions. He suggested having a small team of CSRs identify ways to make the information more accessible.

The team first identified the equipment and models customers asked about most often. Next they created job aids with the information the CSRs needed to reference most frequently. The team also recommended standards for the manuals, including the use of icons, labels, and colors to help speed up the process of finding information. The team also recommended a different set of procedures for calls about the least-asked-about equipment and models. The new procedures allowed the CSR to note the exception and offer to call the customer back after researching the question. They also recommended establishing a different standard call-handling time for questions about these models. Then the team compared the cost of handling the current number of callbacks with the cost of implementing these changes, to see if the number of callbacks would go down enough to justify the change. Russ's solution incorporated defining and getting agreement on the most used information, agreeing on a design for a job aid (documenting what was agreed to) to make the information more easily retrievable, and agreeing on new work protocols.

Capacity- and Capability-Focused Interventions

The next three interventions are about enhancing people's capacities and capabilities (see Figure 7.6). Just like the interventions that deal with consequences and design, these too must be performed after or in conjunction with those that focus on information. These interventions, in particular, require superior interpersonal skills and skill in creating dissonance and staying focused. Expertise in designing instructional programs may also be required.

Family	If you have evidence that	and	then decide
10. *Interventions that reframe*	Old attitudes about work are preventing innovation or growth.	You agree that strategies are needed for breaking old models, letting go of the past, and coming up with new possibilities; people are stuck or keep applying the same solution, with no results, or there is a lot of resistance to change.	• What opportunities are available to get people to let go • Who you want to involve • How you want it done • When it will start • How you will measure success
11. *Interventions that counsel*	People are preoccupied with or distracted by personal and career issues, and this is limiting productivity or adding unnecessary costs.	You agree people are preoccupied with themselves, their future, their family; people's behavior interferes with others' work or calls into question their effectiveness; you agree to recommend programs or services designed to help people take action and feel more in control.	• What resources are available • Who you want to involve, and what they will do • How you want it done • When it will start • How you will measure success
12. *Interventions that develop*	Current performance is suffering or future performance will suffer because people lack skills and knowledge.	You agree people's skills are out of date; people need cross-training so they can be redeployed; there is a need to develop people for the future; you agree to recommend programs designed to build and reinforce the skills and knowledge required for today and tomorrow.	• Who needs development, why they need it, and when they need it by • How to best fulfill the need • How to best develop and deliver the program • How you will measure the development achieved

Figure 7.6. Interventions Job Aid: Capacity- and Capability-Focused Interventions

Interventions That Reframe. Interventions in this family consist of events or messages that produce a new mental image for people. They are performed to help people look at problems in a new way, gain a new perspective, or redefine a situation so that they can solve their own problems. Reframing is done a lot but is rarely recognized as an intervention. Creating a new paradigm is an example of reframing. New paradigms help people let go of old ways of doing business. Turning a disadvantage into an advantage is another example. Games that distort time, relationships, location, and social rules can be examples of reframing. Photographs or drawings done from an unusual vantage point enable people to see things they have never seen before. Organizations use reframing activities when they want to rechannel people's energy toward new possibilities. Therapists use them when they want to help patients develop new mental models that support emotional growth and constructive relationships. Recommend these types of interventions when old attitudes and frames of reference prevent growth.

Interventions That Counsel. Interventions in this family help people deal with family, financial, career, and health issues. Some examples are employee assistance programs, on-site fitness centers, on-site daycare centers, smoking cessation programs, and preretirement and financial planning seminars. Recommend interventions from this family when people are preoccupied with personal and career issues that distract them, reduce productivity, and increase costs.

Interventions That Develop. Interventions in this family improve or expand people's knowledge and skills. Typical examples are training programs, mentoring programs, job-swapping programs, cross-functional teams, community college programs, continuing education courses, conferences, and seminars. Recommend interventions from this family when people's lack of skills and knowledge adversely affects their current or future performance.

Your consulting and needs assessment processes should help you determine the cost of increasing people's capacity to perform and to deal with personal and business issues, and compare that cost to the anticipated gain.

FIELD NOTES: BUILDING COMMITMENT AND REFRAMING A RELATIONSHIP

Mike returned from visiting the supplier's plant. The dirty, run-down conditions and poor morale at the plant indicated that either the company was losing money or the owner was not sufficiently reinvesting in the company. Mike shared his observations about the supplier, particularly concerning the physical neglect of the plant, the substandard quality of the cafeteria, and the inadequate operating budget. He recommended that before his company lent money to the supplier, it should reframe its relationship with the supplier. He recommended requiring the supplier to implement some very specific interventions, including

- Reinvesting an agreed-upon amount of money into the business
- Using the reinvestment funds to upgrade the plant and equipment inside and out
- Funding training for employees
- Performing a morale survey to establish one baseline measure that could be used later to determine if improvement had occurred
- Agreeing to on-site visits
- Making quarterly progress reports

In exchange Mike's company would guarantee the supplier a minimum amount of business over the next five years. Mike also suggested that the two companies establish product performance standards and financial performance goals. If the supplier did not meet those standards or goals within a specified amount of time, the supplier would lose the business. Mike also recommended that his company determine how much improvement the supplier must demonstrate, and by when, to make a loan worthwhile. Mike's solution was a combination of defining new performance standards and making the consequences of not meeting those standards clear. Mike also recommended a significant redefinition of his company's relationship with the supplier, to one in which expectations, measures, and accountability were spelled out. The recommended changes were so significant that they constituted a reframing, as they changed how both companies viewed their relationship.

Congruency-Focused Interventions

The last family of interventions is about congruency (see Figure 7.7). Unlike the interventions that deal with consequences, design, and capacity, these must be performed after or in conjunction with *all* those that precede it. As with the other interventions, you will use your expertise in assessment and measurement and your skill at facilitation.

Interventions That Align. Interventions in this family help ensure that an organization's goals, practices, and resources all support the same vision and mission. Sometimes programs that seem to be appropriate, on track, and working successfully may actually be counterproductive over time. The result could be wasted investment, because programs get aborted or abandoned when the company realizes that they drain resources, shift costs, or undermine other initiatives. An example is an intervention that is designed to promote the values

Figure 7.7. Interventions Job Aid: Congruency-Focused Interventions

Family	*If you have evidence that*	*and*	*then decide*
13. *Interventions that align*	Current messages, behaviors, systems, structures, or environments do not support the organization's goals.	You agree that what people say is not what they do, what people do is not what the organization wants, or how people get the work done is not in keeping with the organization's values or public image; you agree to identify what is out of alignment and to recommend ways to bring it into alignment.	• What is out of alignment • What it will take to bring it back into alignment • Who needs to be involved • How to get them involved • Who will facilitate the session to get buy-in • When it will be done • How you will measure success

of openness and honesty but is implemented in an environment that punishes people for being candid. Another example is work groups that claim to encourage critical debate to avoid mistakes but actually chastise people who offer criticism for not being team players. The result is communication accomplished through innuendo and the rumor mill. Recommend interventions that better align values and norms with goals when current rhetoric and behavior do not support each other. Your processes should allow you to compare the cost of operating under conflicting goals, practices, and so on with the cost of bringing them into alignment.

FIELD NOTES: CERTIFICATION

Russ and the team assigned to support the new product line at the medical equipment manufacturer decided that they wanted a program (an *intervention*) that would (1) improve product reliability by ensuring that the company's field technicians were competent to install and service the equipment and (2) earn customer confidence (the intervention's *measure of success*). The company's field technicians were responsible for installing the equipment and handling preventive maintenance and repairs. Because doctors used the equipment in making diagnoses, it was critical that it perform satisfactorily. The team decided that if the company certified the field technicians (the specific intervention), they might accomplish both of their goals.

The decision to develop a certification program put into motion a whole series of smaller, supportive interventions. First the team had to do a job analysis (*define* the job and the criteria for judging proficiency). In the process the team discovered wide variances in preventive maintenance practices across geographic zones. The team brought together engineers, zone directors, and technicians, who shared their practices and agreed to a common set of procedures (*standardization*). To become certified, technicians would have to demonstrate competence and consistent performance (based on *established measures*). The criteria used to judge competence and consistent performance included level of customer satisfaction (measured by ratings on customer satisfaction surveys); productivity (measured by noting the number of installations within a period of time, the efficiency of the installations, and the average time spent on them); troubleshooting skill (measured using problem simulations); and adherence to procedures (measured by direct observation of the task at a client site). The technicians' performance was documented and communicated (informally) to technicians and zone managers. Technicians had six months to meet the criteria. Those who did were given special recognition (a *reward*); those who did not were offered the opportunity for remediation (*development*) or placement in another job (*enforcement*). The team then looked at the training given new hires. The training did not adequately explain customer expectations or provide practice in procedures and troubleshooting. The team recommended that the training be modified to match the criteria for certification (*alignment*).

FIELD TECHNIQUES: USING THE INTERVENTIONS IF-THEN TABLES

You can use the if-then tables (Figures 7.3 through 7.7) to facilitate discussions about what other elements might be affected by implementing a major intervention. Use them to drive discussions about what else has to change for the intervention to work. The if-then tables can help you evaluate an intervention after it has been implemented and identify why an intervention failed or met with resistance. Here are some guidelines for using the tables:

1. Go over the table row by row. For each problem or "if" statement, ask if this describes your situation.

2. If appropriate, discuss with your team all the things you want your solution to accomplish and how you might judge which actions are more likely to yield the greatest benefit.

3. Use the table with your team to identify the kinds of activities or programs that will help in your situation.

4. Identify what else has to change or be in place for your recommendations to be successful.

5. Identify how you will measure the effectiveness, cost benefit, or success of the intervention.

FIELD TOOLS: THE HIERARCHY-INTERVENTIONS MATRIX

This matrix summarizes for you, your team, and your client, on one page, the relationship between the hierarchy and the interventions (see Figure 7.8). The columns list the elements of the hierarchy you examined during your needs assessment. The rows are the families of interventions.

As the matrix shows, more than one intervention is almost always necessary to produce long-lasting results. Use the matrix to help decide what needs to be done and in what order to do it. Here are some guidelines for using the matrix:

1. Compare what you decided would be the appropriate combination of interventions from the if-then table with what the matrix indicates.

2. Remember that performance problems are caused by a series of interdependent variables, not just one factor.

3. Because most performance problems are the result of a number of smaller breakdowns, the solutions, too, must be done in combination if long-term change is your goal.

4. Discuss with your team how one single large intervention (like implementing a new technology, reengineering a major process, or establishing a certification program) might accomplish most if not all of your goals.

5. Discuss what has to be done for your intervention to produce lasting results.

If one of the ten elements in the hierarchy is a cause of a performance problem, then one or more of the interventions marked in that column can help eliminate the problem.

Families of inter- ventions

Elements of the Hierarchy

Interventions that . . .	Vision and mission	Goals	Cultural environment	Organizational job structures	Procedures and processes	Documentation and standards	Job aids and signage	Physical spaces	Training and development	Resource capacity
Define	X	X	X	X	X	X	X	X	X	X
Inform	X	X	X	X	X	X	X	X	X	X
Document	X	X	X	X	X	X	X	X	X	X
Reward			X							
Measure		X	X	X	X	X	X	X	X	
Enforce		X	X	X	X	X	X		X	
Organize				X	X					
Standardize					X	X	X			X
(Re)Design					X	X	X	X		
Reframe			X							
Counsel										X
Develop						X			X	
Align	X	X	X	X	X	X	X	X	X	X

**Figure 7.8.
The Hierarchy-
Interventions Matrix**

6. Decide what would be a reasonable course of action.

7. Decide who needs to be involved, in what ways they need to be involved, and when they need to be involved.

8. Define everyone's roles and responsibilities.

9. Use this information to build a project plan for designing, implementing, and evaluating the intervention.

⦿ FIELD TECHNIQUES: ELIMINATING BARRIERS TO BECOMING A PERFORMANCE CONSULTANT

To gain practice in identifying the best combination of interventions, use the if-then tables to come up with an action plan to support your own transition to performance consulting. For example:

1. What will you do to gain agreement and understanding among your colleagues and clients concerning what performance consulting is and how it will be done in your organization?

2. How will you communicate your vision and mission to staff, clients, and colleagues? Will you develop a flowchart like Mike's (Figure 1.9) or use something else to document your vision, mission, goals, and processes?

3. How will you measure your performance? Will you measure it in terms of how efficient and effective your processes are, how satisfied your customers are, or your ability to measure your results? Will you use the kinds of measures Mike wants to use (Figure 2.2) or something else?

4. What are the consequences of your success or failure?

5. How have you decided to organize your department or your projects?

6. What standard procedures and processes will you adopt?

7. Will you redesign any elements of your work space or equipment to support the new role?

8. Would reframing your role help your clients understand it and be better able to work with you in new ways?

9. Do you or any of your colleagues want further development or training? If so, what would be the topic or skill? Do you think development would be valuable?

10. How will you align your vision, mission, processes, and practices so that all of your resources are concentrated on the same goal?

SUMMARY

I find it helpful to remember that organizations are always going to do things to shape human performance and improve business results. They can do it with or without a process. As a performance consultant you can offer your clients a process that will allow them to set measures, identify resources, identify barriers, and take control. You can use that same process to help them fully understand the implications of their actions and be successful.

WHERE TO LEARN MORE

Drucker, P., *The Organization of the Future* and *The Leader of the Future* (San Francisco: Jossey-Bass, 1997).

Nelson, B., *1001 Ways to Reward Employees* (available through Knowledge Interact, a Division of Softbank Forums, Colorado Springs, CO).

Rossett, A., and Gautier-Downes, J., *A Handbook of Job Aids* (San Francisco: Jossey-Bass/Pfeiffer, 1991).

In addition to reading what others have said about Taylor and the Gilbreths, I found it enlightening to read their writings myself. This allowed me to draw my own conclusions about the importance of their work. One of the Gilbreths' children, Frank, Jr., chronicled his parents' work in the book *Cheaper by the Dozen* (New York: Bantam Books, 1984).

Chapter 8

Measuring Results

Sometimes people have trouble measuring because they are unclear about what they want to accomplish by doing so. Some people simply don't know how to measure. Nonetheless, managers keep asking for better measures so they can decide which programs to fund and support. All of us are being asked to prove that our programs are worth the investment. Here are some examples:

FIELD NOTES: MEASURING RESULTS

A large data-processing firm wanted to certify its resellers. The resellers had asked for the certification. They claimed that being "brand certified" would give them a competitive edge. Senior management wanted to know how the payoff would be measured.

A company decided to require quality training for *all* of its employees. The company had seven field offices located in three states. The training was scheduled to last from one to one and a half days. The training manager wanted to know how success would be measured.

A VP of HR got his company to support a corporate university because a benchmarking study had found that employees were attracted to and more inclined to stay with companies that have aggressive employee development programs. The company also bought, at the VP's insistence, a new computer system so HR staff at corporate headquarters could transfer information to field HR staff. Up until then they had relied on phone calls and faxes. Senior management now wants the VP to show the return on investment.

In each of these cases people wanted support for their program or intervention. What they hadn't figured out was how to measure its worth or effectiveness. Measurement, when done well, helps people make better decisions about where to direct resources, what programs to fund, and if they should invest more (or less) in current programs. Our role as performance consultants is to help our clients develop better measures and measuring systems.

EXPERIENCES FROM THE FIELD: ABOUT MEASURING

Over the last twenty years I've learned that my clients and I do not share a common language or understanding of evaluation. For example, clients frequently use the words *evaluation* and *measurement* to mean the same thing, but at other times they use them to mean completely different things. It is only by listening and questioning that we can help our clients define what they want to evaluate and why. Here is how I use these and other, related terms:

- *Evaluation* is the act of judging something or placing a value on it. To learn what your clients value, observe what they pay attention to; for instance, if your client keeps talking about something or keeps raising a particular issue, then that subject is important to him or her. Our job as performance consultants is to use our questioning and active listening skills to find out what makes a subject important to our clients.

- *Measuring* is the act of comparing. When clients talk about needing to improve performance, they are motivated by the difference between current performance and some standard or goal they want to obtain. They would not know that their current performance needed improvement if they had not compared it to something and found it deficient in some way. Measuring is done by gathering information about a situation, activity, or process and then comparing the information against a set of criteria that defines a desired standard. As performance consultants our job is to find out if our clients have considered sufficient information and to determine what criteria should be used as a basis for comparison.

- *Criteria* are the gauges or yardsticks people use to weigh, rank, or value what they are comparing. Criteria may be stated, unspoken, or assumed. For example, when people say things like "the training worked," they are measuring the program or intervention they are referring to (in this case, training). What such statements leave unclear is the criteria they are using. The criterion might be that the participants liked the training or that after the training was complete a performance problem went away. When you hear "the safety program fell short of what we wanted" or "people don't get it," the people making the statements are basing their conclusions on some criteria. Our job is to ask questions to find out what information people are using as the basis for their conclusions—what they are using to judge adequacy. Commonly used criteria are time, speed, quantity, weight, accuracy, purity, consistency, earnings, costs, savings, compliance, satisfaction, appearance, appropriateness, and performance.

- *Metrics* are units of measure. Metrics allow for precision and exactness. For example, if the criterion is speed, the metric used might be seconds to the fourth decimal point (as in Olympic swimming and running competitions). For some other purpose the metric for speed might be days, weeks, or even months. The metric for weight might be grams or tons. When product performance is measured by sales volume (the criterion), the metric could be tens of thousands of dollars. If the criterion for product performance changes from sales volume to customer satisfaction, the new metric might be the number of customer complaints over a six-month period.

I've also observed that people measure all the time. Because of this tendency, measuring can become the impetus for formal needs assessments (described in Chapter Six), it can influence the process of identifying appropriate interventions (like what was described in Chapter Seven), and it can affect how a program gets evaluated (which is the focus of this chapter). But what is most important is that everything gets measured for a reason. Here are some examples:

FIELD NOTES: TRANSACTIONS, NEW ACCOUNTS, AND THE PERFORMANCE APPRAISAL FORM

A retailer decided to launch a promotion. The retailer hired a public relations (PR) firm to design the campaign. They agreed that the PR firm would receive a bonus if the promotion was a success, and the store owner agreed that the criterion for measuring the promotion's success would be the number of transactions (cash register sales) recorded during the campaign. This criterion provided only a partial picture of the promotion's effects, however. Promotions often encourage customers to buy items priced at or below cost; therefore a high number of transactions may or may not mean that the store is making money. In fact, it may only be breaking even, or possibly losing money. Transactions by themselves do not give an accurate picture of financial success. Thus although the criterion of number of transactions met the PR firm's needs, it may not have met the store owner's needs. If the store owner's objective was to grow the business, to increase profits, or to build customer loyalty, the owner would not know whether the promotion had met his objectives.

A bank had a $5 million merchandising budget to attract new customers and to encourage current customers to buy additional products (mortgage loans, auto loans, certificates of deposit, and so on). Merchandising is used to attract customers of one product or service to other products or services at the point of sale (in this case the bank). The merchandising budget was for things like signs, banners, window decals, fliers, and lobby displays.

One of the bank's products was free checking with no minimum balance for three years. To determine the ROI of the merchandising effort, the bank asked its branch managers to track the number of new checking accounts opened over a one-month period. Free checking is a loss leader, however; that is, customers who want free checking usually have low-balance accounts, which are the most costly accounts to service. Banks lose money on free checking accounts. Therefore, measuring only the number of new checking accounts did not accurately measure the return on investment for the merchandising campaign.

The director of HR for a municipal government developed a new performance appraisal process. The municipality's employees were all unionized, and the union had negotiated that performance measures and salary could not be linked. The director of HR wanted to prove that there was nevertheless a benefit to adopting a new performance appraisal process, and he convinced management that it would have value and increase productivity despite the provision of the union contract. The director suggested that they measure the effectiveness of the new process based on how many managers used it. The number of managers using the process had no bearing on productivity, however. Other criteria were needed before HR could prove that the cost to develop the process and train managers in how to use it was worth the investment.

These stories illustrate two common measurement problems, insufficient criteria and inappropriate criteria and metrics:

- *Insufficient criteria.* In each case only one criterion (the number of transactions, new checking accounts, and managers who used the process) was used. Other measures the retailer might have used were the number of add-on transactions (transactions for items that were not part of the promotion), the margin (profit) that resulted from those other transactions, and how much the overall sales volume changed. The retailer could then have compared these measures to the cost of the promotion, which included the costs of advertisements and printed collateral materials and the amount of time it took the sales clerks off the floor to be briefed on the promotion. In the case of the new appraisal process, the HR department could have measured whether or not performance had improved, how the process affected development, or if it reduced turnover.

• *Inappropriate criteria and metrics.* In each of these cases the only thing that was tracked was volume over a period of time. None of these measures tracked if costs were eliminated, avoided, reduced, or just shifted to other parts of the organization, and as a result, management got a distorted picture of what happened. For example, new checking accounts may have been opened, but if the balances were low, the cost of servicing those accounts was not recovered, thus increasing overall costs. The bank should have used other criteria that are better indicators of business results.

FIELD TECHNIQUES: GETTING MORE THAN TWO SOURCES OF MEASURES

It takes more than two sources of measures to get an accurate picture of what is working and how well it is working. Therefore, find out

1. Whose needs are being met by the current mode of measurement

2. Why the client chooses to use certain criteria and metrics

3. How the picture would change if different criteria or metrics were used

4. What other criteria or metrics could be added that would give a more accurate picture of the situation

5. How you can capture the information you need in a way that is reasonable and cost-effective

---

FIELD NOTES: MEASURING THE SUCCESS OF A MULTIMEDIA TRAINING PROGRAM

Before she joined the firm, Deborah's department had contracted with a vendor to develop a multimedia component for the new-hire training program. The company asked Deborah to prove that its investment in the multimedia component had been worthwhile. Deborah learned that the new-hire training program was nine weeks long, that on average eight hundred to nine hundred new hires were trained annually, and that forty-five full-time trainers were dedicated to delivering the training. The initial investment for the multimedia component had been $1.2 million. The promise made to management was that the multimedia component would shorten the time required for new-hire training. What happened instead was that the length of the training got longer by two weeks, not shorter.

Deborah knew that the length of the training program was only one measure of its success. A second measure could be the overall cycle time to bring a new employee to proficiency. A third measure could be how the multimedia component affected the indirect costs of the center. Deborah began her search for the other measures. She learned that

- The training course was now longer, because more content had been added. In the past the content covered by the multimedia component had been left to supervisors to cover once an employee was released to his or her job.

- In the past it had taken, on average, another fifteen weeks beyond the training period to bring a new employee to proficiency.

- Proficiency was measured in terms of average call-handling time and order accuracy.

After the company added the multimedia component to the training course, new hires achieved the standards for order accuracy and call-handling time within seven weeks. This meant that the overall cycle time had gone from twenty-four weeks (nine weeks of class time plus fifteen weeks of on-the-job training) to eighteen weeks (eleven weeks of class time plus seven weeks on the job). Achieving order accuracy faster reduced the cost of rework due to errors (an indirect cost). The supervisors' time to coach new hires was reduced by half (an indirect cost). The reduction in cycle time and the reduction in indirect costs proved the value of the multimedia component. If Deborah had just looked at how the multimedia component had affected the length of the class, she would have gotten a distorted picture of its impact.

HOW TO SELECT CRITERIA

One of the hardest parts of measuring anything is knowing what to use as criteria. When should the criteria be money? When should it be time? When should it be compliance, customer satisfaction, volume, or something else? As a performance consultant your goal is to identify sufficient criteria to corroborate the results. You want an accurate picture of the situation. Following are discussions of some possible measurement criteria.

Costs

All interventions affect costs in one or more ways. They can eliminate costs, reduce costs, avoid costs, or shift costs to someone else or to a later time. An intervention affected costs positively if it

- Saved time. (Time is money.)

- Eliminated activities; for example, if it resulted in having to check work fewer times or in reducing the number of steps in a process. (Activities consume resources.)

- Improved product performance (by lengthening the shelf life of a product, for example, or reducing the amount of maintenance it requires).

- Improved processes (by eliminating the need for checking, waiting, or handling, for example) or resulted in products or services that deviated less from the standard.

- Increased human productivity (by increasing work performed per hour).

I pay particular attention to whether or not the intervention shifted costs. This happens when an intervention increases the number of activities that have to be performed by others (such as forcing them to check more things, go through more steps to do their work, wait longer, use more resources, or do things they would not ordinarily have to do). It also happens when others are forced to either use more resources or more expensive resources than they did in the past.

Another thing to consider is the cost of the intervention itself. What did it cost to develop (for interventions such as training programs, redesigns of major processes, and reorganizations), and what did it cost to implement? Be sure to include both direct and indirect costs. In addition to consultant or vendor fees, any resource dedicated to a project is a direct cost. Indirect costs might include administrative and management time. How do these costs compare to the cost of the problem? What other costs did the intervention affect?

Satisfaction

Next I think about how satisfied all the vested parties are with the results of the intervention. The vested parties include consumers, internal customers, management, and the employees performing the job. As a measurement criterion, satisfaction includes more than how happy people are; it includes how they feel about the intervention and about how it was developed, who was involved, and how it was implemented. Another component of satisfaction is how confident the vested parties are that the program will fulfill its promise. A third component of satisfaction is image. In this case you find out how strongly people want to be associated with the intervention. If the intervention is popular, more people will want it known that they played some role in its identification, development, or deployment. If it is unpopular, they will disassociate themselves from it.

Rate of Adoption, or Use

Interventions only work if people do them, use them, or embrace them as part of doing business. Consider measuring who is using the intervention, how many people are using it, and how often they are using it.

Goal Accomplishment

Behind every intervention there should be a need to satisfy, an issue to resolve, an opportunity to seize, or a problem to be avoided. The criterion then becomes what the client will accept as evidence that the intervention has achieved its purpose.

FIELD TOOLS: THE COMMON MEASURES, CRITERIA, AND METRICS JOB AID

Figure 8.1 mirrors the first four columns of the scorecard introduced in Chapter Six for needs assessment. It includes a more detailed list of what commonly gets measured, the criteria used, and possible metrics. Use it with your team and client to come up with more ways to measure what happened, what changed, and what still needs attention. Add any criteria and metrics you would like so that it meets your needs. Discuss what might be a feasible way to measure the project you are working on.

FIELD TECHNIQUES: GETTING EVIDENCE

When clients have difficulty coming up with measurement criteria, I ask them what they will accept as evidence that the program worked, the problem was solved, or things got better. This seems to be an easier question to answer than "What criteria do you want to use?" Evidence is made up of the behaviors and results that have to be present or absent for people to believe things have changed.

FIELD TOOLS: EVIDENCE WORKSHEET

Figure 8.2 has examples of evidence for each intervention. Figure 8.3 is a worksheet you can use to list what you and your client will accept as evidence that your intervention has worked. To use the worksheet, think about the kinds of projects or programs you are working on, and then

1. List what you will take as evidence that your project or program has been successful.

2. Be sure to list corroborating evidence (this is analogous to having more than one measure or set of criteria).

3. Discuss how different people might want different evidence depending on how they see the situation.

4. Discuss what might be a feasible way to get the evidence you are looking for.

FIELD TECHNIQUES: GETTING TO THE OBVIOUS

Clients sometimes assume that the right people know what is being measured, how it is being measured, and why. These are dangerous assumptions. Subordinates, in particular, are inclined to behave like they understand even when they don't. It takes courage to ask questions, particularly if someone of higher

Key measures: what organizations pay attention to and value	Criteria: things commonly used to measure performance	Metrics: what gets counted, weighed, and so on	Ways to get the information or metrics
Customer satisfaction	Perceptions and opinions; complaints and returns; referrals	Ratings of how strongly the opinion is held; number of incidents; cost to resolve the problem	Focus groups; rating scales on surveys; customer service numbers
Employee satisfaction	Morale; grievances; turnover and retention	Mean score on survey; number of incidents per year; percent within x months; cost to recruit	Surveys; focus groups; interviews; exit interviews
Market share	Actual compared to potential or competition	Dollar amount or percentage of sales; number of units sold; cost to increase service	Market research; industry indices
Productivity	Time at task; units produced; calls received; process versus cycle time	Percentage of time; number and average per time; average call-handling time; size of gap; indirect cost to achieve	Time sheets; production records; worksheets
Product performance	Cost; recalls; variance; customer opinion; unscheduled service; waste.	Dollars or cents per unit; number per unit or model; standard deviation; ratings; number, percentage, or ratio; direct and indirect cost of waste	Finance; statistical process control data; focus groups; service calls
People performance	Yield; waste; time at task; attainment of objectives; cost of supervision; rework	Ratio or percentage; percentage of time; percentage of achievement; ratio of managers to employees; direct and indirect cost to achieve	SPC data; time sheets; plans; budgets
Financial performance	Fixed costs; variable costs; margin; rate of growth; cost of sales; cost of service	Ratio; percentage or dollars per unit	Daily reports; actual dollars versus budgeted dollars; sales analyses
Compliance	Formal filings; incidents; reportables	Quantity; dollar value; rate per 1,000 hours; number of incidents	QC reports; complaint calls; citations
Growth	Training; succession plans	Number trained; dollars per employee; training that meets individual development plans; retention (dollars, number, or percentage)	Actual versus budget; changes in the database

Figure 8.1. Measures, Criteria, and Metrics Scorecard

status has the answers. One of the benefits of being a consultant is that you are expected to ask questions. Ask open-ended questions that elicit information, clarification, or additional insight. Stay away from closed questions, except to confirm your understanding of a point or to get directions. Here are some examples of open-ended questions:

- What made you notice there was a problem? (Ask this to find out what they pay attention to and value.)

- What makes you think the situation needs improvement or is not up to par? (Ask this to find out their reason for seeking a change and to determine if they are acting on firsthand or secondhand information.)

- What exactly has changed? (Ask this to find out what they track and if it is the same as what they pay attention to and value. If the answers are the same, it means the client is on track.)

- Can you think of a time when it (whatever is being measured) was okay? What was different then? (Listen for whether the answer is the same as for the previous question or if they are using other criteria as well. Again, this indicates whether the client "has a clue.")

- What would have to be different for you to change your opinion of the situation? (Ask this to find out what the person is using for criteria.)

- What will you accept as evidence that things have improved? (Again, you are trying to get at all of the criteria.)

- How much do things have to improve? How will you know when the change is sufficient? (Ask this to find out the metric: do things have to change 1 percent or 100 percent?)

A good consultant is willing to ask tough questions instead of politically correct ones. You want your clients to reflect on their own thinking and question it. This is important because

- What clients pay attention to and what they want to measure might not give them an accurate picture of performance.

- The criteria and metrics being applied might not be appropriate; they might even be misleading.

- More than one criterion is necessary to get an accurate picture of performance.

Group	Family	Evidence
Information-focused	1. Interventions that define: what you did to achieve clarity	An operational definition exists and is used; mistakes and rework have decreased.
	2. Interventions that inform: what you did to make sure people have the information they need when they need it	Incidents of errors and misunderstandings are down; the cost to go back and clarify or correct is down.
	3. Interventions that document: what you did to make information continuously accessible and retrievable	Documents are used and have reduced cycle times for harder and less frequent tasks.
Consequences-focused	4. Interventions that reward: what you did to make sure the behaviors and results that are desired get rewarded and celebrated	Cost shifting has decreased; margins are up; complaints by employees about being treated unfairly are down.
	5. Interventions that measure: what you put in place to ensure that behaviors and results get measured according to valid criteria	A sufficient number of people have used the measures to improve processes or performance, and this has positively affected costs, service, and so on.
	6. Interventions that enforce: what you put in place to ensure that there are positive and negative consequences to actions and results	Enforcement is up and appropriate.
Design-focused	7. Interventions that organize: what you did to change the structure of work relationships	Cycle times and costs have decreased and satisfaction has increased.
	8. Interventions that standardize: what you did to automate and standardize tasks, processes, and so on	Costs and cycle times have changed positively.
	9. Interventions that (re)design: what you did to make space, equipment, and materials safe, easy to use, and so on	Time lost to accidents, sick leave, and absenteeism has decreased; productivity is up.
Capacity- and capability-focused	10. Interventions that reframe: what you did to help people see new possibilities and move forward	Less time is spent rehashing old issues; more time is spent on tasks that contribute.
	11. Interventions that counsel: what you did to help people deal more effectively with personal issues	The number of people who use the services is up; there has been a positive change in absenteeism and tardiness.
	12. Interventions that develop: what you did to keep people current and prepared for the future	Number of people prepared has increased; bench strength for the future is greater; turnover is lower; job satisfaction is higher
Congruence-focused	13. Interventions that align: what you did to keep purposes and practices in harmony	Customer surveys show less dissonance.

Figure 8.2.
Examples of Evidence

Intervention	If you have evidence that	Then what will you recommend?	What will you accept as evidence that things have improved? What metric will you use?
1. Defining	There is disagreement about goals, no shared understanding, or conflicting objectives.		
2. Informing	People are uninformed, and the consequence is poor performance; people don't get the information they need.		
3. Documenting	Documentation (job aids, manuals, help screens, and so on) is lacking, inadequate, inaccurate, or hard to access.		
4. Rewarding	The wrong behaviors are celebrated; desired performance is overlooked; there are few incentives for people to do better, to do more, or to do things differently.		
5. Measuring	Measures of good performance are lacking or inappropriate.		
6. Enforcing	There are no consequences for poor performance.		
7. (Re)organizing	The way jobs and tasks are structured adds costs, reduces morale, or interferes with service.		
8. Standardizing	Lack of standardization is adding unnecessary costs.		
9. (Re)designing	Equipment, materials, tools, or work space add time, add costs, increase errors, or reduce morale.		
10. Reframing	People are stuck, keep applying the same solution with no results, or resist change.		
11. Counseling	People are preoccupied with themselves, their future, or their family; people's behavior interferes with others' work or calls into question their effectiveness.		
12. Developing	People's skills are out-of-date; there is little opportunity to develop people for the future.		
13. Aligning	What people say is not what they do; what people do is not what the organization wants; how people get the work done is not in keeping with the organization's values or public image.		

Figure 8.3.
Evidence Worksheet

FIELD NOTES: CRITERIA
FOR PERFORMANCE IMPROVEMENT

Mike, who heads his company's shared services department, had to prove that centralizing word processing, financial analysis, and performance analysis had not only been cost-effective but had also more effectively driven costs out of the system. He had already studied the effects of the intervention on one supplier and could place a value on what the system had gained in that case. Now he had to prove that combining these services and following a consulting process had allowed him to better drive costs out of the system.

Mike established two sets of criteria to evaluate his department's effectiveness. The first set gauged how well everyone on his staff modeled the principles they espoused. Mike wanted evidence that his group was respected and was being used as consultants by other departments on initiatives to improve the system's performance. The second set concerned his staff's ability to deploy and institutionalize performance improvement initiatives worldwide that would drive costs out of the system and improve product quality. In the past the company had insisted that its suppliers measure their processes and outputs but had never done so itself. The company had also invested in new programs on a regular basis, only to never implement them. Mike and his staff were putting in place processes for measuring results and holding other departments accountable for implementing the programs they supported. Measures that Mike would accept as evidence of his department's worth included the number of strategic projects his team had been asked to worked on, how often his team had been invited to participate on strategic teams, whether or not the team's clients had actually adopted their recommendations, and lower costs that could be directly linked to their interventions.

Kelly's department made the transition from training to performance improvement. Kelly knew she would have to prove the value of this move. She and her staff began by making sure that their change in mission had supported the company's mission and goals. Next they identified the criteria and metrics they would use to evaluate how the change had affected the company. Their criteria were their ability to measure how efficiently they do their work and whether or not what they did had improved performance as measured by criteria selected by the client. In the past the department had never really had a process for measuring results.

FIELD TECHNIQUES: MEASURING YOUR RESULTS

To gain practice in measuring, think of all that is involved in becoming a performance consultant, adding consulting services to your repertoire, and positioning yourself as an expert in performance improvement. Next, think of how you might assess the impact of your move on yourself, your department, and your organization, using the measurement principles discussed in this chapter:

1. What will you accept as evidence that adding performance consulting has been worth the investment in time and money?

2. What will you use for criteria: cost? satisfaction? adoption? goal accomplishment? outputs? outcomes? consistency among products?

3. If you choose cost, which costs do you want your performance consulting to affect?

   • Whether you are an internal or an external consultant, start with your internal costs (your cost of doing business, or overhead, which is a fixed cost). What was this cost in the past? How will adding consulting services enable you to reduce your fixed costs—by outsourcing services or by being more efficient?

   • How will adding consulting services increase your output? Your fixed costs may remain the same, but if you increase your billable hours or increase the amount of time you have available to consult because you are more efficient, the ratio of fixed costs to outputs will be more favorable.

   • What do you want the effect of your move to consulting to be on your direct or variable costs? Do you want it to enable you to reduce the use of costly outside services, such as consultants and vendors, which in turn will reduce your variable direct costs? If your costs are less than those of consultants and you can bring the same level of expertise to a project, it may be more cost-effective for you to do the work. This could reduce your direct costs.

   • Will the change reduce turnover in your department? What does it cost to recruit competent performers?

   • If you are an external consultant, what costs do you want the move to performance consulting to reduce?

4. If you choose satisfaction as a criterion, whose satisfaction will you measure: your own? your staff's? your colleagues'? your management's? your clients'? your consultants' and vendors'?

5. If you choose adoption or deployment as a criterion, will you count the number of instances clients use your performance consulting services, or the proportion of time you spend on consulting versus other services?

   • Will you count the number of times you are called in early to facilitate defining a problem, evaluating the scope of a problem, and selecting the team to work on a problem?

   • What will you accept as evidence that your services are valued and being used appropriately?

6. If you choose goal accomplishment as a criterion, what was your goal in deciding to become a performance consultant? What will you take as evidence that you are achieving your goal?

By now you should understand that assessment, analysis, and evaluation are closely related. They all involve some element of measurement.

SUMMARY

If the large data-processing firm described at the beginning of this chapter wants to evaluate the cost benefit of certifying its resellers, it will have to answer a few important questions: Does having certified resellers shorten the sales cycle, thus reducing the cost of sales? What is the average length of the sales cycle now? What is the cost of sales? What does it cost now to recruit and train a reseller? Does the certification program reduce the cost of recruitment? Does it contribute to retention?

The company that wants to roll out quality training to all employees should first ask what it wants to change as a result of the training. Is the training intended to help everyone reduce the cost of their work processes? Is it intended to make all staff more customer-oriented? If so, how will that be demonstrated? What impact will it have on the company's ability to compete, increase its market share, retain profitable customers, or retain high-performing employees? Criteria the company might use to measure the impact of the training include a reduction in the cost of expansion, avoidance of costs associated with getting back customers lost to the competition, and a reduction in the cost of recruiting and retaining high-performing employees.

To prove the cost benefit of setting up a corporate university and investing in a new computer system, the VP of HR should find out the current cost of recruiting, training, and retaining qualified HR staff worldwide. Other information that would provide a basis for comparison is the gaps in skills and knowledge among the HR field staff because of the company's inability to efficiently communicate with them. Another useful piece of information would be how satisfied HR's customers are with the department's performance and how much of that satisfaction is due to HR's being qualified or informed.

Measuring begins with getting information on how current performance affects cost, satisfaction, and goal accomplishment. Once you know this you can get information about what changed as a result of the interventions. You want to find out if the intervention improved performance. The information you need to determine this is how much the intervention affected cost, satisfaction, adoption, and goal accomplishment. If you do not have any information about current performance, you can still measure performance after the intervention. You just need to be clear concerning what you and your client will accept as evidence of worth and value.

WHERE TO LEARN MORE

Brown, M. G., *Keeping Score: Using the Right Metrics to Drive World-Class Performance* (New York: AMACOM, 1996). This is an excellent little book on how to measure and metrics that drive performance.

Hale, J., and Westgaard, O., *Achieving a Leadership Role for Training* (New York: Quality Resources Press, 1995). This book describes how to apply the Baldrige criteria and ISO 9000 principles to managing the function of training and performance improvement. It has numerous examples of criteria and ways to measure performance.

Chapter 9

Measuring People Performance

*E*very day, managers are asked to evaluate their staffs' performance. Management wants better measures so they can decide who to promote and how to reward performance fairly. HR, in particular, wants better methods for linking compensation to performance.

FIELD NOTES: PERFORMANCE REVIEWS

Merit reviews were coming up. People would soon find out what their salary increases would be. The compensation department had set guidelines limiting what people could receive. It was an emotional time for managers, who were left with the burden of evaluating people's performance within the context of a limited budget.

A professional association outsourced its training to a group of independent instructors. The association used a two-part process to evaluate these instructors: first the instructors evaluated one another, and then the students evaluated the instructors. The result was that every instructor received the most positive evaluation possible, every time. The association struggled with how to get a more accurate evaluation of the instructors.

The lack of adequate measures results in managers' having inadequate information to fairly and accurately evaluate people's performance. The irony is that people measure one another all the time. In the workplace, however, the criteria may not be clear. Worse, they may be inappropriate, insufficient, or misleading. Performance measures communicate what the organization values. They tell people what the organization thinks is important and what it expects. Therefore an important part of our job as performance consultants is to help our clients find and fairly apply better measures of behaviors and results.

More often than not, what people say they measure and what they actually measure are not the same thing. The most frequently overlooked evaluation criteria concern activities that only get noticed when they are not done or are done poorly, when they shift costs to others or to a later time, or when they destroy relationships.

Administrative duties, for example, often get noticed only when they do not get done or are done poorly. Furthermore, they do not usually earn a person extra points, even when they are done well. But poor performance in this area shifts costs to managers or to administrative staff. Late, incomplete, or inaccurate paperwork by one group actually shifts costs to another group, whose own work gets delayed.

Not communicating what all the criteria are misleads employees. Other examples of criteria that get overlooked are

- *Safety.* People do not get extra points for being safe or driving safely. However, they may get punished for being unsafe, doing things unsafely, or having an accident.

- *Honesty.* People rarely get extra points for being honest. However, they may experience negative consequences if they misrepresent something, such as work records, product performance, expenses, and so on.

- *Professional demeanor* (including social skills and the ability to rapidly establish credibility). People do not usually get evaluated higher because they dress well, speak well, or possess social graces. However, they may be overlooked for plumb assignments, promotions, or rewards if they lack a professional demeanor.

- *Quality of relationships* (the relationships required to gain cooperation, access to information, sponsorship of one's ideas, and so on). It is assumed that people will get along. However, when people insult others or erode important or long-standing relationships, someone else has to come in and mend hurt feelings. Again, the consequences are unnecessary added costs.

- *Ability to handle ambiguity and lack of certainty.* In some jobs people are presented with the same variables day after day. Other jobs require people to work with a great deal of ambiguity and uncertainty about what might happen next. For example, they may have to work with people from different cultures, with different social norms, and with different business protocols.

FIELD NOTES: EVALUATING SALES REPS

Steve was the sales training manager for the medical equipment manufacturer where Russ worked. He worked with Russ to devise ways to reduce costs and improve people performance. The VP of sales asked Steve to find a better way to evaluate the performance of the company's sales reps. In the past they had evaluated sales reps based only on how skilled they were at the company's sales call process and how often they followed it. The sales call process was a proven approach to consultative selling. It was well documented, and every rep was trained in it. Each sales manager went on sales calls with their reps two to four times a year to evaluate how well each rep followed the process. They recorded their evaluations on a quarterly review form, which asked them to rate how often the reps used the process, using a five-point scale ranging from "Never" to "Always."

When the VP of sales met with Steve, he did not talk about the *validity* of specific metrics, criteria, or measures; he was concerned only with whether the sales managers used the *same* criteria to evaluate the reps. He thought that basing evaluations on the sales call process reduced variance in the managers' ratings. This proved not to be the case, however. A rep who was evaluated highly by one manager could be rated as poor by another manager on the same criterion. Steve decided to talk to the sales managers separately to find out exactly how they evaluated the reps' use of the sales call process, to determine if this criterion provided an accurate picture of the reps' performance.

Steve reported the following to the VP of sales:

- *The criterion used to evaluate the reps was both inappropriate and insufficient.* It was inappropriate because it did not take into account how much time the customer was willing to spend with the rep, the relationship the rep had established with the customer, what the rep and the customer agreed to during the previous sales call, or how the customer felt about the product. It was insufficient because it was only a single variable; therefore it gave a limited picture of performance. Steve told the VP there might be other activities they could measure that contribute as much if not more to results than following the sales call process. Additional criteria Steve suggested included territory management, number of customer calls, product knowledge, and customer satisfaction with the product.

- *There was a mismatch between the criterion and the metric.* The sales managers could not honestly say whether or not a rep followed the sales call process 100 percent of the time. They only observed each rep for one or two days a quarter. During the visit the manager and rep would jointly call on four to eight customers. The managers could judge performance based only on what they saw. To draw a conclusion about what happened the rest of the time, they had to rely on what the rep told them.

- *There were hidden criteria*. The sales managers were applying other criteria in evaluating the reps that were not universally known or agreed to by the other managers. For example, one or more of the managers considered some combination of (1) the number of sales calls made weekly, (2) whether or not the sales reps worked with reps from other departments to ensure a coordinated effort, (3) the reps' product knowledge, (4) whether the reps completed paperwork on time, (5) how well they controlled expenses, (6) the reps' driving record, and (7) achievement of the company's sales goal. Not all of the managers considered these criteria or applied them consistently for all reps, however.

Steve also concluded that the sales managers' performance was not evaluated in terms of assessing, coaching, and developing high performers. Therefore, instead of focusing on how to evaluate the reps, Steve recommended a series of interventions aimed at improving the sales managers' ability to more fairly and consistently evaluate the reps' performance. The interventions included

- Rewarding the sales managers for consistently using agreed-upon criteria
- Measuring the sales managers' compliance with applying the criteria
- Measuring the sales managers' skill at coaching, developing, and evaluating reps
- Defining and documenting criteria for evaluating the sales managers' performance

Steve recommended that the VP of sales meet with his zone managers (the sales managers' bosses) to

- Jointly determine what they expected of the sales managers
- Jointly determine ways to measure the sales managers' performance
- Agree on the criteria and metrics
- Agree on how to share their expectations and criteria with the sales managers

FIELD TECHNIQUES: SELECTING USABLE CRITERIA

One of the harder aspects of evaluating people performance is identifying and agreeing on the right criteria. The first step is to find out the reason for the evaluation. Once you have done that you can develop the performance criteria. Figure 9.1 lists some of the more common reasons for evaluating performance and gives examples of possible criteria.

Figure 9.1. Reasons and Criteria for Evaluating Performance

Reasons	*Possible criteria*
To determine developmental needs	• Growth • How long it takes a person to achieve proficiency • The cost of development
To assess level of competence	• Level of productivity • How well work relationships function • Work or project cycle time • The cost to raise the level of competence
To determine bonuses or merit increases	• Goal accomplishment • What it cost to achieve the goal • The impact achieving the goal had on others
To assess readiness to take on more responsibility	• Quality of the work produced • The time it takes to produce at the current level • What might be put at risk if more responsibility were added

Once I know how a client wants to use evaluation criteria, I can facilitate the process of identifying what criteria to use. I use the nominal group technique (NGT) early in the consulting relationship to surface hidden criteria and help the group come to consensus on what they will use as evidence of adequate performance. The NGT has a couple of advantages over other group processes. It limits the influence of people with higher status and the more vocal members of the group. The process gives everyone an equal chance to contribute. You can even analyze the results statistically by computing the mean (average) number of points and the standard deviation. Answers that receive points that are one or more standard deviations above the mean are considered significant. Figure 9.2 has directions for conducting a nominal group session.

Once I have discovered what the client expects I can develop a worksheet to document and communicate its criteria. I find it helpful to separate quantitative measures from qualitative measures. Quantitative measures are similar to productivity in that they include things like frequency and volume (they can be counted easily). Qualitative measures include customer satisfaction, product knowledge, and reasoning—factors that require some type of scale to measure them. For the qualitative measures I use a combination of Likert scales and behavioral descriptions, similar to what Mike used to evaluate his consultants (Figure 2.2). Just like conducting a nominal group session, the process of documenting quantitative and qualitative measures results in clarity and helps achieve consensus. Figure 9.3 has guidelines for developing people performance worksheets.

Figure 9.2. Directions for the NGT

1. Explain the purpose of the meeting (that is, what you want the group to accomplish).

2. Present the question (you may have a series of questions, but ask only one question at a time).

3. Ask everyone to silently generate a list of answers to the question. Recommend that they keep their answers short and avoid compound answers.

4. Once everyone is done, ask them to share one answer at a time. Record their answers on flipchart paper, and hang each page where it can be seen by everyone. Keep going around the table until everyone has exhausted his or her list. Ask everyone to withhold their comments and questions until all of the responses are listed.

5. Once everyone's answers are listed, the group may choose to combine those that are alike. Don't let them combine answers to make compound or complex statements, however.

6. Next, ask each person to privately pick five answers from the whole list that he or she feels are the most important.

7. When everyone has picked five, ask them to rank the five, from 1 for least important to 5 for most important.

8. Read each answer one at a time, and ask how many points everyone gave to that answer. Record the number of points next to the response. When all of the points are recorded, read aloud those responses that received the greatest number of points. These are the ones the group considers the most important.

Figure 9.3. Guidelines for Creating People Performance Worksheets

1. Separate the quantitative evaluation criteria from the qualitative criteria.

2. Create a separate worksheet for each set of criteria.

3. Label and date each performance worksheet.

4. Make enough rows on each worksheet to list the names of all the people being evaluated.

5. For both worksheets, create enough columns for all of the criteria, plus a column for comments. If appropriate, include a key indicating what information goes in each column.

6. For the qualitative worksheet, add columns to record performance ratings. Create rating scales for each factor. The scales can be behaviorally anchored or based on performance checklists. Remember to add a column for comments.

7. If appropriate, develop a set of instructions on how to fill in the worksheet, what criteria to use for the ratings, and how to interpret the information.

FIELD NOTES: EVALUATING SALES REPS

Steve learned from his interviews that the sales managers, their bosses (the zone managers), and the VP of sales were in agreement on using the performance criteria to

- Identify the reps' developmental needs
- Determine which reps were worth investing more time in and which were too costly to support
- Determine which reps might be considered for a management position
- Determine bonuses and merit increases

The zone managers were not in agreement on how to evaluate the sales managers, however. Steve decided to use the nominal group technique to get the zone managers to identify and rank the criteria they use to evaluate sales managers. The zone managers, the VP of sales, the head of consumer products, and two sales managers participated. Figure 9.4 lists the results.

The VP of sales assigned a team to develop worksheets the zone managers could use to evaluate the sales managers. The team consisted of Steve, two of the zone managers, and the two sales managers who participated in the nominal group session.

Figure 9.4. Performance Criteria for the Sales Managers

The question: What factors should be considered when evaluating a sales manager's performance?

Responses, in order of importance	Points awarded
1. Number of shared expectations sessions done and agreed to	26
2. Ability to give regular, focused, specific feedback	15
3. Number of developmental plans that meet needs	14
4. Performance (compared with objectives)	8
5. Unbiased quantitative and qualitative analysis	7
6. Knowledge of business factors affecting territory	7
7. Ability to immediately verbalize each reps' strengths and weaknesses	4
8. Product sales volume	3
9. Number of observations	3
10. Consistency between verbal and written feedback	2
11. Soliciting feedback from reps	0
12. Staying on top of administrative duties	0
13. Having clear goals	0
14. Exit interview data	0
15. Including regular feedback on field observation forms	0
16. What I see happening in a coaching situation	0
17. Business acumen	0
18. Making realistic evaluations	0
19. Initiating relationships with counterparts in other departments	0
20. Confronting negative behavior	0
21. Giving consistent messages to reps	0

The process of using the NGT and developing the worksheets helped the zone managers clarify what they valued. Steve was able to facilitate discussions about what behaviors they attend to and how they interpret those behaviors. Then Steve worked with his team to come up with the metrics for each of the criteria. The metrics would be behaviors that would give evidence of adequate performance. The zone managers could use these worksheets when they met with sales managers to talk about expectations. The worksheets also served as models for other worksheets the sales managers could use to evaluate reps' performance.

The first worksheet had the quantitative measures. Steve wanted to raise the zone managers' awareness of which reps the sales managers spent time with and what effect that had on performance. He used the qualitative worksheet to define the behaviors and results to be used to evaluate the sales managers. The sales managers were rated separately on eight factors. A five-point rating scale was used, with 1 most favorable and 5 least favorable. A rating of 2 meant the sales manager met expectations. The worksheets are reproduced in Figures 9.5 and 9.6.

**Figure 9.5.
Quantitative Measures
Summary Worksheet**

SM's names	1. #		2. # of joint calls			3. # of plans		4. Sales by product family: actual v. goal								5. Turnover	6. Comments
								Z		X		M		Q			
	f	p	l	m	h	d	s	a	g	a	g	a	g	a	g		
1																	
2																	
3																	
4																	
5																	
6																	
7																	
8																	
9																	

f = full product line, p = partial product line; l = low performer, m = medium performer, h = high performer, d = developmental, s = strategic, a = actual, g = goal

1. # of Reps: Record the number of Reps that report to each Sales Manager (SM) and how many of those Reps represent the full product line versus a more limited line of products.

2. # of days spent doing Joint Sales Calls: Record how many days each SM spent jointly calling on customers with low-, medium-, and high-performing Reps. Pay particular attention to:
   • Whether or not the joint sales calls were 1 or 2 days in length.
   • How the joint sales calls are distributed across low, medium, and high performers. It may be appropriate to have fewer 2-day joint calls depending on the performance or developmental needs of the Rep. However, the distribution should become less skewed over time. If distribution remains skewed, find out why. You rate the effectiveness of working directly with the Rep during calls on the Qualitative Measures Summary Worksheet.

3. # of Plans: Record the number of Developmental and Strategic plans each SM has for their Reps. Developmental plans are designed to improve skills that lead to better performance. Strategic plans are designed to build business. You rate the quality and appropriateness of those plans on the second worksheet.

4. Actual versus goal: Record the year-to-date sales for products Z, X, M, and Q compared to the goal.

5. Turnover: Record the amount of turnover each SM has experienced. This gives you a basis for discussing the reasons behind the turnover. Reducing turnover by 20% is a corporate objective.

6. Comments: Use this column for notes regarding necessary action steps, explanations, or overall ratings.

JC: Joint sales calls led to changes in behavior that improved business results.	*DP:* Plans meet reps' individual and business needs and were achieved.	*PO:* Objectives are current, appropriate, and aligned with the business needs and were met.	*KP:* Knows the products; is considered an expert; knows the competition and the field of therapy.
1. Extra calls led to significant improvements in reps' performance.	1. Reps are consistently high performing, and all have strategic plans.	1. All reps met objectives, which had a positive effect on the business.	1. Selected to instruct new sales managers and reps in the products.
2. Did 100 percent (all reps) or per plan, distribution is fair.	2. Have plans for all reps or objectives, and all plans meet needs.	2. Reps met objectives appropriate to their level of experience.	2. Completed all product training priority assessments at 85 percent.
3. Did 90 percent, or distribution skewed for this quarter.	3. Have plans for 90 percent or less, or only 90 percent of plans meet needs.	3. 90 percent of reps met objectives.	3. Completed all product assessments at 85 percent except for one major product.
4. Did 80 percent, or distribution skewed for more than one quarter.	4. Have plans for 80 percent or less, or only 80 percent meet needs.	4. 80 percent of reps met objectives.	4. Completed all product assessments at 85 percent except for two major products.
5. Did 70 percent or less, or distribution skewed for more than two quarters.	5. Have plans for 70 percent or less, or only 70 percent meet needs.	5. 70 percent of reps met objectives.	5. Has not completed any product assessments.
RFF: Feedback is consistently regular, frequent, specific, timely.	*UQQ:* Evaluations are based on corroborated facts.	*KBF:* Knows business factors affecting the territory.	*AM:* Administrative practices don't impact others negatively and are current.
1. Exceptional skills inspired and led to business results.	1. Bases analysis on all variables and customer feedback.	1. Regularly shares local market factors and plans to address them.	1. Suggestions on administrative processes produced enhancements, efficiency.
2. All get regular, frequent, specific, timely, and constructive feedback.	2. Bases analysis on objectives attainment, quality of sales call process, and call activity.	2. Initiates relationships with other sections and counterparts.	2. Administrative duties performed on time and accurately.
3. Confronts negative behavior sometimes, and gives specific feedback 70 to 90 percent of time.	3. Bases analysis on quality of sales call process and call activity but not on objectives.	3. Knows roles and goals of customer, division, and territory well.	3. Has to be reminded about 30 percent of the time to get reports in or to do them correctly.
4. Feedback has some action steps for improvement with time lines or is not specific or relevant to issue.	4. Bases analysis on call activity or sales process alone.	4. Focuses efforts on processes alone; ignores or doesn't identify market factors.	4. Reminded more than 30 percent to 50 percent of the time; others can't meet their expectations.
5. Written and verbal feedback are not consistent.	5. Bases analysis on gut instinct and experience alone.	5. Relies excessively on feelings or past knowledge.	5. Reminded more than 50 percent of the time.

Figure 9.6. Qualitative Measures Summary Worksheet

Period covered: _____										
1. Manager's name:	2. Ratings								3. Average rating	4. Comments
	JC	DP	PO	KP	RFF	UQQ	KBF	AM		
1										
2										
3										
4										
5										
6										
7										
8										
9										

Ratings Key: JC = joint sales calls; DP = development plans; PO = performance against objectives; KP = knows the products; RFF = regular, frequent feedback; UQQ = unbiased quantitative and qualitative analysis; KBF = knows business factors affecting the territory; AM = administrative management.

Ratings: Rate each sales manager on a scale of 1 to 5, from most to least positive. See attached form for the behavioral anchors for each factor.

Average rating: Total the ratings for all eight factors, and divide by eight to get the average rating.

Figure 9.6. Qualitative Measures Summary Worksheet, *cont'd.*

EXPERIENCES FROM THE FIELD: EVALUATING THE JOB

Sometimes there is more to be gained from evaluating a job than from evaluating a person's job performance. Every job has dimensions. Those dimensions are the inputs to the job and the processes used to produce the expected outputs and outcomes (see Figure 9.7).

Once I identify the inputs, processes, outputs, and outcomes, I can measure them. Examples of the types of measures you can use for each of these dimensions are in Figure 9.8.

Identifying how to measure job dimensions helps when hiring and assigning people to a job. When the right people get hired or assigned, the need for a lot of interventions goes away. Knowing the dimensions also helps you determine what to use when measuring the effect of an intervention. Figure 9.9 is a job aid you can use to evaluate a job.

Figure 9.7.
Dimensions
of a Job

1. Job *inputs:* the requests, information, and people that demand that a job be performed. The criteria used to measure inputs are volume, complexity, clarity, and maturity. Measure inputs to determine
   - The complexity of a job or task, the volume of work expected for it, the quality and clarity of directions given, what needs the job is expected to satisfy, and who depends on the outputs
   - How skilled people have to be at managing the inputs
   - How well an intervention improved either the inputs or people's ability to manage them

2. Job *processes:* the procedures, systems, equipment, and technology used to perform the job. The criteria used to measure processes are response time, cycle time, efficiency, and cost. Measure processes to determine
   - The effectiveness and sufficiency of the processes in terms of response time, cycle time, efficiency, and cost
   - How skilled people have to be at managing the processes
   - How well an intervention improved the processes

3. Job *outputs* (also called productivity measures): the product(s) of the processes. The criteria used to measure outputs are volume, customers served, and worth. Measure outputs to determine
   - How much work a person did and for whom the work produced worthy results
   - How well an intervention increased either the volume of outputs or the ratio of value-adding outputs to non-value-adding outputs

4. Job *outcomes:* the consequences of the outputs. The criteria used to measure outcomes are satisfaction, accomplishment, aftermath, cost, compliance, and image. Measure outcomes to determine
   - The value and worth of what a person accomplished
   - How well an intervention improved, enhanced, or increased the consequences of what was accomplished

FIELD TECHNIQUES: EVALUATING A JOB

Follow these steps to evaluate a job:

1. Explain to the client that before you can recommend ways to evaluate a person's performance, you want to understand the person's job better.

2. Arrange to interview a few people currently in the job. It is even better if you can observe them in the job.

3. Start by asking people in the job what its typical tasks are. If there are a lot of tasks, ask if they fall into families or can be grouped under general headings.

4. Once you have a sense of what tasks make up the job, ask what causes the person in the job to perform these tasks. Explain that you want to find out what or who creates the need for the job. If you were able to observe the person directly, you should have seen some of the people or systems that signaled the need for the job to be performed.

Inputs	Processes	Outputs	Outcomes
Measures at this level are about *what* people in the job have to deal with:	Measures at this level are about *how* people do the task:	Measures at this level are about *how much* people did:	Measures at this level are about the *results* or consequences of what people did, in terms of
• How much work is there?	• Does something cue the person to respond, and if so in what priority?	• How much got done?	• Feelings:
• Is it routine or unique?		• How many requests were handled?	– How confident and satisfied are people with the results?
• What's the driver behind the request (personal, business, legal)?	• Is the process mapped or defined?	• Does what got done break out by customer or some other factor?	• Accomplishment:
	• How long does it take to complete or carry out the request (cycle time), on average?	• How much was done for each type of request?	– Was the goal achieved?
• How clear, complete, or accurate is the information the person has to work from?			• Aftermath:
	• How many resources are used to carry out the task (efficiency)?	• How much time was spent on each type of request?	– Was there any unforseen fallout?
			• Compliance:
• Who generates the request? Who is the customer?	• What does it cost to do the task or respond?	• Which customers were served? Which were not served?	– What regulations were met or not met?
		• How were the results used?	•Money:
			– Were direct and indirect costs incurred or avoided?
		• What effect did the results have on others?	– What was the return on investment?
			• Image:
			– How did goal achievement affect the status of the job, department, or person?

Figure 9.8. Examples of Measures for Job Dimensions

5. Ask the client to name the job's processes. The more hesitant he or she is about answering this question (or if he or she cannot think of any processes), the more likely it is that the job's processes have not been defined. This means it will be harder to evaluate the person's performance.

6. Ask the client to describe the job's products and the effects of those products on others. Be sure to ask who uses the job's outputs, as these are the people who can help you come up with criteria for measuring the outputs and even the outcomes.

7. As you interview or observe (either individuals or a group), fill in the form (Figure 9.9). Once you feel you have a fair picture of the job, share the form with the people you interviewed to see if anything needs to be added.

Inputs	Processes	Outputs	Outcomes
What do people in the job have to deal with?	*How* do people perform the job?	*How much* gets done?	What are the *results* or consequences of what gets done?
Criteria:	Criteria:	Criteria:	Criteria:
• Volume	• Response time	• Quantitative measures	• Satisfaction
• Complexity	• Cycle time	• Customers serviced	• Accomplishment
• Clarity	• Efficiency	• Worth	• Aftermath
• Maturity	• Cost		• Cost
			• Compliance
			• Image

Figure 9.9.
Job Evaluation
Job Aid

8. Once you and your client are in agreement about the characteristics of the job, ask if there is anything about the job that could be changed to support improved performance.

9. Ask if the purpose of the intervention is to help people deal with the realities of the job or to change some aspect of it to eliminate the cause of poor performance.

10. Focus on those things that will be most likely to help people perform better if they are changed or improved.

FIELD TECHNIQUES: MEASURING VARIABILITY IN A JOB, FOCUSING ON INPUTS

Frequently job environments differ significantly for different people with the same job title. However, since the jobs' titles, descriptions, and salary grades are the same, people assume that the jobs are the same as well.

Inputs are all the stimuli that cause a task or job to be performed. Sometimes inputs are customer requests. Sometimes they are the outputs of another work group. Measure inputs to find out what people have to manage to do their job effectively. The criteria used to measure a job's inputs are volume, complexity, clarity, and maturity.

Volume

As a measurement criterion, volume concerns how much work the person in the job is expected to handle within a given time period. Work can be defined as requests, orders, or units. Here are some examples:

• For a medical doctor, volume is the number of office appointments, patients to see in the hospital, test results to be reviewed, patient consultations, and so on over the course of an hour, a day, or a week.

- For an HR generalist, volume is the number of employee complaints to respond to and investigate, the number of positions to fill, the number of terminations to process, the number of new-hire orientations to conduct, the number of meetings to attend, and so on.

- For a building engineer, volume is the square footage of the building to be maintained, the number of floors and entrances to monitor, the number of heating and cooling systems to service, and so on.

Complexity

As a measurement criterion, complexity is about the number and variety of variables that the person in a job has to handle. The opposite is simplicity. Having many customers adds some complexity. If those customers have different needs and expectations, the complexity is even greater. It is also about how many inputs are routine compared to how many are unique. For example:

- For a medical doctor, complexity increases as the variety, uniqueness, and gravity of patient diseases go up.

- For an HR generalist, complexity increases as the number of departments, management levels, employees, and services go up. It also increases as situations become more unusual.

- For a building engineer, complexity increases as the number of contractors goes up, the variety of equipment manufacturers increases, control systems become more sophisticated, and the need to comply with rigorous environmental standards goes up.

Clarity

As a measurement criterion, clarity concerns how much direction a person is given in his or her job. The opposite is ambiguity. Clarity increases with well-defined rules and procedures; it decreases when people are given only broad guidelines. Like complexity, the need for clarity depends on whether the input is routine or unique. The more unique the inputs, the more the person has to use professional judgment in deciding what to do. For example:

- For a medical doctor, the procedures for treating some illnesses and injuries are proven and quite straightforward. Other illnesses and injuries require more professional judgment.

- For an HR generalist, some procedures, such as enrolling new hires in the company's benefits program, are well defined and do not allow for any deviation. Other tasks, such as investigating harassment or drug abuse charges, may be less well defined and have only broad guidelines. They require greater sensitivity and judgment.

- For a building engineer, procedures for preventive maintenance may be well-defined because the activity is routine. There may only be general guidelines for troubleshooting and decommissioning a system, however.

Maturity

As a measurement criterion, maturity concerns the length and functionality of relationships. Maturity increases as people gain experience in a job. It increases with the sophistication of customers and suppliers. It increases as people begin to trust one another's expertise and experiences. For example:

- For a medical doctor, maturity refers to how well the doctor functions with his or her staff. Maturity also refers to how long patients have had a relationship with the doctor.

- For an HR generalist, maturity refers to how well labor and management get along and to what degree employees and management rely on HR's expertise.

- For a building engineer, maturity refers to the engineer's relationship with suppliers and service contractors. It also refers to the engineer's relationship with the people who work or live in the building.

FIELD NOTES: EVALUATING INPUTS

Steve asked the sales managers to describe what the sales reps do and how they do it. He discovered that although the reps all have the same job title, they work in very different job environments. For example, some of the reps sold as many as fifteen products; others sold only five. Some had what were considered friendly markets; others had hostile markets. Some had inherited well-established relationships with customers; others had to spend a significant amount of time cold-calling. Some were assigned very concentrated geographic areas, such as big cities; others were given very large geographic areas, like the state of Idaho.

The zone managers and the sales managers needed to decide whether they wanted to apply the same evaluation criteria to reps with significantly different job inputs. If they did decide to apply the same criteria, they needed to decide how the metrics might differ.

Russ, at the medical equipment manufacturer, was asked to develop a curriculum for the company's HR generalists. Management believed that the generalists lacked skills. Russ met with some of the generalists and discovered that

- Some were assigned to manufacturing plants, reported to the plant manager, and ran a one-person shop.
- Some worked in regional offices, reported to a VP of HR, and worked with specialists in compensation and benefits.
- Some worked out of zone offices, still reported to a VP of HR in the regional office, but served field sales and service personnel.
- Some spent from 10 to 30 percent of their time on non-HR duties, such as managing the cafeteria, reinforcing security, acting as a receptionist, and co-ordinating large-scale meetings.

Different work environments require different evaluation criteria. The best way for Russ to improve the generalists' performance might be to help management establish fair and reasonable criteria for each work environment. Then he could conduct a skill gap analysis to uncover real deficiencies in skills and knowledge, based on the new criteria sets.

FIELD TECHNIQUES: MEASURING EFFICIENCY, FOCUSING ON JOB PROCESSES

Processes are how a job or task gets done. Processes include the procedures, systems, equipment, and technology used to perform the job or produce an output (an idea, a recommendation, a product, and so on). Measure processes to determine if they support the required work cost-effectively. The criteria used to measure processes are response time, cycle time, efficiency, and cost.

Response Time

As a measurement criterion, response time concerns how efficiently a process signals people to respond. Response time is affected by how well or how poorly the process communicates priority or urgency. For example:

- For a medical doctor, good intake procedures identify patients in need of immediate medical attention.
- For an HR generalist, informal communication networks help identify problems before they escalate into more serious situations.
- For a building engineer, appropriate equipment sensors signal the need for maintenance before a major breakdown occurs.

Cycle Time

As a measurement criterion, cycle time refers to how long it takes to complete a task. Cycle time goes up when a person has to wait for inputs or for work to be checked by someone else, and it goes up as more steps are added. Well-designed processes have minimal, if any, checking and wait time and few non-value-adding steps. For example:

- For a medical doctor, efficient hospital admissions procedures lead to more rapid treatment.
- For an HR generalist, procedures for investigating problems and submitting recommendations to management lead to quicker resolution of problems.
- For a building engineer, procedures that quickly restore a building system to full functioning lead to faster job outcomes.

Efficiency

As a measurement criterion, efficiency is about how well resources are used during a process. Resources include people, time, equipment, space, and materials. The more resources dedicated to rework and checking, the less efficient the process. For example:

- For a medical doctor, reducing operator and equipment error decreases the need to redo tests.
- For an HR generalist, reducing the number of dead ends investigated before getting to the cause of a problem leads to faster problem resolution.
- For a building engineer, grouping similar tasks to avoid repetition of effort leads to faster service.

Cost

As a measurement criterion, cost refers to the number of resources a process consumes. The more unnecessary resources consumed (and the more expensive the resources), the greater the cost. For example:

- For a medical doctor, prescribing generic drugs and not running unnecessary tests reduces costs.
- For an HR generalist, outsourcing certain services can reduce costs, if the services consume more resources when provided internally.
- For a building engineer, using materials with longer shelf lives reduces the number of service calls.

FIELD NOTES: EVALUATING PROCESSES

While developing a curriculum for his company's HR generalists, Russ discovered that they spend the majority of their time on employee relations and staffing and recruiting. Employee relations and staffing and recruiting are processes. Because Russ defines his own job in terms of processes, he took the same approach to defining the generalists' jobs. He recommended that a team be set up to define these processes and that measures be created to evaluate their effectiveness.

⊙ FIELD TECHNIQUES: MEASURING PRODUCTIVITY, FOCUSING ON JOB OUTPUTS

Outputs are what a person produces, including things like products, reports, ideas, recommendations, sales calls, classes taught, and so on. Measuring outputs determines how much work people do, how well they do it (by comparing actual outputs to possible outputs), for whom they do it, and which activities lead to worthy results. The criteria used to measure outputs are quantity, customers served, and worth.

Quantity

As a measurement criterion, quantity refers to how much work was actually done compared to either what was expected or what the process is capable of producing. When a process is capable of producing more than what is being produced, then it is being underutilized. Underutilization of a process may be due to insufficient demand or the availability of other processes that accomplish the same results (this may indicate redundancy). For example:

- For a medical doctor, the number of hours billed can be compared to the number of hours available. If billed hours are less than available hours, it would indicate insufficient quantity.

- For an HR generalist, the amount of paperwork completed can be compared to the amount that needed to be done.

- For a building engineer, the number of building systems serviced during a time period can be compared to the number that could have been serviced.

Customers Served

As a measurement criterion, customers served concerns who got served and who did not. Some customers demand so much attention that they prevent servicing of other customers. Not servicing customers may result in lost business. For example:

- For a medical doctor, it is important to be able to service patients with urgent needs and still be able to service those wanting routine checkups.
- For an HR generalist, it is important to be able to service the home office staff without sacrificing the needs of the field staff.
- For a building engineer, it is important to meet the needs of every tenant in a building, as opposed to just some tenants.

Worth

As a measurement criterion, worth concerns the value of what was produced. For example:

- For a medical doctor, providing preventive treatments avoids more serious situations or complications.
- For an HR generalist, preparing programs that are proven to reduce the number of charges of harassment improves the workplace environment.
- For a building engineer, proper maintenance of building equipment and systems avoids breakdowns and possible damage to tenants' equipment, materials, and inventory.

FIELD NOTES: EVALUATING OUTPUTS

Chris, a performance consultant at Mike's company, headed the finance group that did financial analyses for product managers. In the past Chris's group had been evaluated only in terms of customer satisfaction. Since the group was now expected to evaluate their own processes and their ability to add value, they decided to start by looking at what they did, how much time they spent doing it, and which customers consumed most of their time.

Chris went back to her group's work records and found out that 60 percent of their time was spent with U.S. product managers. Half of that time was spent providing quick answers to financial questions (the financial help-desk function). The other half of that time was spent producing standard financial reports, which Chris wasn't sure the U.S. managers really used. About 25 percent of the group's remaining time was spent on international issues, and another 15 percent was spent on global issues. All of their international and global work was strategic in nature (such as determining how to more effectively compensate dedicated suppliers or reduce packaging costs). They realized that what drove the help-desk activities was the product managers' lack of skills and knowledge in financial analysis. They also believed that the help desk was not the best use of their time, and they had doubts about the value of some of their recurring reports. Chris went back to her mission and vision (see Figure 1.12) and used that information to establish goals and measures for her group and for each group member (see Figure 9.10).

Figure 9.10. The Finance Group's Measures

> *Goal No. 1:* To increase our customers' awareness of our services. The criterion to measure our success is an increase in activities that directly support our vision and mission and our global strategic initiatives.
>
> *Goal No. 2:* To increase our ability to influence and add value. The criteria to measure whether or not we increase our level and sphere of influence will be
>
> 1. The number of approved projects and activities that we identified as strategic and are supported by the supply chain managers.
> 2. The number of strategic initiatives in which we play a leadership role.
> 3. The number of relationships we establish with influential stakeholders that result in those stakeholders' supporting our vision and mission.
> 4. The ratio of time spent on help desk and routine matters compared to time spent on global strategic initiatives.
>
> *Goal No. 3:* To measure the effectiveness and efficiency of our projects. The criteria to measure effectiveness and efficiency will be
>
> 1. Timeliness: how often was our work delivered on time, and how often was it timely enough to make a difference to the system even if it was not perfect (the 80–20 rule)?
> 2. Customer satisfaction: how often did we meet our customers' expectations, and to what degree did our work satisfy their needs?
> 3. Worth: what is our ability to provide evidence of our cost benefit to the system?
> 4. Implementation: how often were our recommendations actually implemented or acted on by the customer?

⌖ FIELD TECHNIQUES: DETERMINING REWARDS AND BONUSES, FOCUSING ON OUTCOMES

Outcomes are the consequences of doing or not doing the job. The consequences can affect customers, employees, and the organization. The criteria used to measure outcomes are satisfaction, accomplishment, the aftermath (negative fallout), cost, compliance, and image.

Satisfaction

As a measurement criterion, satisfaction refers to how satisfied customers, bosses, and other vested parties are in what was done and how confident they are that it will meet their needs. For example:

- For a medical doctor, it refers to patients' level of satisfaction with their treatment and their level of confidence in the doctor's ability to accurately diagnose future illnesses.

- For an HR generalist, it refers to employees' and management's level of satisfaction with staffing and recruitment, employee relations, compensation, benefits, and training.

- For a building engineer, it refers to tenants' and owners' level of satisfaction with the engineer's services in terms of flexibility; the building's ergonomics, security, and attractiveness; and how disruptions in utilities were handled.

Accomplishment

As a measurement criterion, accomplishment refers to the degree to which a goal or objective was achieved. For example:

- For a medical doctor, successfully treating a patient indicates accomplishment.
- For an HR generalist, getting managers to do annual performance reviews indicates accomplishment.
- For a building engineer, meeting an energy conservation goal indicates accomplishment.

The Aftermath

As a measurement criterion, the aftermath of an intervention, action, process, and so on refers to any unexpected or undesirable consequences. Examples are shifting costs to other work units, damaging relationships, or putting something else at risk. For example:

- For a medical doctor, a course of treatment may have long-term negative consequences for a patient's health.
- For an HR generalist, dealing with the aftermath of a process might mean confronting an emotionally laden situation without jeopardizing labor or management relationships.
- For a building engineer, an energy efficiency program might produce an uncomfortable environment for tenants, causing their productivity to suffer.

Cost

As a measurement criterion, cost refers to the financial consequences of achieving or not achieving a goal. It includes the financial impact on direct or indirect costs, fixed or variable costs, cash flow, return on investment, return on capital employed, profits before taxes, or other economic variables. For example:

- For a medical doctor, it could include the impact of the practice's management on fixed costs, direct costs, and profits before taxes.
- For an HR generalist, it could include the effect of staffing and recruitment practices on the cost of retention, recruitment, benefits, and salaries.
- For a building engineer, it could include the effect of preventive maintenance practices on direct costs and the market value of the property.

Compliance

As a measurement criterion, compliance concerns whether or not regulatory or organizational requirements were violated in accomplishing the goal. For example:

- For a medical doctor, compliance with state medical board requirements is essential.
- For an HR generalist, processes must comply with labor laws and the organization's guidelines.
- For a building engineer, building modifications must comply with EPA and OSHA regulations.

Image

As a measurement criterion, image concerns how accomplishing a goal affected community relations, industry standing, and reputation. For example:

- For a medical doctor, image includes the doctor's professional reputation and community standing.
- For an HR generalist, image includes the HR department's reputation and status within the organization.
- For a building engineer, image includes the engineer's technical and management reputation among tenants, owners, and peers.

HOW PERFORMANCE GETS TRANSLATED INTO MERIT REVIEWS

Another breakdown in measuring people performance comes when it is time for salary discussions and merit increases. The problem is complicated by compensation policies that limit the number (percentage) of people who can get the maximum raise. Looking only at goal attainment is not enough. Managers need to consider all the factors: the inputs, process, and outputs. Managers should also pay attention to all of the criteria used to measure outcomes.

FIELD TECHNIQUES: FAIRLY APPLYING CRITERIA FOR MERIT REVIEWS

One technique I recommend to clients is to create a list of questions that the manager and employee can both go over before conducting the merit review. Ideally the list should be reviewed at the beginning of the annual pay cycle. The list should include the criteria the manager takes into account when deciding on a person's merit increase. What is helpful about the list of questions is the emphasis on outputs and outcomes, particularly worth, costs, and aftermath. The list makes public the behaviors and results that the organization values. It helps managers move the discussion from "I met my goals" to "at what cost?" Figure 9.11 has an example of such a list of questions.

To create a similar job aid for managers and employees, meet with your team and clients to discuss what the real criteria are for merit reviews and what they should be. Make sure you discuss those often-overlooked, assumed factors such as cost, relationships, compliance, and teamwork. Then build your own merit review form. Ask managers to try it. Find out if and how it affected the quality and focus of their discussions with employees.

FIELD TECHNIQUES: MEASURING YOUR OWN PERFORMANCE

At this point you should have a more thorough understanding of what the job of performance consultant is. You can begin by asking what the purpose of the job is. Is the position of performance consultant developmental? If the answer is yes, what position are you being prepared for? Is it your goal to improve your competence? If the answer is yes, then what will you and others take as evidence that your competence has improved?

Develop your own quantitative and qualitative evaluation worksheets. Develop the supporting performance checklists or behaviorally anchored scales to evaluate your performance. Use the dimensions of a job (Figures 9.7 and 9.8) to describe your inputs, processes, outputs, and outcomes. Decide what becoming a performance consultant is supposed to accomplish and what you can do to become the best at performance consulting.

SUMMARY

Better criteria help managers and employees evaluate performance and identify ways to improve it. Without defined criteria, judgments about performance are arbitrary and unfair. To help identify relevant criteria, examine the job. Start by identifying and evaluating the job's inputs to determine

- The complexity of the job, the volume of work it is expected to handle, the quality and clarity of direction given to those who hold it, whose needs it is expected to satisfy, and who depends on the outputs
- How skilled people are at managing the inputs
- How well an intervention improved either the inputs or people's ability to manage them

Next, evaluate the job's processes to determine

- If they are effective and sufficient, in terms of response times, cycle times, efficiency, and cost
- How skilled people are at using the process
- How well an intervention improved them

Here are some questions to help managers be more consistent in what they consider when determining merit raises. The manager should answer the questions before meeting with the individual. The intent is to get the manager to consider what was or was not accomplished, how important to the organization the accomplishment was, and the impact that the person's actions and results had on resources and others' ability to perform. To complete this form, read each question with the staff person you are rating in mind. Assess that staff person using the scale provided. The scale reflects a continuum, ranging from marginal performance, with opportunity for improvement, to high performance, where the person is meeting or exceeding expectations. Select the numerical position on the scale as appropriate. An example of the scale follows:

No	Somewhat	Not relevant	Mostly	Yes
1	2	3	4	5

Factors pointing to opportunities for improvement ↔ Factors indicating the employee met or exceeded expectations

Comments:
_____

1. Did the person accomplish the objectives of the work plan (business volume, customer satisfaction, personal development, staff development, and so on)?

No	Somewhat	Not relevant	Mostly	Yes
1	2	3	4	5

Comments:
_____

2. How difficult were the work plan's objectives to achieve; that is, were they stretch goals?

No	Somewhat	Not relevant	Most were hard	Very Difficult
1	2	3	4	5

Comments:
_____

3. Did the person overcome barriers that interfered with the achievement of the objectives?

None	Minor ones	Don't know	Significant ones	Major ones
1	2	3	4	5

Comments:
_____

4. To what degree did the person use unplanned resources to carry out the work plan?

Used a lot of unplanned resources	Used some	Don't know	Used very few	Used no unplanned resources
1	2	3	4	5

Comments:
_____

5. Did the person use resources wisely when carrying out the work plan?

No	Not enough	Not relevant	Mostly	Yes
1	2	3	4	5

Comments:
_____

6. How much did accomplishment of the objectives interfere with others' ability to accomplish their work plan?

A great deal	Somewhat	Not relevant	Very little	Not at all
1	2	3	4	5

Comments:
_____

Figure 9.11. Merit Review Criteria

7. Did the person achieve the goals considered the top priorities of the work plan?

No	Somewhat	Not relevant	Mostly	Yes
1	2	3	4	5

Comments: _____

8. Was the person's work plan strategically aligned with the department's initiatives, and did the results contribute to the department's goals?

Not at all	Somewhat	Not relevant	Mostly	A great deal
1	2	3	4	5

Comments: _____

9. Did the person contribute to helping others accomplish their goals?

Not at all	Somewhat	Not relevant	A lot	Led to breakthroughs
1	2	3	4	5

Comments: _____

10. Did the person accomplish goals beyond what was on the work plan?

Not at all	Somewhat	Not relevant	Mostly	Led to breakthroughs
1	2	3	4	5

Comments: _____

Figure 9.11. Merit Review Criteria, *cont'd.*

Evaluate the expected and actual job outputs to determine

- How much work a person did, for whom the person did it, and if that work led to beneficial results
- How well an intervention increased either the volume or percentage of outputs that led to beneficial results

Finally, evaluate the outcomes of the job's outputs to determine

- The consequences of what was or was not accomplished
- How well an intervention improved or enhanced the consequences of what was accomplished

WHERE TO LEARN MORE

Shrock, S., and Coscarelli, W., *Criterion Referenced Test Development* (Washington, DC: International Society for Performance Improvement, 1989). This is excellent for learning about the use of scales to evaluate performance.

To learn more about the nominal group technique and controlling group bias, check out the writings of A. L. Delbecq and A. H. Van de Ven. They have done extensive research on controlling bias in decision making.

About the Author

*J*udith Hale has dedicated her career to helping management professionals develop effective, practical ways to improve individual and organizational performance. She has used the techniques, processes, and job aids described in this fieldbook in her own consulting work, which has spanned twenty-four years. Judith's clients speak of the practicality of her approach and the proven results it yields. She is able to explain complex ideas so that people understand their relevance and can apply them to their own situation. She is able to help others come to a shared understanding about what to do and how to commit to action.

Her consulting firm, Hale Associates, was founded in 1974 and enjoys long-term relationships with a variety of major corporations. The services her firm provides include consultation on alignment, assessment, certification, evaluation, integration of performance improvement systems, performance management, and strategic planning.

Her book *Achieving a Leadership Role for Training* describes how training can apply the standards espoused by the International Standards Organization and Baldrige to its own operation. She was the topic editor for *Designing Work Groups, Jobs, and Work Flow* and *Designing Cross-Functional Business Processes* and the author of the chapter "The Hierarchy of Interventions" in the *Sourcebook for Performance Improvement.* Judith also wrote *The Training Manager Competencies: The Standards,* as well as *The Training Function Standards* and *Standards for Qualifying Trainers,* and she put together the *Workbook and Job Aids for Good Fair Tests.*

Judith was president of the Chicago chapter of the National Society of Performance and Instruction (NSPI) and served on NSPI's President's Advisory

Council. NSPI named her Outstanding Member of the Year in 1987. She has also served as president of the International Board of Standards for Performance and Instruction and president of the Chicago chapter of the Industrial Relations Research Association (IRRA). She was a commercial arbitrator with the American Arbitration Association and has been a member of the American Society for Training and Development (ASTD) for many years. She was nominated for ASTD's Gordon Bliss Award in 1995. She taught graduate courses in management for fourteen years for the Insurance School of Chicago and received the school's Outstanding Educator award in 1986.

Judith speaks regularly at ASTD International, ASTD Technical Skills, Computer Training & Support, the International Society for Performance Improvement, and Lakewood's annual training conferences.

Judith holds a B.A. from Ohio State University (communication), an M.A. from Miami University (theater management), and a Ph.D. from Purdue University (instructional design, with minors in organizational communication and adult education).

Index

215

WORKSHEET FIGURES ON DISK

The minimum configuration needed to utilize the files included on this disk is a system with one 3.5" floppy disk drive capable of reading double-sided high-density IBM formatted floppy disks and word processing or desktop publishing software able to read Microsoft Word 6.0/95 files. Document memory needs will vary, but your system should be capable of opening file sizes of 50+K. No monitor requirements other than the ones established by your software need be met.

Each of the figures in your textbook that are marked with a disk icon have been saved onto the enclosed disk as a Microsoft Word 6.0/95 file. These files can be opened with many Windows- and Macintosh-based word processors or desktop publishers for viewing or editing as you see fit. The files were originally created and saved as a Word 6.0/95 DOC file by Microsoft Word 97. Not all software will read the files exactly the same, but the DOC format is an honest attempt by Jossey-Bass/Pfeiffer to preserve the composition of the figures, including fonts, borders, italics, bold face, bullets, and so on, as accurately as possible.

Copy all DOC files to a directory/folder in your system. To read the files using your Windows-based document software, select File from the main menu followed by Open to display the Open dialog box. Set the correct drive letter and subdirectory shown in the Open dialog box by using the Look in control. In the Files of type text box, enter *.doc to display the list of DOC files available.

Each file name is coded to its figure in the text to make it easy for you to find the one you want. For example, Figure 2.3 has been named FIG02-03.doc. You can open the file by either double-clicking your mouse on the file name that you want to open or by clicking once on the file name to select it and then once on the Open command button.